AN INTRODUCTION TO THE PHILOSOPHY OF MIND

E. J. LOWE

University of Durham

CAMBRIDGE
UNIVERSITY PRESS

PUBLISHED BY THE PRESS SYNDICATE OF THE UNIVERSITY OF CAMBRIDGE
The Pitt Building, Trumpington Street, Cambridge, United Kingdom

CAMBRIDGE UNIVERSITY PRESS
The Edinburgh Building, Cambridge CB2 2RU, UK
40 West 20th Street, New York NY 10011–4211, USA
10 Stamford Road, Oakleigh, VIC 3166, Australia
Ruiz de Alarcón 13, 28014 Madrid, Spain
Dock House, The Waterfront, Cape Town 8001, South Africa
http: // www.cambridge.org

First published 2000
Reprinted 2001

Printed in the United Kingdom at the University Press, Cambridge

Typeset in Baskerville 11/12.5 pt [WV]

A catalogue record for this book is available from the British Library

Library of Congress cataloguing in publication data
Lowe, E. J. (E. Jonathan)
An introduction to the philosophy of mind / E. J. Lowe.
p.   cm.
Includes bibliographical references and index.
ISBN 0 521 65285 5 (hardback). – ISBN 0 521 65428 9 (paperback)
1. Philosophy of mind. I. Title.
BD418.3.L69 1999
128'.2–dc21   99–21498   CIP

ISBN 0 521 65285 5 hardback
ISBN 0 521 65428 9 paperback

Contents

vii

Preface

At a time when many introductory books on the philosophy of mind are available, it would be fair to ask me why I have written another one. I have at least two answers to this question. One is that some of the more recent introductions to this subject have been rather narrow in their focus, tending to concentrate upon the many different 'isms' that have emerged of late – reductionism, functionalism, eliminativism, instrumentalism, non-reductive physicalism and so forth, all of them divisible into further sub-varieties. Another is that I am disturbed by the growing tendency to present the subject in a quasi-scientific way, as though the only proper role for philosophers of mind is to act as junior partners within the wider community of 'cognitive scientists'. It may be true that philosophers of an earlier generation were unduly dismissive – and, indeed, ignorant – of empirical psychology and neuroscience, but now there is a danger that the pendulum has swung too far in the opposite direction.

Perhaps it will be thought that my two answers are in conflict with one another, inasmuch as the current obsession with the different 'isms' does at least appear to indicate an interest in the *metaphysics* of mind, a distinctly philosophical enterprise. But there is no real conflict here, because much of the so-called 'metaphysics' in contemporary philosophy of mind is really rather lightweight, often having only a tenuous relation to serious foundational work in ontology. In fact, most of the current 'isms' in the philosophy of mind are generated by the need felt by their advocates to propound and justify a broadly *physicalist* account of the mind and its capacities, on the questionable assumption that this alone can render talk about the mind scientifically respectable. Many of the esoteric disputes between philosophers united by this common assumption have arisen simply because it is very unclear just what 'physicalism' in the philosophy of mind really entails. In the chapters that follow, I shall try not to let that relatively sterile issue dominate and distort our philosophical inquiries.

This book is aimed primarily at readers who have already benefited from a basic grounding in philosophical argument and analysis and are beginning to concentrate in more detail upon specific areas of philosophy, in this case the philosophy of mind. The coverage of the subject is broad but at the same time, I hope, sharply focused and systematic. A start is made with a look at some fundamental metaphysical problems of mind and body, with arguments for and against dualism providing the focus of attention. Then some general theories of the nature of mental states are explained and criticised, the emphasis here being upon the strengths and weaknesses of functionalist approaches. Next we turn to problems concerning the 'content' of intentional states of mind, such as the question of whether content can be assigned to mental states independently of the wider physical environments of the subjects whose states they are. In the remaining chapters of the book, attention is focused successively upon more specific aspects of mind and personality: sensation, perception, thought and language, reasoning and intelligence, action and intention, and finally personal identity and self-knowledge. The order in which these topics are covered has been deliberately chosen so as to enable the reader to build upon the understanding gained from earlier chapters in getting to grips with the topics of later chapters. Rather than include separate guides to further reading for the topics covered by the book, I have avoided unnecessary duplication by constructing the notes for each chapter in such a way that they serve this purpose as well as providing references.

The book is not partisan, in the sense of espousing an exclusive approach to questions about the mind in general –

such as any particular form of physicalism or dualism – but at the same time it does not remain blandly neutral on more specific issues. Developments in empirical psychology are taken into account, but are not allowed to overshadow genuinely philosophical problems. Indeed, my approach is a problem-oriented one, raising questions and possible answers, rather than aiming to be purely instructive. I have tried to write the book in a simple and non-technical style, with a view to making it accessible to as wide a readership as possible. At the same time, I hope that professional philosophers specialising in the philosophy of mind will find it of interest more than just as a teaching aid.

I am grateful to a number of anonymous referees who provided valuable suggestions and advice at various stages in the preparation of this book. I only regret that limitations of space have prevented me from adopting all of their suggestions. I am also very grateful to Hilary Gaskin of Cambridge University Press for her encouragement and help throughout the process of planning and writing the book.

1

Introduction

What is the philosophy of mind? One might be tempted to answer
that it is the study of philosophical questions concerning the
mind and its properties – questions such as whether the mind
is distinct from the body or some part of it, such as the brain,
and whether the mind has properties, such as consciousness,
which are unique to it. But such an answer implicitly assumes
something which is already philosophically contentious,
namely, that 'minds' are *objects* of a certain kind, somehow
related – perhaps causally, perhaps by identity – to other
objects, such as bodies or brains. In short, such an answer
involves an implicit *reification* of minds: literally, a making of
them into 'things'. Indo-European languages such as English
are overburdened with nouns and those whose native tongues
they are have an unwarranted tendency to suppose that
nouns name things. When we speak of people having both
minds and bodies, it would be naïve to construe this as akin
to saying that trees have both leaves and trunks. Human
bodies are certainly 'things' of a certain kind. But when we
say that people 'have minds' we are, surely, saying something
about the properties of people rather than about certain
'things' which people somehow own. A more circumspect way
of saying that people 'have minds' would be to say that people
are *minded* or *mindful*, meaning thereby just that they feel,
see, think, reason and so forth. According to this view of the
matter, the philosophy of mind is the philosophical study of
minded things just insofar as they are minded. The things
in question will include people, but may well also include
non-human animals and perhaps even robots, if these too can

1

be minded. More speculatively, the things in question might even include disembodied spirits, such as angels and God, if such things do or could exist.

Is there some single general term which embraces all minded things, actual and possible? Not, I think, in everyday language, but we can suggest one. My suggestion is that we use the term 'subject' for this purpose. There is a slight inconvenience attached to this, inasmuch as the word 'subject' also has other uses, for instance as a synonym for 'topic'. But in practice no confusion is likely to arise on this account. And, in any case, any possible ambiguity can easily be removed by expanding 'subject' in our intended sense to 'subject *of experience*' – understanding 'experience' here in a broad sense to embrace any kind of sensation, perception or thought. This agreed, we can say that the philosophy of mind is the philosophical study of subjects of experience – what they are, how they can exist, and how they are related to the rest of creation.[1]

EMPIRICAL PSYCHOLOGY AND PHILOSOPHICAL ANALYSIS

But what is distinctive about the *philosophical* study of subjects of experience? How, for instance, does it differ from the sort of study of them conducted by empirical psychologists? It differs in several ways. For one thing, the philosophy of mind pays close attention to the *concepts* we deploy in characterising things as being subjects of experience. Thus it is concerned with the analysis of such concepts as the concepts of perception, thought and intentional agency. The philosophical analysis of a concept is not to be confused with a mere account of the meaning of a word as it is used by some speech community, whether this community be the population at large or a group of scientists. For example, an adequate analysis of the concept of *seeing* cannot be arrived at simply by examin-

---

[1] I say more about the notion of a 'subject of experience' in my book of that title, *Subjects of Experience* (Cambridge: Cambridge University Press, 1996): see especially chs. 1 and 2.

ing how either ordinary people or empirical psychologists use the word 'see'. Of course, we cannot completely ignore everyday usage in trying to analyse such a concept, but we must be ready to criticise and refine that usage where it is confused or vague. The philosophical study of any subject matter is above all a critical and reflective exercise which – the opinion of Wittgenstein notwithstanding – almost always will not and should not leave our use of words unaltered.[2]

No doubt it is true that good empirical psychologists are critical and reflective about their use of psychological words: but that is just to say that they too can be philosophical about their discipline. Philosophy is not an exclusive club to which only fully paid-up members can belong. Even so, there is such a thing as expertise in philosophical thinking, which takes some pains to achieve, and very often the practitioners of the various sciences have not had the time or opportunity to acquire it. Hence it is not, in general, a good thing to leave philosophising about the subject matter of a given science exclusively to its own practitioners. At the same time, however, it is incumbent upon trained philosophers to inform themselves as well as they can about a domain of empirical scientific inquiry before presuming to offer philosophical reflections about it. A scientific theory of vision, say, is neither a rival to nor a substitute for a philosophical analysis of the concept of seeing: but each will have more credibility to the extent that it is consistent with the other.

METAPHYSICS AND THE PHILOSOPHY OF MIND

The philosophy of mind is not only concerned with the philosophical analysis of mental or psychological concepts, how-

---

[2] It is in the *Philosophical Investigations*, trans. G. E. M. Anscombe, 2nd edn (Oxford: Blackwell, 1958), § 124, that Ludwig Wittgenstein famously says that 'Philosophy may in no way interfere with the actual use of language . . . [i]t leaves everything as it is'. As will be gathered, I strongly disagree with this doctrine, which has, in my view, had a malign influence on the philosophy of mind. At the same time, I readily concede that Wittgenstein himself has contributed much of value to our understanding of ourselves as subjects of experience.

ever. It is also inextricably involved with *metaphysical* issues. Metaphysics – which has traditionally been held to be the root of all philosophy – is the systematic investigation of the most fundamental structure of reality. It includes, as an important sub-division, *ontology*: the study of what general categories of things do or could exist. The philosophy of mind is involved with metaphysics because it has to say something about the ontological status of subjects of experience and their place within the wider scheme of things. No special science – not even physics, much less psychology – can usurp the role of metaphysics, because every empirical science pre-supposes a metaphysical framework in which to interpret its experimental findings. Without a coherent general concep-tion of the whole of reality, we cannot hope to render compat-ible the theories and observations of the various different sciences: and providing that conception is not the task of any one of those sciences, but rather that of metaphysics.

Some people believe that the age of metaphysics is past and that what metaphysicians aspire to achieve is an imposs-ible dream. They claim that it is an illusion to suppose that human beings can formulate and justify an undistorted pic-ture of the fundamental structure of reality – either because reality is inaccessible to us or else because it is a myth to suppose that a reality independent of our beliefs exists at all. To these sceptics I reply that the pursuit of metaphysics is inescapable for any rational being and that they themselves demonstrate this in the objections which they raise against it. For to say that reality is inaccessible to us or that there is no reality independent of our beliefs is just to make a *meta-physical* claim. And if they reply by admitting this while at the same time denying that they or any one else can justify metaphysical claims by reasoned argument, then my response is twofold. First, unless they can give me some *reason* for thinking that metaphysical claims are never justifiable, I do not see why I should accept what they say about this. Secondly, if they mean to abandon reasoned argument alto-gether, even in defence of their own position, then I have nothing more to say to them because they have excluded themselves from further debate.

Metaphysics is unavoidable for a rational thinker, but this is not to say that metaphysical thought and reasoning are either easy or infallible. Absolute certainty is no more attainable in metaphysics than it is in any other field of rational inquiry and it is unfair to criticise metaphysics for failing to deliver what no other discipline – not even mathematics – is expected to deliver. Nor is good metaphysics conducted in isolation from empirical inquiries. If we want to know about the fundamental structure of reality, we cannot afford to ignore what empirically well-informed scientists tell us about what, in their opinion, there is in the world. However, science only aims to establish what *does* in fact exist, given the empirical evidence available to us. It does not and cannot purport to tell us what *could* or *could not* exist, much less what *must* exist, for these are matters which go beyond the scope of any empirical evidence. Yet science itself can only use empirical evidence to establish what does in fact exist in the light of a coherent conception of what could or could not exist, because empirical evidence can only be evidence for the existence of things whose existence is at least genuinely *possible*. And the provision of just such a conception is one of the principal tasks of metaphysics.[3]

The point of these remarks is to emphasise there cannot be progress either in the philosophy of mind or in empirical psychology if metaphysics is ignored or abandoned. The methods and findings of empirical psychologists and other scientists, valuable though they are, are no substitute for metaphysics in the philosopher of mind's investigations. Nor should our metaphysics be slavishly subservient to prevailing scientific fashion. Scientists inevitably have their own metaphysical beliefs, often unspoken and unreflective ones, but it

---

[3] I explain more fully my views about metaphysics and its importance in my *The Possibility of Metaphysics: Substance, Identity and Time* (Oxford: Clarendon Press, 1998), ch. 1.

would be a complete abdication of philosophical responsibility for a philosopher to adopt the metaphysical outlook of some group of scientists just out of deference to their importance as scientists. We shall have occasion to heed this warning from time to time in our examination of the problems which the philosophy of mind throws up.

A BRIEF GUIDE TO THE REST OF THIS BOOK

I have organised the contents of this book so as to begin, in chapter 2, with some fundamental metaphysical problems concerning the ontological status of subjects of experience and the relationship between mental and physical states. Then, in chapters 3 and 4, I move on to discuss certain general theories of the nature of mental states and some attempts to explain how mental states can have *content* – that is, how they can apparently be 'about' things and states of affairs in the world which exist independently of the individuals who are the subjects of those mental states. In chapters 5, 6 and 7, I look more closely at certain special kinds of mental state, beginning with *sensory* states – which even the lowliest sentient creatures possess – and then progressing through *perceptual* states to those higher-level cognitive states which we dignify with the title *thoughts* and which, at least in our own case, appear to be intimately connected with a capacity to use *language*. This leads us on naturally, in chapter 8, to examine the nature of *rationality* and *intelligence* – which we may like to think are the exclusive preserve of living creatures with capacities for higher-level cognition similar to our own, but which increasingly are also being attributed to some of the machines that we ourselves have invented. Then, in chapter 9, I discuss various accounts of how intelligent subjects put their knowledge and powers of reasoning into practice by engaging in *intentional action*, with the aim of bringing about desired changes in things and states of affairs in the world. Finally, in chapter 10, we try to understand how it is possible for us to have *knowledge of ourselves and others* as subjects of experience existing both in space and through time:

that is, how it is possible for intelligent subjects of experience like ourselves to recognise that this is precisely *what we are*. In many ways, this brings us back full circle to the metaphysical problems of self and body raised at the outset, in chapter 2.

2

Minds, bodies and people

A perennial issue in the philosophy of mind has been the so-called *mind–body problem*: the problem of how the mind is related to the body. However, as I indicated in the previous chapter, this way of putting the problem is contentious, since it suggests that 'the mind' is some sort of *thing* which is somehow related to the body or some part of the body, such as the brain. We are invited to consider, thus, whether the mind is *identical* with the brain, say, or merely causally related to it. Neither proposal seems very attractive – the reason being, I suggest, that there is really no such thing as 'the mind'. Rather, there are *minded* beings – subjects of experience – which feel, perceive, think and perform intentional actions. Such beings include human persons, such as ourselves, who have bodies possessing various physical characteristics, such as height, weight and shape. The mind–body problem, properly understood, is the problem of how subjects of experience are related to their physical bodies.

Several possibilities suggest themselves. In describing them, I shall restrict myself to the case of *human persons*, while recognising that the class of subjects of experience may be wider than this (because, for instance, it may include certain non-human animals). One possibility is that a person just *is* – that is, is identical with – his or her body, or some distinguished part of it, such as its brain. Another is that a person is something altogether distinct from his or her body. Yet another is that a person is a composite entity, one part of which is his or her body and another part of which is something else, such as an immaterial spirit or soul. The latter two views are traditionally called forms of 'substance dualism'. A 'substance', in this context, is to be understood, quite simply, as any sort of persisting *object* or *thing* which is capable of undergoing changes in its properties over time. It is important not to confuse 'substance' in this sense with 'substance' understood as denoting some kind of *stuff*, such as water or iron. We shall begin this chapter by looking at some arguments for substance dualism.

CARTESIAN DUALISM

Perhaps the best-known substance dualist, historically, was René Descartes – though it is not entirely clear which of the two forms of substance dualism mentioned above he adhered to.[1] Often he writes as if he thinks that a human person, such as you or I, is something altogether distinct from that person's body – indeed, something altogether non-physical, lacking all physical characteristics whatever. On this interpretation, a human person is an immaterial substance – a spirit or soul – which stands in some special relation to a certain physical body, *its* body. But at other times he speaks more as if he thinks that a human person is some sort of combination of an immaterial soul and a physical body, which stand to one another in a rather mysterious relation of 'substantial union'. I shall set aside this second interpretation, interesting though it is, largely because when philosophers today talk about 'Cartesian dualism' they usually mean the former view, according to which a person is a wholly immaterial substance

[1] Descartes's views about the relationship between self and body receive their best-known formulation in his *Meditations on First Philosophy* (1641), to be found in *The Philosophical Writings of Descartes*, ed. J. Cottingham, R. Stoothoof and D. Murdoch (Cambridge: Cambridge University Press, 1984). In recent times, one of Descartes's best-known and severest critics has been Gilbert Ryle: see his *The Concept of Mind* (London: Hutchinson, 1949), ch. 1. For a controversial critique of the received view that Descartes was a 'Cartesian dualist', see Gordon Baker and Katherine J. Morris, *Descartes' Dualism* (London: Routledge, 1996). It is unfortunate that many modern philosophers of mind tend to distort or oversimplify the historical Descartes's views, but this is not the place for me to engage with them over that issue.

possessing mental but no physical characteristics. But it is important, when considering this view, not to confuse the term 'substance' in the sense in which we have just been using it with the sense in which it denotes a kind of stuff. Cartesian dualism does not maintain that a person is, or is made of, some sort of ghostly, immaterial stuff, such as the 'ectoplasm' beloved of nineteenth-century spiritualists. On the contrary, it maintains that a person, or self, is an altogether simple, indivisible thing which is not 'made' of anything at all and has no parts. It contends that you and I are such simple things and that we, rather than our bodies or brains, are subjects of experience – that is, that we rather than our bodies or brains have thoughts and feelings. In fact, it contends that we and our bodies are utterly unlike one another in respect of the sorts of properties that we possess. Our bodies have spatial extension, mass, and a location in physical space, whereas we have none of these. On the other hand, we have thoughts and feelings – states of consciousness – whereas our bodies and brains lack these altogether.

What reasons did Descartes have for holding this seemingly strange view of ourselves – and how good were his reasons? He had several. For one thing, he considered that our bodies were simply incapable of engaging in intelligent activity on their own account – incapable of *thinking*. This is because he believed that the behaviour of bodies, left to themselves, was entirely governed by mechanical laws, determining their movements as the effects of the movements of other bodies coming into contact with them. And he couldn't see how mechanically determined behaviour of this sort could be the basis of such manifestly intelligent activity as the human use of speech to communicate thoughts from one person to another. With the benefit of hindsight, we who live the age of the electronic computer may find this consideration less than compelling, because we are familiar with the possibility of machines behaving in an apparently intelligent fashion and even using language in a way which seems to resemble our own use of it. Whether it is right to think of computers as really being capable of intelligent behaviour on their own account, or merely as cleverly constructed devices which can *simulate* or *model* intelligent behaviour, is an open question, to which we shall return in chapter 8. But, certainly, there is no simple and obvious argument from our own capacity for intelligent behaviour to the conclusion that we are not to be identified with our bodies or brains.

THE CONCEIVABILITY ARGUMENT

The argument that we have just considered and found wanting is an empirical argument, at least to the extent that it appeals in part to the laws supposedly governing the behaviour of bodies. (Descartes himself thought that those laws had an *a priori* basis, but in this he was almost certainly mistaken.) However, Descartes also had, more importantly, certain *a priori* arguments for his belief that there is, as he puts it, a 'real distinction' between oneself and one's body. One of these is that he claims that he can 'clearly and distinctly perceive' – that is, coherently conceive – the possibility of himself existing without a body of any kind, that is, in a completely disembodied state. Now, if it is *possible* for me to exist without any body, it seems to follow that I cannot be *identical* with any body. For suppose that I were identical with a certain body, *B*. Given that it is possible for me to exist without any body, it seems to follow that it is possible for me to exist without *B* existing. But, clearly, it is *not* possible for me to exist without *me* existing. Consequently, it seems that I cannot, after all, be identical with *B*, because what is true of *B*, namely, that I could exist without it existing, is not true of me.

However, the force of this argument (even accepting its validity, which might be questioned) depends upon the cogency of its premise: that it is indeed possible for me to exist without any body.[2] In support of this premise, Descartes

---

[2] One possible reason for questioning the argument is that it assumes that it is an *essential* property of any body, *B*, that it is a body, that is, that *B* would not have existed if it had not been a body. I myself find this assumption plausible, but it

claims that he can at least conceive of himself existing in a disembodied state. And, to be fair, this seems quite plausible. After all, many people report having had so-called 'out of body' experiences, in which they seem to float away from their bodies and hover above them, seeing them from an external point view in the way in which another person might do so. These experiences may not be veridical: in all probability, they are hallucinatory experiences brought on by stress or anxiety. But they do at least indicate that we can *imagine* existing in a disembodied state. However, the fact that we can *imagine* some state of affairs is not enough to demonstrate that that state of affairs is even logically possible. Many of us find little difficulty in imagining travelling back in time and participating in historical events, even to the extent of changing what happened in the past. But on closer examination we see that it is logically impossible to change the past, that is, to bring it about that what has happened has not happened. So too, then, we cannot conclude that it really is possible to exist without a body from the fact that one can imagine doing so.

Of course, Descartes doesn't claim merely that he can *imagine* existing without a body: he claims that he can 'clearly and distinctly perceive' that this is possible. But then, it seems, his claim simply amounts to an assertion that it really *is* possible for him to exist without a body and doesn't provide any independent *grounds* for this assertion. On the other hand, is it fair always to insist that a claim that something is possible must be susceptible of proof in order to be rationally acceptable? After all, any such proof will have to make appeal, at some stage, to a further claim that something or other is possible. So, unless *some* claims about what is possible are acceptable without proof, no such claims will be acceptable at all, which would seem to be absurd. Even so, it may be felt that Descartes's particular claim, that it is possible for him to exist without a body, is *not* one of those possibility

has been challenged by Trenton Merricks: see his 'A New Objection to A Priori Arguments for Dualism', *American Philosophical Quarterly* 31 (1994), pp. 80–5.

claims which is acceptable without proof. The upshot is that this argument of Descartes's for the 'real distinction' between himself and his body, even though it could conceivably be sound, lacks persuasive force: it is not the sort of argument that could convert a non-dualist to dualism.

THE DIVISIBILITY ARGUMENT

Descartes has another important argument for the 'real distinction' between himself and his body. This is that he, as a subject of experience, is a simple and indivisible substance, whereas his body, being spatially extended, is divisible and composed of different parts. Differing in these ways, he and his body certainly cannot be one and the same thing. But again, the crucial premise of this argument – that he is a simple and indivisible substance – is open to challenge. Why should Descartes suppose this to be true? There are two ways in which his claim might be attacked, one more radical than the other. The more radical way is to challenge Descartes's assumption that he is a *substance* at all, whether or not a simple one. By a 'substance', in this context, recall that we mean a persisting object or thing which can undergo changes in its properties over time while remaining one and the same thing. To challenge Descartes's assumption that he is a substance, then, is to question whether, when Descartes uses the first-person pronoun, 'I', he succeeds in referring to some single thing which persists identically through time – indeed, more radically still, it is to question whether he succeeds in referring to some *thing* at all. Perhaps, after all, 'I' is not a referring expression but has some other linguistic function.[3] Perhaps the 'I' in 'I think' no more serves to pick out a certain object than does the 'it' in 'It is raining'. Although some philosophers have maintained precisely this, it seems an

[3] For an example of a philosopher who holds that 'I' is not a referring expression at all, see G. E. M. Anscombe, 'The First Person', in S. Guttenplan (ed.), *Mind and Language* (Oxford: Clarendon Press, 1975), reprinted in G. E. M. Anscombe, *Metaphysics and the Philosophy of Mind: Collected Philosophical Papers, Volume II* (Oxford: Blackwell, 1981). I discuss this view more fully in chapter 10.

implausible suggestion. It seems reasonable to suppose that what I have been calling 'subjects of experience', including human persons, do indeed exist and that the first-person pronoun is a linguistic device whose function it is to refer to the subject who is using it. And it also seems reasonable to suppose that subjects of experience persist through time and undergo change without loss of identity. Anyway, I shall assume for present purposes that this is so, though we shall return to the issue when we come to discuss personal identity in chapter 10. In short, I shall consider no further, here, the more radical of the two ways in which Descartes's claim that he is a simple substance might be challenged.

The other way in which this claim might be challenged is to accept that Descartes, and every subject of experience, is a 'substance', in the sense of the term that we have adopted, but to question whether he is a *simple* and *indivisible* substance. Why should Descartes have supposed that he himself is simple and indivisible? After all, if he were to lose an arm or a leg, would he not have lost a part of himself? Descartes's answer, no doubt, is that this would only be to lose a part of his *body*, not a part of *himself*. But this presupposes that he is not identical with his body, which is the very point now in question. What is required is an independent reason to suppose that Descartes's loss of his arm or leg is no loss of a part of *himself*. However, there is perhaps some reason to suppose that this is true, namely, that the loss of an arm or a leg makes no essential difference to oneself as a subject of experience. There are, after all, people who are born without arms or legs, but this makes them no less *people* and subjects of experience. However, even if we accept this line of argument, it doesn't serve to show that *no* part of one's body is part of oneself. For one cannot so easily contend that a loss of part of one's *brain* would make no essential difference to oneself as a subject of experience. Nor do we know of any people who have been born without brains. Of course, if Descartes were right in his earlier claim that he could exist in a completely disembodied state, then this would lend support to his view that even parts of his brain are not parts of himself. But we have yet to be persuaded that that earlier claim is true. So it seems that, at this stage, Descartes's claim that he himself is a simple and indivisible substance is insufficiently compelling. This is not say that the claim may not be true, however, and I shall give it more consideration shortly.

NON-CARTESIAN DUALISM

So far we have failed to identify any compelling argument for the truth of Cartesian dualism, so perhaps we should give up dualism as a lost cause – especially if there are in addition some compelling arguments *against* it. But before looking at such counterarguments, we need to sound a note of caution. We shouldn't imagine that in rejecting Cartesian dualism we must automatically reject *every* form of 'substance dualism'. There is, in particular, one form of substance dualism which is untouched by any consideration so far raised, because it doesn't appeal to the kind of arguments which Descartes used in support of his position. According to this version of substance dualism, a person or subject of experience is, indeed, not to be identified with his or her body or any part of it, but nor is a person to be thought of as being an immaterial spirit or soul, nor even a combination of body and soul. On this view, indeed, there need exist no such things as immaterial souls. Rather, a person or subject of experience is to be thought of as a thing which possesses *both* mental *and* physical characteristics: a thing which feels and thinks but which also has shape, mass and a location in physical space. But why, it may be asked, should such a thing not simply be identified with a certain physical body or part of it, such as a brain?

At least two sorts of reason might be adduced for denying any such identity. The first is that mental states, such as thoughts and feelings, seem not to be properly attributable to something like a person's brain, nor even to a person's body as a whole, but only to a person himself or herself. One is inclined to urge that it is *I* who think and feel, *not* my brain or body, even if I need to *have* a brain and body in order to be able to think and feel. (I shall say more in defence of this view in chapter 10.) The second and, I think, more immediately compelling reason is that the *persistence-conditions* of persons appear to be quite unlike those of anything such as a human body or brain. By the 'persistence-conditions' of objects (or 'substances') of a certain kind, I mean the conditions under which an object of that kind continues to survive as an object of that kind. A human body will continue to survive just so long as it consists of living cells which are suitably organised so as to sustain the normal biological functions of the body, such as respiration and digestion; and much the same is true of any individual bodily organ, such as the brain. However, it is not at all evident that I, as a person, could not survive the demise of my body and brain. One needn't appeal here, as Descartes does, to the supposed possibility that I could survive in an altogether disembodied state. That possibility is indeed very hard to establish. All that one need appeal to is the possibility that I might *exchange* my body or brain for another one, perhaps even not composed of organic tissue at all but of quite different materials. For example, one might envisage the possibility of my brain cells being gradually and systematically replaced by electronic circuits, in such way as to sustain whatever function it is that those cells serve in enabling me to feel and think. If, at the end of such a process of replacement, I were still to exist as the same subject of experience or person as before, then I would have survived the demise of my present organic brain and so could not be identical with it. (Again, I shall discuss this sort of argument more fully in chapter 10.)

If this reasoning is persuasive, it supports a version of substance dualism according to which a person is *distinct* from his or her body, but is nonetheless something which, like the body, possesses physical characteristics, such as shape and mass. An analogy which may be helpful here is that provided by the relationship between a bronze statue and the lump of bronze of which it is composed. The statue, it seems, cannot be identical with the lump of bronze, because the statue may well have come into existence later than the lump did and has persistence-conditions which are different from those of the lump: for instance, the statue would cease to survive if the lump were squashed flat, but the lump would continue to survive in these circumstances. However, the statue, although distinct from the lump, is none the less like it in having physical characteristics such as shape and mass: indeed, while it is composed of that lump, the statue has, of course, exactly the same shape and mass as the lump does. So too, it may be suggested, a person can have exactly the same shape and mass as his or her body does, without being identical with that body. However, the analogy may not be perfect. The statue is *composed* by the lump. Do we want to say that a person is, similarly, *composed* by his or her body? Perhaps not, for the following reason.

First, let us observe that, so long as the lump composes the statue, every part of the lump is a part of the statue: for example, every particle of bronze in the lump is a part of the statue. However, the reverse seems not to be the case: it doesn't seem correct to say that every part of the statue is a part of the lump of bronze. Thus, for instance, if the statue is a statue of a man, then the statue's arm will be one of its parts and yet it doesn't seem correct to say that the statue's arm is a part of the lump of bronze, even though it is correct to say that a part of the lump of bronze *composes* the arm. For the part of the lump of bronze which composes the statue's arm is not *identical* with the statue's arm, any more than the whole lump of bronze is identical with the statue. So the statue and the lump do not have exactly the same parts – which, of course, is an additional reason for saying that they are not identical with one another. Indeed, if they *did* have exactly the same parts, this would be a good reason for saying that they *were* identical with one another, because it is a widely accepted principle of mereology – the logic of part–whole relations – that things which have exactly the same parts are identical with one another.[4] Suppose that this prin-

---

[4] For a comprehensive modern treatment of mereology, see Peter Simons, *Parts: A Study in Ontology* (Oxford: Clarendon Press, 1987). I discuss part–whole relations more fully in my *Kinds of Being: A Study of Individuation, Identity and the Logic of*

ciple is correct, then, and turn to the case of a person and his or her body. If a person is *composed* by his or her body but not identical with it, then, it seems, by analogy with the statue and the lump of bronze, every part of the body must be a part of the person but not every part of the person can be part of the body: that is to say, the person must have certain parts *in addition to* parts of his or her body. However, it is very far from evident what these supplementary parts of the person could be, given that we have abandoned any suggestion that a person has an immaterial soul. It will not do to cite such items as a person's *arm*, for this *is*, of course, a part of the person's body. In this respect, the analogy with the statue and the lump of bronze breaks down, because the statue's arm plausibly is *not* a part of the lump. So, on the plausible assumption that a person has no parts which are not parts of his or her body – and yet is not identical with his or her body – it seems that we must deny that a person is *composed* by his or her body.

ARE PERSONS SIMPLE SUBSTANCES?

Now, if the preceding line of reasoning is correct, then we can reach a more remarkable conclusion, namely, that Descartes was right, after all, in thinking that he is a simple substance, altogether lacking any parts. The argument is simply this. First, we have argued that a person is not *identical* with his or her body nor with any part of it, on the grounds that persons and bodily items have different persistence-conditions. Secondly, we have argued that a person is not *composed* by his or her body nor – we may add – by any part of it. Our reason for saying this is that there appear to be no parts that a person could have *other than* parts of his or her body. However, if a person were to have as parts *only* parts of his or her body, then, according to the mereological principle

---

Sortal Terms (Oxford: Blackwell, 1989), ch. 6. Of course, we should not assume that principles of mereology, even if they are widely accepted ones, are immune to criticism.

mentioned earlier, it would follow, after all, that that person *would* be identical either with his or her body as a whole or with some part of it (depending on whether the parts in question were *all* the parts of the body or just *some* of them). And we have already ruled out any such identity. Consequently, a person can have *no parts at all* of which he or she is composed: a person must be a simple substance. But notice that this argument proceeds in the opposite direction to that in which Descartes argues. He argues from the premise that a person is a simple substance (together with certain other premises) to the conclusion that a person is not identical with his or her body, whereas we have just argued from the premise that a person is not identical with his or her body (together with certain other premises) to the conclusion that a person is a simple substance.

Of course, some philosophers might see the foregoing argument as a *reductio ad absurdum* of one or more of its premises, most likely the premise that a person is not identical with his or her body nor with any part of it. They will urge that it is just obvious that a human person has parts and that the only parts of a person are bodily parts, arguing thence to the conclusion that a person is identical with his or her body or some distinguished part of it. However, I don't think it really is obvious that a person has parts. That, perhaps, is why it is not easy for us to make clear sense of the notion of 'dividing a person in two'. If we remove any part of a person's body, it seems that either we are left with one person who is the same whole person as before or else we are left with no person at all. There are, of course, various science-fiction scenarios in which a single person is envisaged as dividing into two distinct persons, perhaps as a consequence of brain-bisection and transplantation. But whether we can really make sense of such stories is a matter for debate, to which we shall return in chapter 10. Again, there are actual cases of so-called 'multiple personality' syndrome in which, apparently, several different persons or subjects of experience manifest themselves within a single human body – and these different subjects are sometimes described as having resulted from the fragmentation of what was originally a single subject or person. But how literally one can interpret such descriptions of these cases is also a matter for debate. Uncontentious examples of the division of one person into two or more different persons are simply not available. When a human mother gives birth to a child, it is indeed uncontentious that we begin with one person and end up with two: but it is certainly not uncontentious that this happens as a result of one person, the mother, dividing into two.

However, there is another objection to the claim that persons are simple substances, at least if this is combined with the claim that persons share with their bodies such physical characteristics as shape and height. For if persons are spatially extended, must they not be divisible into distinct parts – for instance, must I not have a left half and a right half? If that is so, does it not follow that anyone who maintains that a person is a simple substance must agree with Descartes that persons lack physical characteristics and thus are *immaterial* substances? No, it doesn't follow. For to accept that I have a left half and a right half is not to accept that these are parts of me into which I am divisible and which together compose me, in the way in which my body is composed of cells into which it is divisible. My 'left half' and 'right half' are not items which could, even in principle, exist independently of me, in the way in which individual cells of my body could exist independently of it: they are not, as we might put it, independent substances in their own right and so not items of which I am *composed*. Rather, they are mere abstractions, whose identity depends essentially upon their relation to me as the single person whose 'halves' they are.

I don't expect anyone to be completely convinced, on the basis of what I have said so far, that the non-Cartesian version of substance dualism sketched above is correct.[5] But I

---

[5] For a fuller exposition of the kind of non-Cartesian substance dualism talked about here, see my *Subjects of Experience* (Cambridge: Cambridge University Press, 1996), ch. 2. This position is similar in some ways to the view of persons defended by P. F. Strawson in his book *Individuals: An Essay in Descriptive Metaphysics* (London: Methuen, 1959), ch. 3, although Strawson would not happily describe himself as a 'dualist'.

hope at least to have demonstrated that questions concerning the ontological status of subjects of experience and their relations to their bodies are complex ones which require careful thought. Off-hand dismissals of substance dualism, treating 'Cartesian' dualism as the only version of it that is available, are not helpful. (I shall return to some of the issues raised here in chapter 10, when I discuss problems of personal identity.)

CONCEPTUAL OBJECTIONS TO DUALISTIC INTERACTION

Cartesian substance dualism is a form of *interactionist* dualism: that is, it maintains that mental states of a subject or person may and often do interact causally with physical states of that person's body, both causing such states and being caused by them. And in this respect the theory is fully in agreement with common sense. Unless we are philosophers, we unquestioningly believe that, for instance, damage to one's foot can cause one to feel pain and that a desire to raise one's arm can have the effect of that arm's going up. But for many critics of Cartesian dualism, its interactionism is its Achilles' heel. These critics hold that, because Cartesian dualism regards mental states as states of a wholly non-physical substance, it faces grave difficulties in maintaining that such states are causes and effects of physical states. What, exactly, are these supposed difficulties? They are of two types, one conceptual and the other empirical.

The alleged conceptual difficulties centre upon the contention that we cannot really make sense of there being causal transactions between items as radically different in nature from one another as the dualist conceives mental and physical states to be. The Cartesian dualist treats the two kinds of states as having virtually nothing in common – apart, perhaps, from their existence in time and their alleged capacity to enter into causal relationships. According to the Cartesian dualist, thoughts and feelings, being states of an immaterial substance altogether lacking location in physical space, must themselves lack location in physical space. So how, it may be

asked, can such mental states act upon or be acted upon by
the physical states of a particular body? Perhaps the assumption here is that causation must always be *local*: that there
can be no 'action at a distance', much less action between
something located in physical space and something which
lacks physical location altogether. Another assumption may
be that whenever a causal transaction takes place, some
property of the cause must be transmitted to the effect – as,
for example, when motion in one billiard ball gives rise to
motion in another upon impact, or when heat in a poker gives
rise to heat in some water into which the poker is plunged.
And then the objection to Cartesian dualism would be that,
since it treats mental and physical states as having virtually
no properties in common and hence no properties which
could be transmitted between them, it leaves itself no scope
for saying that there can be causal transactions between
mental and physical states.

These objections are not particularly convincing. The idea
that causation must be 'local' was effectively abandoned by
the Newtonian theory of gravitation, some 300 years ago.
And although the theory was criticised by contemporaries as
being 'occult' on this account, these criticisms were rightly
soon laid aside. It is true that some modern physicists propose that gravitational force is carried by particles known as
'gravitons', which would imply that gravitational effects are,
after all, 'local' rather than being the results of 'action at a
distance'. But the point is that this proposal is just part of
an empirical theory – one which has yet to be strongly confirmed – not a consequence of a *conceptual* constraint on the
intelligibility of the notion of gravitational attraction. Similarly, the claim that in any causal transaction some property
must be transmitted from cause to effect does not express a
conceptual truth. Indeed, it even appears to have many
scientific counterexamples. For instance, motion in a body
may be produced by a cause which does not itself involve
motion, as when an electrically charged object moves under
the influence of an electromagnetic field. Of course, it may
be said that even here something *is* transmitted from cause

to effect, namely, *energy*, which may be converted from one form to another (for instance, from potential energy into kinetic energy). But the point, once again, is that this is not a consequence of a *conceptual* constraint on the intelligibility of the notion of such a causal transaction, but at most a consequence of an empirically well-confirmed theory concerning transactions of this kind.

David Hume long ago gave the decisive answer to all such conceptual objections to the possibility of dualistic mental–physical causation. This is that there are simply no *a priori* constraints on what *kinds* of states or events can enter into causal relationships with one another. As Hume himself puts it at one point: 'to consider the matter *a priori*, any thing may produce any thing'.[6] We discover what *does* produce what by *empirical* means, not least by observing that certain kinds of states or events are 'constantly conjoined' with other kinds of states or events. We can agree with Hume about this, even if we do not agree with him about how we should *define* causation (if, indeed, we think that it can be defined at all). Commentators dispute amongst themselves over precisely how Hume himself thought that causation should be defined, but the 'Humean' definition is widely taken to be something like this: to say that state S_1 caused (or was a cause of) state S_2 is to say that S_1 was followed by S_2 and that every state of the same kind as S_1 is followed by a state of the same kind as S_2.[7] We may concur with critics of this 'Humean' definition of causation in terms of 'constant conjunction' that it fails to capture important features of our concept of causation – for instance, that it fails to capture our conviction that, if state S_1 caused state S_2, then, other things being equal, if S_1 had

---

[6] See David Hume, *A Treatise of Human Nature* (1739–40), ed. L. A. Selby-Bigge and P. H. Nidditch (Oxford: Clarendon Press, 1978), Book I, Part IV, Section V: the sentence quoted in the text is taken from p. 247 of this edition.

[7] For a thought-provoking examination of Hume's views about causation in general, denying that Hume himself accepted a 'constant conjunction' theory of causation of the sort described in the text, see Galen Strawson, *The Secret Connexion: Causation, Realism, and David Hume* (Oxford: Clarendon Press, 1989). For an alternative account of Hume's position, see Tom L. Beauchamp and Alexander Rosenberg, *Hume and the Problem of Causation* (New York: Oxford University Press, 1981).

not existed, S_2 would not have existed either. But I think that we should, none the less, agree with Hume that, as I put it a moment ago, there are no *a priori* constraints on what *kinds* of states can be causally related to one another.

EMPIRICAL OBJECTIONS TO DUALISTIC INTERACTION

So let us turn to the empirical objections to Cartesian interactionism. These are best approached by seeing first why some of Descartes's contemporaries raised objections of this kind against his account of psychophysical causation. Descartes supposed that interaction between the non-physical self and its body takes effect in a specific organ situated in the middle of the brain, the pineal gland. This seemed to him the most probable seat of mind–brain interaction, not only because of the gland's central location, but also because it is unique, whereas many other brain-structures are duplicated in the brain's two hemispheres. Hence, he thought, the pineal gland could readily serve as a unitary control-centre for the whole brain and nervous system. (With the benefit of hindsight, we now know that the pineal gland serves no such purpose, but Descartes's hypothesis was not unreasonable in his own day.) Descartes regarded the nervous system as something like a network of pipes and valves operating in accordance with hydraulic principles, with the nerve filaments conducting quantities of so-called 'animal spirits' to and fro throughout the body. These animal spirits were thought to be a rarefied and highly motile fluid, capable of flowing freely and rapidly through tiny pores in the nerve filaments. (Thus, the term 'spirits', in this context, was certainly not intended to denote something *immaterial* in nature.) Descartes believed that, when these animal spirits flowed through the nerve filaments in the region of the pineal gland, the non-physical self could subtly alter their direction of flow, thus giving rise to variations in their movements. These variations, after being conveyed by nerve filaments to the body's extremities, could ultimately bring about concomitant variations in the movements of a person's limbs. In the reverse direction, movements in the animal spirits at the body's extremities, brought about by impact with external objects, could be conveyed to the central region of the brain and there – so Descartes supposed – cause a person to undergo appropriate experiences, such as those of pain or pleasure.

An important feature of Descartes's theory was that it held that the self acted upon its body only by altering the *direction* of motion of the animal spirits, not by imparting new motion to them. Indeed, Descartes believed that the total 'quantity of motion' in the physical universe never changes, but is only redistributed amongst material bodies as they interact with each other upon impact. Thus, in a collision between two material bodies, one which was formerly at rest might begin to move, but only at the expense of the other body losing some of its 'quantity of motion'. The principle that Descartes was advocating here was an early form of *conservation law*. Modern physics recognises several such laws, the most important being the law of the conservation of momentum and the law of the conservation of energy. Unfortunately – as Descartes's near-contemporary Leibniz appreciated – Descartes's conservation law is incompatible with these modern laws.[8] In particular, Descartes did not seem to realise that one cannot alter the *direction* of motion of a material body without altering its *momentum*, which is a conserved quantity according to the modern laws. A body's momentum is the product of its mass and its velocity. And velocity is a *vector* rather than a scalar quantity. What this means is that if a body is undergoing a change in its direction of motion, then it is undergoing a change of velocity and hence a change of momentum, even if it is moving at a constant speed. Thus, for example, a body which is moving in a circular path at a

---

[8] Leibniz's criticisms of Cartesian interactionism are interestingly discussed by R. S. Woolhouse in his 'Leibniz's Reaction to Cartesian Interactionism', *Proceedings of the Aristotelian Society* 86 (1985/86), pp. 69–82 and by Daniel Garber in his 'Mind, Body, and the Laws of Nature in Descartes and Leibniz', *Midwest Studies in Philosophy* 8 (1983), pp. 105–33. I myself go more fully into some of the issues raised in the text concerning the conservation laws of physics in my *Subjects of Experience*, pp. 56–63.

constant rate is none the less constantly undergoing a change in its velocity. The modern laws of motion, first postulated by Newton, state that a massive body can only undergo a change of velocity if it is acted upon by a corresponding force. Hence, it appears that these laws imply that any change of direction in the motion of the animal spirits – which Descartes thought could be brought about by the non-physical self – would in fact have to be a consequence of some *force* acting upon the animal spirits: and it is hard to see how the Cartesian self, being non-physical, could be the source of any such force. In the light of this apparent difficulty, Leibniz himself rejected interactionism in favour of *parallelism* – the doctrine that mental and physical states never interact causally, but merely 'keep in step' with one another in accordance with a divinely preordained plan. However, an alternative and perhaps more plausible response is to accept that mental and physical states interact causally, but to reject the dualist claim that mental states are quite distinct from physical states. Instead, one could espouse the *physicalist* claim that mental states just *are* – that is, are identical with – certain physical states, most plausibly certain neural states of the brain.

THE CAUSAL CLOSURE ARGUMENT

Of course, the preceding line of argument against Cartesian interactionism not only appeals to quite specific empirical premises, in the form of the conservation laws of modern physics, but also has as its target the quite specific mechanism of mind–brain interaction proposed by Descartes himself. Thus, it leaves at least two possible escape-routes for the would-be dualist advocate of mind–brain interaction. One is to challenge the presumed correctness of the laws in question, though this might seem a foolhardy venture in view of their well-entrenched status in modern physics. The other is to propose some quite different system of causal interaction between mental and physical states. This then raises the question of whether the physicalist might not be able to present some much more general line of empirical argument against dualist interactionism, which would rule out any conceivable system of mind–brain interaction of a dualist character. In the view of many present-day physicalists, just such a line of argument is indeed available and it is one which is, moreover, fairly simple in form.[9] The argument has three premises, as follows.

(1) At every time at which a physical state has a cause, it has a fully sufficient physical cause. (Call this premise *the principle of the causal closure of the physical*.)

(2) Some physical states have mental states amongst their causes. (Call this premise *the principle of psychophysical causation*.)

(3) When a physical state has a mental state amongst its causes, it is rarely if ever causally overdetermined by that mental state and some other physical state. (Call this premise *the principle of causal non-overdetermination*.)

These premises call for a few explanatory comments. Premise (1) means that if P is a physical state which has a cause existing at a certain time t, then there is a non-empty set of physical states, all of them existing at t, such that (a) each of these states is a cause of P and (b) collectively these states are causally sufficient for P. (To say that a number of physical states are *collectively causally sufficient* for another physical state, P, is to say that, given that all of those states exist, it follows of causal necessity that P also exists.) Premise (2) is self-explanatory. Premise (3) rules out the possibility that, whenever a mental state M is a cause of a physical state P, there is another physical state Q such that (a) Q is a cause of P and yet (b) even if one of the two states M and Q had not existed, the other would still have sufficed, in the circumstances, to cause P to exist. Causal overdetermination of the kind generally ruled out by premise (3) can be illustrated (using a non-psychophysical example) as follows. Suppose

[9] A good example of a version of this argument may be found in David Papineau's recent book, *Philosophical Naturalism* (Oxford: Blackwell, 1993), ch. 1.

that two assassins independently shoot at the same time and both bullets inflict fatal wounds upon their victim, who promptly dies: in this case, the victim's death is causally over-determined by the two acts of shooting, since (a) each act is a cause of the death and yet (b) even if one of the acts had not existed, the other would still have sufficed, in the circum-stances, to cause the death. Premise (3) rules out the pos-sibility that, as a general rule, mental states cause physical states rather in the way in which one of these acts of shooting causes the death, that is, in such a way that the physical effects of those mental states simultaneously have independ-ent but fully sufficient physical causes.

I shall consider in a moment the question of how plausible these three premises are, but first we must see what they are supposed to entail. Physicalists take them to entail the following conclusion:

(4) At least some mental states are identical with certain physical states.

How does (4) follow from premises (1), (2) and (3)? In the following way, it would seem. Suppose, in accordance with premise (2), that M is a mental state, existing at a time t, and that M is a cause of a certain physical state, P. From premise (1), we can infer that there is a non-empty set of physical states, all of them existing at t, which are collectively causally sufficient for P. Call these physical states $P_1, P_2, \ldots P_n$. Finally, suppose, in accordance with premise (3), that P is not causally overdetermined by M and any one of these physical states. That is to say, suppose it is not the case that there is one of these physical states, say P_i, such that if either one of the states M and P_i had not existed, the other would still have sufficed, in conjunction with the remaining physical states in the set, to cause P to exist. Then it would seem that we have no option but to *identify* the mental state M with one or other of the physical states $P_1, P_2, \ldots P_n$. For suppose that M is *not* identical with any of these states. We have assumed that M is a cause of P but we have also assumed that the physical states $P_1, P_2, \ldots P_n$ are collectively causally sufficient for P. Hence we can apparently infer that even if M had not existed but all of $P_1, P_2, \ldots P_n$ had still existed – which must be a possibility given that M is not identical with any of $P_1, P_2, \ldots P_n$ – then $P_1, P_2, \ldots P_n$ would still have sufficed to cause P to exist. But this is to imply that P is causally overdetermined by M and one or more of $P_1, P_2, \ldots P_n$, contrary to what we have hitherto assumed. Hence we must reject the supposition that M is not identical with any one of $P_1, P_2, \ldots P_n$ and conclude that (4) is true.

OBJECTIONS TO THE CAUSAL CLOSURE ARGUMENT

I shall not question the validity of the foregoing argument, but we need to examine its premises carefully before accepting it. Obviously, advocates of dualist interactionism, who are the targets of the argument, will not want to query premise (2), since they accept it themselves. But they might well be wary of accepting premise (3), once they see what it leads to. Perhaps they would be well advised to maintain that systematic causal overdetermination is a pervasive feature of psychophysical causation.[10] It is not obvious that this is an untenable position to adopt, although to adopt it merely in order to evade the unwelcome conclusion of the physicalist's argument would be blatantly *ad hoc*. To make this position credible, the dualist needs to find some independent reason for supposing that such causal overdetermination is commonplace – and it is far from clear what that reason might be. The dualist's best hope, then, would seem to lie in challenging premise (1), the principle of the causal closure of the physical. As I have stated the principle here, it is an extremely strong one which – the dualist might urge – cannot plausibly be claimed to be an indisputable implication of currently accepted empirical science. Premise (1) must be carefully distinguished from a weaker and correspondingly more plausible principle, namely,

---

[10] For a defence of such a position, see Eugene Mills, 'Interactionism and Overdetermination', *American Philosophical Quarterly* 33 (1996), pp. 105–17.

(1*) Every physical state has a fully sufficient physical cause.

To distinguish them, we could call (1) and (1*), respectively, the *strong* and the *weak* principle of the causal closure of the physical. I should perhaps point out that, despite these titles, there is one respect in which (1*) is, in fact, stronger than (1). This is that (1*) implies, as (1) does not, that there are no *uncaused* physical states. That assumption is not altogether uncontroversial, as we shall see when we come to discuss the issue of free will and determinism in chapter 9. It also raises cosmological and theological questions of whether there was a 'first' cause. However, I shall set aside any such concerns here. (In particular, I shall ignore the fact that modern quantum physics suggests that at least some physical states do *not* have fully sufficient physical causes. Perhaps, however, it is safe to ignore this fact in the present context, given that quantum physics is chiefly concerned with physical phenomena on the atomic scale, rather than at the level of neural structure and function in the brain.) We shall see in a moment precisely in what sense (1) *is* stronger than (1*).

If we replace (1) by (1*) in the physicalist argument examined above, we can no longer draw the physicalist conclusion, (4), that at least some mental states are identical with physical states. The explanation of this involves the fact that causation is a transitive relation. Causation is transitive inasmuch as if a state S_1 is a cause of a state S_2, and S_2 is a cause of a state S_3, then it follows that S_1 is a cause of S_3. Moreover, if S_1 is a *fully sufficient* cause of S_2, and S_2 is a *fully sufficient* cause of S_3, then S_1 is a *fully sufficient* cause of S_3. However – and this is the crucial point – if S_1 and S_2 are thus *both* fully sufficient causes of S_3, because S_1 is a fully sufficient cause of S_2 and S_2 is a fully sufficient cause of S_3, this does not imply that S_3 is *causally overdetermined* by S_1 and S_2. Consequently, the following situation is perfectly consistent with the truth of principles (1*), (2) and (3): M may be a mental state which is *not* identical with any physical state and yet which is also a cause of a certain physical state, P. In this case, principle (2) is obviously satisfied. But principle (1*), the weak principle of the causal closure of the physical, may also be satisfied in respect of the physical state P. All that is required is that the mental state M should itself have a fully sufficient physical cause, say Q: if it does, then, by the transitivity of causation, Q is a cause of P and, moreover, may evidently either itself be, or else be part of, a *fully sufficient* physical cause of P. Furthermore, for the reason just explained, nothing here implies that P is *causally overdetermined* by M and any other cause of P, so that principle (3) is also satisfied. Thus, even an advocate of dualist interactionism could happily accept the weak principle of the causal closure of the physical, (1*). Indeed, a dualist who espoused a doctrine of *emergentism* concerning the mental would have a positive reason for endorsing (1*). Emergentists hold that mental states have not always existed in the spacetime universe and that at one time all states of the universe were purely physical – for instance, at the time of the so-called 'Big Bang' when the universe was created. They further hold that mental states have come into existence as a result of the natural evolution of highly complex biological entities, rather than through any kind of divine intervention by a being who exists 'outside' the spacetime universe, such as God. Consequently, they hold that all mental states ultimately have fully sufficient causes which are purely physical in character. What we can now see is that this emergentist doctrine is consistent not only with dualist interactionism, but also with the weak principle of the causal closure of the physical.[11]

The question that we must ask ourselves now is whether we have any reason to suppose that not only the weak but also the *strong* principle of the causal closure of the physical is correct. The difference between them is precisely this: the strong principle requires that at *every* time at which it has a cause, any physical state has a fully sufficient physical cause, whereas the weak principle requires only that at *some* time at which it has a cause, any physical state has a fully sufficient

[11] I defend an emergentist doctrine of dualist interactionism in my *Subjects of Experience*, ch. 3.

physical cause. The sort of consideration which supports the weak principle – namely, that, as far as we know, the spacetime universe at its beginning contained only physical states and has not been subject to intervention from 'outside' since then – certainly does not serve to support the strong principle. Moreover, we need to appreciate what a *very* strong claim the strong principle makes. It implies, for instance, that if a physical state has a cause *one nanosecond* before it comes into existence, then it has a fully sufficient physical cause *at that time*. It is not at all clear to me what currently available empirical evidence could be taken to support such a strong claim quite generally. But perhaps we should not be surprised that it is only possible to mount a decisive argument against dualist interactionism if one starts from a premise, like (1), which already embodies strong physicalist presumptions. Knock-down arguments in philosophy often appear, upon closer examination, to be implicitly question-begging. That is why fundamental philosophical disputes, such as that between dualism and physicalism, stubbornly refuse to go away. Many dualist philosophers find it so incredible that a mental state, such as a feeling or a thought, could just *be* – that is, be identical with – a physical state, such as a state of neuronal activity in the brain, that they would find it more compelling to argue from (2), (3) and the *negation* of (4) to the *negation* of (1) than to argue, as the physicalist does, from (1), (2) and (3) to (4). Both arguments are valid, if either is: the only question is which set of premises is the more plausible and the more defensible. But that question, I think, is at present still an open one.

OTHER ARGUMENTS FOR AND AGAINST PHYSICALISM

The causal closure argument is not the only general argument that has been advanced in favour of identifying mental states or events with physical states or events. Another well-known argument in favour of this identity thesis has been advanced by Donald Davidson.[12] Like the causal closure argument, Davidson's argument has three premises, the first of which is similar to premise (2) of the causal closure argument:

(5) Some mental events interact causally with physical events. (Davidson calls this premise *the principle of causal interaction*.)

Davidson's remaining two premises are these:

(6) Events related as cause and effect fall under strict deterministic laws. (Davidson calls this premise *the principle of the nomological character of causality*.)

(7) There are no strict deterministic psychophysical laws. (Davidson calls this premise *the principle of the anomalism of the mental*.)

Davidson's conclusion, similar to the conclusion (4) of the causal closure argument, is that at least some mental events are identical with physical events. To see how the argument works, suppose that a certain mental event, M, causes a certain physical event, P, in line with premise (5). It follows, by premise (6), that M and P must be characterisable in terms which allow them to fall under a strict deterministic law. But according to premise (7), there are no such laws under which M falls in virtue of being characterisable in mentalistic terms, so that it would seem that M must also be characterisable in *physical* terms and thus qualify as a physical event. Interesting though Davidson's argument is, I shall not examine here his reasons for advancing premises (6) and (7), which are evidently controversial – even more so, indeed, than premises (1) and (3) of the causal closure argument. It

---

[12] See Donald Davidson, 'Mental Events', in L. Foster and J. W. Swanson (eds.), *Experience and Theory* (London: Duckworth, 1970), reprinted in Davidson's *Essays on Actions and Events* (Oxford: Clarendon Press, 1980). Davidson's version of the identity theory is couched in terms of *events* rather than *states*, because he regards causation as a relation between events: but for our present purposes nothing of significance turns on the distinction between events and states.

is debatable whether, whenever one event causes another, there is always some general causal law under which this particular causal interaction may be subsumed as an instance.[13] And it is debatable whether, even in physics, there are strict – that is, exceptionless – and deterministic laws of causal interaction.[14] In view of these doubts, physicalists might be better advised to pin their hopes on the causal closure argument, contestable though it is.

On the other side, there are general arguments which have been advanced *against* the thesis that mental events or states are identical with physical events or states.[15] Some physicalists have urged that, just as science has revealed to us that water is simply H_2O and that heat in a gas is simply the mean kinetic energy of its constituent molecules, so neuroscience will one day reveal to us that pain, say, is simply a certain neural state, such as the stimulation of C-fibres. These physicalists believe, then, that the discovery that pain just is – that is, is identical with – a certain neural state will be an empirical or *a posteriori* one, resembling discoveries that science has already made in many other fields of enquiry. However, there seems to be an important disanalogy between the proposed identification of pain with something like C-fibre stimulation and the other 'scientific' identifications exemplified a moment ago. Take the identification of water with H_2O. We can readily understand why it took empirical enquiry to establish this identity, because we can easily imagine encountering a substance which to all outward appear-

---

[13] For scepticism on this point, see G. E. M. Anscombe, 'Causality and Determination', in her *Metaphysics and the Philosophy of Mind*. Of course, the 'Humean' definition of causation in terms of 'constant conjunction', discussed earlier in this chapter, does imply the truth of Davidson's premise (6): but that definition is itself highly controversial.

[14] For doubts on this score, see Nancy Cartwright, *How the Laws of Physics Lie* (Oxford: Clarendon Press, 1983).

[15] The thoughts which follow are partly inspired by Saul A. Kripke's *Naming and Necessity* (Oxford: Blackwell, 1980), first published in G. Harman and D. Davidson (eds.), *Semantics of Natural Language* (Dordrecht: D. Reidel, 1972): see especially pp. 144–55. I should remark that, while I am ignoring for present purposes the distinction between 'type-type' and 'token-token' identity theories, this is something that I shall have more to say about in chapter 3.

ance *looks* just like water, but which turns out upon investigation to have a quite different chemical constitution. This pseudo-water, as we might call it, would not *be* water, given that the chemists are right in telling us that water is in fact H_2O. But now suppose, in like manner, that future neuroscientists tell us that pain just *is* the stimulation of C-fibres. And suppose, too, that we were to encounter a mental state, perhaps in some creature belonging to an alien species, which *felt* just like pain but which, none the less, could *not* be identified with the stimulation of C-fibres – because, say, this creature simply does not have C-fibres. Then it follows, if the analogy is sound, that we should have to say that what this creature feels is not, after all, *pain* at all, but only 'pseudo-pain'. But that seems absurd, because what *feels* like pain surely *is* pain. And the same absurdity would threaten to beset us *whatever* physical state the neuroscientists proposed to identify with pain, thus calling into question the intelligibility of *any* such identification. It is very tempting to conclude from this that a mental state such as pain simply *cannot* be identified with any physical state whatever.

Of course, it might be urged on behalf of the physicalists that if neuroscientists *do* one day discover that pain just is the stimulation of C-fibres, then for that very reason we shall *not* be able to encounter a creature having a mental state which feels just like pain even though it lacks C-fibres. The fact that we can *imagine* encountering such a creature is no guarantee that such a creature really *could* exist because – as we saw when we were discussing Descartes's 'conceivability argument' for the distinction between himself and his body – even something which is logically impossible may be 'imaginable'. However, physicalists who respond in this manner at least owe us an explanation of why it should be that imagination is especially prone to mislead us in this sort of case. Indeed, they owe us a good deal more than that, because what is at issue is the very intelligibility of identifying pain with some physical state. Until that issue is resolved, it seems idle to speculate about what we could or could not encounter *if* neuroscientists discover that pain 'just is' the stimulation of C-fibres, since such speculation appears to presume that we can, after all, make sense of such a discovery being made. More generally, the point is that anyone who wishes to propose a certain kind of theoretical identification owes us a demonstration that such an identification is in principle *possible* – and it is not at all clear that physicalists in the philosophy of mind have yet succeeded in doing this. Here is another analogy: no one would be remotely satisfied if some Pythagorean philosopher were to tell us that he had discovered a wealth of empirical evidence supporting the thesis that the things which we think of as being material objects really 'just are' *numbers*. We should demand, first, that he explain to us how such an identification even *makes sense*. To many of their opponents, physicalists who propose that mental states really 'just are' physical states seem to be in much the same sort of position as this hypothetical Pythagorean.[16]

CONCLUSIONS

In this chapter, we have looked at a number of fundamental metaphysical problems in the philosophy of mind, beginning with the question of how persons, or subjects of experience, are related to their physical bodies. We saw that 'Cartesian' substance dualism, which holds that persons are wholly immaterial things capable of existing independently of the bodies which they may happen to 'inhabit', has no very compelling argument in its favour. But we also saw that there are reasons for doubting that persons can simply be *identified* with their bodies, or with any distinguished part of their bodies, such as their brains. It may be that a person is related to his or her body somewhat in the way in which a bronze statue is related to the lump of bronze which composes it –

---

[16] For this analogy, see P. T. Geach, *Truth, Love and Immortality: An Introduction to McTaggart's Philosophy* (London: Hutchinson, 1979), p. 134. I say more about the conceptual difficulties involved in trying to identify mental states and events with physical states and events in my *Kinds of Being*, pp. 113–14 and pp. 132–3.

though even this analogy would appear to be imperfect. Perhaps we should see personal 'embodiment' as a unique kind of relationship in its own right, one which can be reduced neither to a mere causal relationship, nor to identity, nor to composition. (Perhaps, indeed, this is what the historical Descartes had in mind in talking of the relation of 'substantial union' between self and body.) It would be facile to suppose that a reductionist account of the relationship of embodiment *must* be available, even in principle. *Some* relationships, after all, must be primitive and irreducible and we may in the end have to accept that embodiment is one of these. On the other hand, we should not be too quick to accept this conclusion, either, while we continue to lack a convincing argument that a reductionist account is unattainable. At present, then, it seems that we should retain an open mind about this question.

The other main question which we examined was whether mental states ought to be identified with physical states, such as states of neuronal activity in the brain, given the plausible assumptions that mental states stand in causal relations to such physical states and yet that systematic causal overdetermination is not a feature of psychophysical causation. Here we saw that, while there is no satisfactory *a priori* argument against interactionist dualism, Descartes's own favoured system of psychophysical causation seems to fall foul of the currently accepted conservation laws of physics. However, we also saw that it is rather more difficult to rule out interactionist dualism in a perfectly general way, by appealing to some version of the principle of the causal closure of the physical, because only a rather strong version of that principle will suffice for this purpose and such a version of it cannot claim to be strongly supported by currently available empirical evidence. Once again, then, it seems that we should keep an open mind about this question – especially in view of the issues raised, in the last section, about the very intelligibility of identifying mental states with physical states. That we have come to no firm conclusion about either of the main questions addressed in this chapter should not disconcert us unduly, however. These questions are amongst the most difficult in the whole of philosophy and it would be surprising if we had been able to resolve them conclusively when so many other able thinkers have failed to do so.

3

Mental states

In the previous chapter, we focused on two important meta-physical questions in the philosophy of mind. One was the question of whether persons or subjects of experience are identical with their physical bodies, or certain parts of those bodies, such as their brains. The other was the question of whether the mental states of persons, such as thoughts and feelings, are identical with certain physical states of their bodies, such as states of neuronal activity in their brains. Many materialists would endorse positive answers to both of these questions, although later in this chapter we shall encounter a species of materialism which denies that mental states, as we ordinarily conceive of them, really exist at all. But before we examine that position, it is worth remarking that, so long as one is a *realist* about mental states – that is, so long as one considers that states of thinking and feeling really do exist – one can, for many purposes, afford to remain neutral with regard to the question of whether or not mental states are identical with physical states. There are many issues in the philosophy of mind which we can usefully discuss without presuming to be able to resolve that question. And this is just as well, knowing as we now do how thorny a question it is. One of these issues is that of how we can best *characterise* and *classify* the various different kinds of mental state which, if we are realists, we believe to exist. So far we have been talking about mental states quite generally, without differentiating between them in any significant fashion. But in a detailed description of the mental lives of persons we need to be able to distinguish, in principled ways, between sensations, perceptions, beliefs, desires, intentions, fears, and many other kinds of mental state: and providing a satisfactory account of these distinctions is no easy matter. It is to the difficulties besetting that task that we shall turn in this chapter.

PROPOSITIONAL ATTITUDE STATES

Let us begin by considering those mental states that philosophers like to call *propositional attitude states*. For brevity, I shall refer to them as 'attitudinal states'. These include beliefs, desires, intentions, hopes and fears, to name but a few. A common feature of such states is that we may ascribe them to subjects of experience by using statements of the form '*S* ϕs that *p*'. Here '*S*' denotes a particular subject or person, '*p*' stands for some proposition – for example, the proposition that it is raining – and 'ϕ' represents any so-called verb of propositional attitude, such as 'believe', 'hope' or 'fear'. Such verbs are called 'verbs of propositional attitude' because each of them is considered to express a particular *attitude* which a subject may have towards a proposition. (What propositions *are* and how subjects *can* have 'attitudes' towards them are matters which we shall take up more fully in the next chapter.) Thus, the following sentences can all be used to ascribe attitudinal states to subjects: 'John believes that it is raining', 'Mary hopes that she has an umbrella', and 'Ann fears that she will get wet'. In each case, the 'that' clause expresses the *propositional content* of the attitudinal state which is being ascribed. A number of questions immediately arise concerning attitudinal states and our knowledge of them. For instance: what, exactly, makes a *belief*, say, different from a *hope* or a *fear*? One and the same subject may simultaneously possess two different attitudinal states with the same propositional content: for example, Ann may both *fear* that she will get wet and *believe* that she will get wet. What does this difference of 'attitude' to one and the same proposition amount to? Again, how do we *know* what attitudinal states another person possesses – indeed, how do we know what attitudinal states *we ourselves* possess? Notice here that knowledge itself is an attitudinal state, so that knowledge of someone's attitudinal states appears to be a 'second-order' attitudinal state – as in the case of John's knowing that Ann fears that she will get wet, or John's knowing that he himself believes that it is raining.

We may be inclined to think that there is no special problem about identifying our own attitudinal states, at least at the times at which we possess them. Surely, if I have any beliefs, desires, hopes or fears right now, then *I*, at least, must know what they are, even if no one else does. Descartes certainly seems to have assumed that this is so. But *how* do I know? Perhaps it will be suggested that I know by a process of 'reflection' or 'introspection', which somehow reveals to me what I am thinking and feeling. After all, if someone *asks* me whether I believe or desire such-and-such, I am usually able to reply fairly spontaneously, so it seems that I must have some sort of direct access to my own attitudinal states. On the other hand, perhaps the feeling of having such a direct or 'privileged' access to one's own attitudinal states is just an illusion. Perhaps I find out what I believe, for example, by hearing myself *express* my beliefs in words, whether out loud to other people or just *sotto voce* to myself. This would make my knowledge of my own beliefs no different in principle from my knowledge of other people's beliefs, which I commonly discover by hearing them express them. Of course, sometimes I can form a good idea of someone's beliefs on the basis of their *non*-verbal behaviour, as when I judge that John believes that it is raining when I see him open his umbrella. But perhaps the same is true, at times, with regard to my knowledge of my own beliefs – as when I surprise myself by the fact that I have taken a certain turning at a road junction and realise that I must believe that it will take me to my desired destination. (We shall explore the nature of self-knowledge more fully in chapter 10.)

BEHAVIOURISM AND ITS PROBLEMS

There are some philosophers who are extremely sceptical about the reliability – or, indeed, the very existence – of introspection as a source of knowledge about our own mental states. At its most extreme, this scepticism finds expression in the doctrine known as *behaviourism*. Behaviourists hold that the only sort of evidence that we can have concerning anyone's mental states, including our own, lies in people's outwardly observable behaviour, both verbal and non-verbal. 'Scientific' behaviourists take this view because they think that a science of mental states – which is what scientific psychology in part claims to be – ought only to rely upon objective empirical evidence which can be corroborated by many independent observers, whereas introspection is necessarily a private and subjective affair. But more radical behaviourists – those who are sometimes called 'logical' behaviourists – would go even further than this. They maintain that *what it is* to ascribe a mental state to a person is nothing more nor less than to ascribe to that person some appropriate *behavioural disposition*.[1] A 'behavioural disposition', in the sense understood here, is a person's tendency or propensity to behave in a certain way in certain specified circumstances. Thus, for instance, a logical behaviourist might suggest that to ascribe to John a belief that it is raining is simply to ascribe to him a disposition to do such things as: take an umbrella with him if he leaves the house, turn on the windscreen wipers if he is driving the car, assert that it is raining if he is asked what the weather is like – and so on. The list must, of course, be an open-ended one, since there is no limit to the ways in which someone might evince the belief in question. This sort of account is intended to apply not only to what we have been calling 'attitudinal' states, but also to what we might call *sensational* states, such as pain and nausea. To be in pain – for example, to feel a sharp twinge in one's big toe – is not to have some attitude towards a proposition: pains do not have 'propositional content'. But the logical behaviourist will once again contend that to ascribe to John

---

[1] A sophisticated version of logical behaviourism is developed by Gilbert Ryle in his *The Concept of Mind* (London: Hutchinson, 1949). See especially p. 129, for Ryle's account of belief.

a feeling of pain in his big toe is simply to ascribe to him a disposition to do such things as: wince and groan if the toe is touched, hobble along if he has to walk, assert that his toe hurts if he is asked how it feels – and so on. The list is, once again, an open-ended one.

Now, the very fact that such lists of behaviour are necessarily open-ended ones presents a problem for logical behaviourism. Take the list of activities associated with John's belief that it is raining. What can possibly be meant by saying that John has a disposition to do 'such things' as are on this list? What *unifies* the items on the list, other than the fact that they are the sorts of things that one might reasonably expect a person to do who believes that it is raining? It seems that one must *already understand* what it means to ascribe to someone a belief that it is raining in order to be able to generate the items on the list, so that the list cannot be used to *explain* what it means to ascribe to someone such a belief. Even setting aside this difficulty, however, there is another and still more serious problem which besets the logical behaviourist's account. Take again John's belief that it is raining. The problem is that someone may perfectly well possess this belief and yet fail to do *any* of the things on the associated list in the appropriate circumstances. Thus John may believe that it is raining and yet leave his umbrella at home when he goes out, fail to switch on the windscreen wipers when he is driving, deny that it is raining when he is asked about the weather, and so on. This is because how a person who possesses a certain belief behaves in given circumstances does not depend solely upon what that belief is, but also upon what *other* attitudinal states that person may happen to possess at the same time, such as his or her desires. John may, for instance, be unusual in that he *likes* to get wet in the rain and so never takes an umbrella with him when he believes that it is raining. Indeed, *whatever* behaviour the logical behaviourist attempts to represent as being characteristic of someone who believes that it is raining, it is possible to envisage a person who holds that belief and yet is *not* disposed to behave in that way, if only because such a person might have a very strong desire to deceive others into thinking that he or she does not hold that belief. The same is true with regard to a person's sensational states: one may feel a pain in one's big toe and yet suppress the kinds of behaviour which the logical behaviourist says are definitive of feeling such a pain, because one is determined to be stoical about it or does not want to appear weak. So we see that there can in fact be no such thing as behaviour that is uniquely characteristic of someone who possesses an attitudinal state with a given propositional content or a sensational state of a certain type. And consequently it is impossible to explain *what it means* for someone to possess such a state in terms of his or her supposed behavioural dispositions. 'Logical' behaviourism is clearly doomed to failure.

However, the failure of logical behaviourism still leaves untouched the weaker form of behaviourism mentioned earlier, which is espoused by 'scientific' behaviourists. This merely maintains that the only *evidence* on whose basis attitudinal and other mental states can be ascribed to subjects is behavioural evidence, that is, publicly available evidence of how people behave in various circumstances. We could perhaps call this 'epistemic' behaviourism, because it concerns our *knowledge* of mental states rather than the nature of those states themselves. Logical behaviourism entails epistemic behaviourism, but not *vice versa* – which is why I have described epistemic behaviourism as being the weaker doctrine. However, epistemic behaviourism, unlike logical behaviourism, does not offer us any account of what mental states *are*, so it needs to be supplemented by such an account – an account which must, of course, be consistent with what the epistemic behaviourist has to say concerning our *evidence* for the existence of mental states. Is a satisfactory account of this sort available? Many contemporary philosophers of mind would say that it is, in the form of a doctrine known as *functionalism*.

FUNCTIONALISM

Functionalism acknowledges the fact that it is impossible to identify types of mental state with types of behavioural disposition, but it still wishes to characterise mental states by reference to behaviour, albeit only indirectly. It tries to achieve this by characterising mental states in terms of the *causal roles* they are thought to play in determining how a subject behaves in different circumstances.[2] (Another term for 'causal role' in this sense is 'functional role': hence the name 'functionalism'.) According to functionalism, three different kinds of causal relationship can be involved in the make-up of a mental state's causal role. (Here, it should be emphasised, we are primarily talking about *types* of mental state, although by implication also about particular instances, or *tokens*, of those types: I shall say more about the type/token distinction in due course.) First, there are characteristic ways in which states of a subject's environment can cause that subject to have a certain type of mental state, as when injury to one's leg causes one to feel pain in it, or when light falling upon one's eyes causes one to experience a visual sensation. Secondly, there are characteristic ways in which a certain type of mental state can interact causally with other mental states of the same subject, as when a feeling of pain in one's leg causes one to believe that the leg has been injured, or when a visual experience causes one to believe that one is seeing something. And third, there are characteristic ways in which a certain type of mental state can contribute causally to the bodily behaviour of its subject, as when a belief that one's leg has been injured, together with a desire to relieve the consequent pain, can cause one to rub the affected part of the leg or withdraw the leg from harm's way. Thus, to a first approximation, the functionalist might say that the causal role of a feeling of pain in one's leg is to signal the occurrence of a physical injury to the leg, cause one to believe that such an injury has occurred, and thereby help to bring it about that one acts in such a way as to repair the damage done and avoid any further injury of a similar kind.

---

[2] One of the founders of functionalism was Hilary Putnam: see his 'The Nature of Mental States' (1967), reprinted in W.G. Lycan (ed.), *Mind and Cognition: A Reader* (Oxford: Blackwell, 1990).

We see, then, that functionalism is committed to regarding mental states as really existing states of subjects which can properly be referred to in causal explanations of the overt behaviour of the persons whose states they are. But it recognises that how a person behaves in given circumstances can never be accounted for simply in terms of the fact that he or she possesses a mental state of this or that type, since an adequate explanation of behaviour will always need to take into account the causal interactions which can occur between different mental states of the same subject. Consequently, functionalists acknowledge that the behavioural evidence for ascribing mental states to a subject is always open to many alternative interpretations and that often the best that we can hope to do, in the light of a given subject's circumstances and pattern of behaviour, is to assign a reasonably high degree of probability to the hypothesis that that subject possesses a certain *combination* of mental states of various types, on the grounds that such a combination of mental states would most plausibly explain the subject's behaviour in these circumstances. Suppose, for example, that John exhibits the following behaviour when, on a particular occasion, it starts to rain as he is walking to work: he unfolds his umbrella and puts it up. Part of an explanation of this behaviour might be that John *believes that it is raining*. However, it will be reasonable to ascribe this belief to John in partial explanation of his behaviour only if it is also reasonable to ascribe to John certain other mental states which are suitably causally related to that supposed belief of his – for instance, a *sensation* of wetness on his skin, a *desire* to remain dry, a *memory* that he has brought his umbrella with him, and a *hope* that putting up an umbrella in these circumstances will help to keep him dry. However, in the light of John's behaviour in other circumstances, it might well be the most likely hypothesis in the present case that his current behaviour is indeed the result of his possessing this particular combination of mental states.

In many respects, mental states as characterised by functionalism are rather like 'software' states of a computer, which may likewise be characterised in terms of their relations to the computer's 'inputs', other software states of the computer, and the computer's 'outputs'. By a 'software' state of a computer, I mean, for instance, its storing of a particular piece of information – which, on the proposed analogy, may be likened to a subject's possession of a certain belief. Such a software state may be contrasted with a 'hardware' state of the computer, such as an electromagnetic state of certain of its circuits, which might correspondingly be likened to a neural state of a person's brain. The computer's 'inputs' are, for example, keystrokes on its keyboard, while its 'outputs' are, for example, patterns displayed on its video screen: and these again might be likened, respectively, to stimulations of a subject's sensory organs and movements of his or her body. Indeed, for many functionalists, this is more than just an analogy, since they think of the human brain as being, in effect, a biological computer fashioned through eons of evolution by processes of natural selection. According to this view, just as the biological function of the heart is to circulate blood through the body and thereby keep it oxygenated and nourished, so the biological function of the brain is to gather information from the body's environment, 'process' that information in accordance with certain 'programmes' which have been 'installed' in it either by genetic evolution or else through processes of learning, and finally to use that information to guide the body's movements about its environment. How seriously or literally we can take this as an account of what the brain really does is a matter we shall discuss more fully in chapter 8. But as a model for the functionalist's conception of mental states the analogy with software states of a computer is certainly an apt one. Indeed, as a matter of historical fact, it would appear that the computational model provided an important source of inspiration for functionalism.[3]

---

[3] See again Putnam, 'The Nature of Mental States', and also Alan M. Turing, 'Computing Machinery and Intelligence', *Mind* 59 (1950), pp. 433–60, reprinted in Margaret A. Boden (ed.), *The Philosophy of Artificial Intelligence* (Oxford: Oxford University Press, 1990).

FUNCTIONALISM AND PSYCHOPHYSICAL IDENTITY THEORIES

It is important to appreciate that functionalism is noncommittal on the question of whether mental states can be *identified* with physical states of a subject's brain – and this is often held to be one of its advantages. Identity theories, in this context, fall into two classes: those which maintain that every *type* of mental state can be identified with some *type* of physical state (type–type identity theories) and those which maintain only that every *token* mental state can be identified with some *token* physical state (token–token identity theories). The type/token distinction, which is of perfectly general application, can be illustrated by the following example. If it is asked how many letters I write when I write the word 'tree', the correct answer is either *three* or *four*, depending on whether one is concerned with letter-*types* or letter-*tokens*, because what I write includes one token of each of the letter-types 't' and 'r', but two tokens of the letter-type 'e'. Now, in contemporary philosophy of mind, type–type identity theories have been called into question on the grounds that types of mental state are, plausibly, 'multiply realisable'. For instance, it is urged that it is implausible to suggest that pain of a certain type is identical with a certain type of neuronal activity, because it seems conceivable that creatures with very different types of neural organisation might nonetheless be capable of experiencing pains of exactly the same type. The computer analogy once again seems apt, for in a similar way it is possible for two computers to be in the same 'software' state even while possessing very different 'hardware' states – for example, they might be running the same programme but implementing it on very different computing machinery. But rejection of any type–type theory of mental and physical states is consistent with acceptance of a token–token theory, that is, a theory according to which any token mental state, such as a pain that I am now feeling in my left big toe, is identical with some token physical state, such as a certain state of neuronal activity now going on in my brain. Such a combination of views – rejection of type–type identity together with acceptance of token–token identity – is commonly referred to as (a species of) *non-reductive physicalism* and is usually advanced in conjunction with the doctrine that mental state types, while not being *identical* with physical state types, do none the less *supervene* upon physical state types.[4] What this doctrine asserts, roughly speaking, is that no two people exemplifying exactly the same *physical* state types could differ in respect of the *mental* state types which they exemplify, although it is allowed that two people exemplifying exactly the same *mental* state types could differ in respect of the *physical* state types which they exemplify (in line with the thesis of the multiple realisability of mental state types). More specifically, it may be held that a person's mental state types at any given time supervene upon that person's *brain*-state types at that time.

Functionalism is fully consistent with non-reductive physicalism of this kind. But it is not committed to that position, since it is equally consistent with a type–type identity theory and even, indeed, with a thoroughgoing dualism of mental and physical states. This is because functionalism only attempts to characterise mental states in terms of the patterns of causal *relations* which they need to bear to other states, both mental and physical, in order to qualify as mental states of this or that type: it consequently leaves entirely open the question of what, if any, *intrinsic* properties mental states must have. (An intrinsic property is one which something has independently of how it is related to other things: for example, in the case of material objects, *shape* is an intrinsic property, whereas *position* and *velocity* are relational.) According to functionalism, the states of an immaterial soul may qualify as mental states, provided that they exhibit a

---

[4] For an excellent discussion of the notion of supervenience, see John Heil, *The Nature of True Minds* (Cambridge: Cambridge University Press, 1992), ch. 3. See also the important work of Jaegwon Kim in this area, collected in his *Supervenience and Mind: Selected Philosophical Essays* (Cambridge: Cambridge University Press, 1993). The topic of supervenience is too complex and large, however, for me to do it justice in the present book.

suitable pattern of causal relationships, as may the states of a bundle of human neurones, or the states of a piece of computing machinery, or even the states of a pile of pebbles on a beach. But this extreme liberality, although initially attractive, does harbour difficulties for functionalism, as we shall soon see.

It may be wondered how functionalism could really be consistent with a *type–type* identity theory of mental and physical states: if all that is required of a state, in order for it to qualify as a mental state of a given type, is that it should exhibit a suitable pattern of causal relationships with other states, both mental and physical, then it is hard to see how a certain *type* of mental state could simply be identical with a certain *type* of physical state – for what could rule out the possibility of *another* type of physical state having tokens which exhibited the same pattern of causal relationships? Here, however, we need to distinguish between two different possible ways of interpreting functionalism. Functionalism, we have seen, characterises mental states in terms of their distinctive 'causal roles'. Thus, for example, it may be said that *pain* states are typically caused by physical damage to a subject's body, cause the subject to desire relief, and give rise to appropriate avoidance behaviour. But here one can ask: should we identify the *type* of mental state to which a token pain state belongs in terms of the causal role which characterises pain, or should we instead identify it in terms of the type of state which 'plays' that role in the person whose pain state this is? An analogy which may help us to understand this distinction is the following. Consider the role of the bishop in chess, as defined by the rules governing its movements. And suppose that we have before us a particular wooden chessman of a certain shape, which is a bishop. We might think of identifying the *type* to which this particular chessman belongs in terms of that role – in which case we must allow that other chessmen, made of different materials and possessing different shapes, may none the less qualify as chessmen of exactly the same type as this one, provided only that they are all played with in accordance with the rules governing the movements of the bishop. Alternatively, however, one might think of identifying the type to which our particular chessman belongs in terms of the type of material object which plays the role of the bishop in the chess set of which this chessman is a member. Analogously, then, if we conceive the type to which a token pain state belongs as being whatever type of state it is that plays the causal role of pain in its subject, it is perfectly possible to maintain that, for example, pain in *human* subjects is identical with a certain type of neuronal state whereas pain in differently constituted subjects is identical with a quite different type of physical state.[5] At this point the reader could be forgiven for feeling confused by these distinctions between type-states and token-states and between roles and the states which 'play' them. There is, indeed, a considerable danger that debates conducted in these terms will generate more darkness than light. So I shall not attempt to adjudicate between the two different interpretations of functionalism just outlined, but shall rest content with the conclusion that one can espouse some form of functionalism while simultaneously adopting virtually any position whatever as regards the question of how mental states are related ontologically to physical states.

THE PROBLEM OF CONSCIOUSNESS

Functionalism, we have seen, is in many respects a very liberal doctrine. For that reason, it may seem surprising that anyone should want to disagree with it. And yet it has vigorous opponents, some of whose arguments against it are extremely compelling. The most influential of these arguments turn on the claim that functionalism, far from provid-

---

[5] For a proposal along these lines, see David Lewis, 'Mad Pain and Martian Pain', in Ned Block (ed.), *Readings in Philosophy of Psychology, Volume I* (London: Methuen, 1980), reprinted in David Lewis's *Philosophical Papers, Volume I* (New York: Oxford University Press, 1983). See also, in the former volume, Ned Block's helpful introductory essay, 'What is Functionalism?'. I should perhaps emphasise that functionalism is a family of views rather than a single doctrine, some of its proponents regarding it more as an account of our *concepts* of mental states than as a theory of the nature of mental states themselves.

ing an adequate account of the character of mental states, leaves out what is most striking about being a subject of such states: the very fact of *consciousness*. As Thomas Nagel has put it, there is 'something it is like' to be a subject of experience – whereas, plausibly, there is nothing whatever it is like to be a pebble, nor even a pile of many pebbles.[6] And yet, as I remarked earlier, functionalism allows that even a pile of pebbles could be a subject of mental states, provided that its states exhibited a suitable pattern of causal relations to each other and to other states of suitable types. This does not seem to make sense. How could something possess states of belief, desire, hope and pain and yet be as devoid of consciousness as a stone?

To this it may be replied that states of consciousness are no different from other mental states in being amenable to a functionalist characterisation. A state of consciousness, on this view, is simply one which exhibits a certain characteristic pattern of causal relations to other states, both mental and physical. In particular, it may be suggested that states of consciousness are distinguished from some other kinds of mental state in that they are 'second-order' states, involving a subject's knowledge, or awareness, of certain other mental states of itself. However, this suggestion – which we shall explore more fully in chapter 10 – does not seem to do justice to the phenomenon at issue. For it remains very hard to see how a pile of pebbles, for instance, could qualify as possessing states of consciousness just in virtue of possessing, not only certain 'first-order' states exhibiting suitable patterns of causal relations, but in addition certain 'second-order' states suitably causally related to some of those 'first-order' states. To this the functionalist may reply that he does not have any reason to suppose that a pile of pebbles really *could* possess states exhibiting this degree of causal complexity, but that if we

---

[6] See Thomas Nagel, 'What is it Like to be a Bat?', *Philosophical Review* 83 (1974), pp. 435–50, reprinted in his *Mortal Questions* (Cambridge: Cambridge University Press, 1979). For a broad survey of many aspects of the problem of consciousness, see Jonathan Shear (ed.), *Explaining Consciousness: The Hard Problem* (Cambridge, MA: MIT Press, 1997).

thought one did then we would have no good grounds for *denying* that it possessed states of consciousness. In support of this he may urge that it is only evidence of such causal complexity, based on what we know of their observable behaviour, that justifies us in attributing states of consciousness to other human beings, so that to deny consciousness to the hypothetical pile of pebbles in the circumstances envisaged would be to succumb to narrow-minded prejudice, of the sort that would even deny consciousness to non-human animals. I shall reserve judgement on this general issue until later in the chapter, after we have looked at some more specific objections to functionalism.

QUALIA AND THE INVERTED SPECTRUM ARGUMENT

A more specific argument against functionalism, but one which again focuses on the problem of consciousness, is the famous 'inverted spectrum' argument.[7] Opponents of functionalism point out that some of our conscious mental states have distinctive *qualitative* features. For example, when I look at a red surface in normal lighting conditions, I have a visual experience of a certain distinctive kind, which differs qualitatively from the kind of experience I have when I look at a green surface in the same lighting conditions. Red surfaces *look* or *appear* to me a certain way in these circumstances, a way which is quite different from the way that green surfaces appear to me in these circumstances. Some philosophers of mind make the point by saying that my visual experiences of red and green surfaces involve different colour *qualia*. ('Qualia' is the plural form of the singular noun 'quale'.) There is a certain danger attached to speaking in this way of visual qualia: namely, the danger that we may be tempted to *reify* qualia and treat them as 'private' or 'inner' objects of visual experience. This is an issue to which we shall return

---

[7] For the inverted spectrum argument, see Ned Block and Jerry A. Fodor, 'What Psychological States are Not', *Philosophical Review* 81 (1972), pp. 159–81, reprinted in Block (ed.), *Readings in Philosophy of Psychology, Volume 1*.

in chapter 5, when we come to discuss sense-datum theories of sensation. For present purposes, we do not really need to talk in terms of 'qualia' at all – we can simply talk in terms of how variously coloured surfaces *look* or *appear* to subjects in various circumstances. The important point is that it seems perfectly conceivable that, for instance, the way that *red* surfaces look *to me* in normal lighting conditions might be the way that *green* surfaces look *to you* in normal lighting conditions – and, more generally, that our colour experiences might be systematically 'inverted' with respect to one another.

Now, if this were the case, both of us would nonetheless have exactly the same powers of colour-discrimination and, other things being equal, both of us would apply colour terms to objects in exactly the same way: we would agree, for instance, that tomatoes, British postboxes, and sunsets are properly described as being 'red', while grass, emeralds, and 'go' signs are properly described as being 'green'. Indeed – and this is the crucial point – it seems that we would be *functionally equivalent* in respect of our colour experiences. That is to say, my colour experiences and your colour experiences would exhibit exactly the same pattern of causal relations to environmental states, other mental states, and behaviour: they would have exactly the same 'causal role'. But this apparently means that functionalism can recognise no difference at all between my colour experiences and your colour experiences, in the hypothetical case of spectrum inversion. And yet it seems that, in that hypothetical case, our colour experiences do in fact differ in the most striking way imaginable. The obvious conclusion to draw is that functionalism fails to characterise colour experiences adequately, because it leaves entirely out of account their most striking feature: their *qualitative character*. Indeed, it may be remarked that this failing of functionalism was entirely predictable, in view of the fact, mentioned earlier, that functionalism provides a purely *relational* characterisation of mental states, saying nothing whatever about their *intrinsic* properties: for the qualitative character of a visual experience would seem to be precisely that – an intrinsic property of the experience.

SOME POSSIBLE RESPONSES TO THE INVERTED SPECTRUM ARGUMENT

There are various ways in which friends of functionalism may want to respond to this argument, other than by resorting to an outright denial of the existence of 'qualia' altogether.[8] Some may contend that the hypothesis of spectrum inversion is not even intelligible, on the grounds that we could, in the nature of the case, never have objective empirical evidence that such an inversion had occurred: for we only know about each other's visual experiences on the basis of our observable behaviour, both verbal and non-verbal – for instance, on the basis of how we *describe* our visual experiences to each other in words. But, by hypothesis, we would be indistinguishable in respect of all such behaviour, in the supposed case of spectrum inversion. However, this response looks like an appeal to a crude form of verificationism – the discredited doctrine that statements which cannot in principle be verified or falsified empirically are on that account meaningless.[9] It may be urged that one understands perfectly well what it would be for a case of *inter*personal spectrum inversion to obtain, not least because one can perfectly well imagine *intra*personal spectrum inversion occurring in one's own case: that is to say, one can imagine waking up one morning to discover that red things, such as tomatoes, have suddenly begun to look the way that green things, such as grass, looked the day before, and *vice versa*. The interpersonal case, it may be said, is to be understood as involving in the case of two

---

[8] Some philosophers do go to the extreme of denying the existence of qualia altogether: see Daniel C. Dennett, 'Quining Qualia', in A. J. Marcel and E. Bisiach (eds.), *Consciousness in Contemporary Science* (Oxford: Clarendon Press, 1988), reprinted in Lycan (ed.), *Mind and Cognition*.

[9] For a well-known exposition of verificationism, see A. J. Ayer, *Language, Truth and Logic*, 2nd edn (London: Victor Gollancz, 1946).

different people exactly what is involved in the case of a single person in the intrapersonal case.

Another possible response for the functionalist is to argue that, when we look into the details of the hypothetical case of interpersonal spectrum inversion, we shall see that, in fact, it is most implausible to suppose that the subjects concerned would *really* be functionally equivalent in respect of their colour experiences. It may be pointed out, for example, that there are causal relations between our colour experiences and our emotional responses: things which look red to us tend to evoke agitated or angry feelings, perhaps, whereas things which look green to us tend to evoke calm feelings – and these different emotional responses tend to be reflected in our behaviour. Consequently, it may be suggested, if red things looked to me the way that green things looked to you and *vice versa*, then we would probably tend to have different emotional responses and therefore different patterns of behaviour in the presence of red things and likewise in the presence of green things. However, this presupposes that it is the *qualitative character* of our colour experiences which makes them tend to evoke certain emotional responses in us, rather than, for example, the *beliefs* which we tend to associate with those colour experiences – for instance, the belief that we commonly experience green things in calm situations, as when we are walking in the countryside. It would seem, indeed, that the functionalist is really committed to the latter sort of explanation of the causal connections, if such there be, between colour experiences and emotional responses. But according to that sort of explanation, two people with inverted colour experiences should *not*, after all, be expected to have different emotional responses to colour and consequently different patterns of behaviour.

Yet another possible response for the functionalist is to argue that, insofar as visual experiences have what may be called 'qualitative character', this is in fact entirely a matter of their *intentional* or *representational* content – that is, a matter

of what those experiences represent the world as being like.[10]
For example, on this view, to say that my colour experiences
of red things have a distinctive qualitative character is just
to say that those experiences represent such things to me as
having a certain property – namely, redness. Of course, we
know that colour experiences can be misleading in this
respect: sometimes a colour experience represents something
to me as having the property of redness, when in fact the
thing that I am seeing really has some other colour. But –
say the supporters of the view in question – this should not
tempt me into saying that, in such cases, I am still experiencing a visual quality or 'quale' which is quite distinct from
the physical colour of the thing before my eyes. Rather, I am
experiencing that physical colour, but my visual experience
is *mis*representing it as being another physical colour. If this
view is right, then it would appear that it really does make
no sense to suppose that a case of 'spectrum inversion' could
occur, for the implication is that there is nothing more to be
said about the qualitative character of a colour experience
than can be captured in an account of the representational
content of that experience – and hence that two people whose
colour experiences have the same representational contents
must have colour experiences which are qualitatively identical. But it would seem that two people whose *beliefs* do not
differ in content on account of their respective colour experiences cannot be enjoying colour experiences with different
representational contents. And the inverted spectrum hypothesis assumes that the beliefs of the two people involved
do indeed not differ in content on account of the supposed
differences between their respective colour experiences – for
if their beliefs did differ in content on this account, the difference could be expected to show up in differences between
their verbal and non-verbal behaviour, contrary to the

---

[10] For a view along these lines, see Michael Tye, *Ten Problems of Consciousness: A
Representational Theory of the Phenomenal Mind* (Cambridge, MA: MIT Press, 1995),
ch. 5.

assumption that they are functionally equivalent in respect of their colour experiences. However, the opponent of functionalism may, I think, justly react to this line of argument by saying that its conclusion simply demonstrates the inadequacy of the proposed 'representational' account of the qualitative character of visual experiences. There is, plausibly, *more* to a 'red' colour experience than simply the fact that it represents the world to one as containing something red: for, plausibly, the experience only has this representational capacity in virtue of a certain feature of the experience which is *intrinsic* to it, namely, what we have been calling its qualitative character. The qualitative character of the experience cannot simply *consist* in its representational capacity, since the representational capacity is partly to be *explained* in terms of the qualitative character. And then the point is that, while a colour experience needs to have *some qualitative character or other* in order to be able to represent the world to one as containing something red, *different* qualitative characters would serve equally well for this purpose, and do so in the hypothetical case of spectrum inversion.

Finally, the functionalist could perhaps just *accept* that his account of the nature of certain kinds of mental state leaves something out – their intrinsic qualitative characters – but argue that the qualitative character of such a state is a relatively unimportant feature of the state, because it is causally inert: if it were *not* causally inert, it would contribute to the causal role of the state – and yet the lesson of the inverted spectrum argument seems to be that the qualitative character of a mental state makes no difference to its causal role, since states with quite different qualitative characters can have exactly the same causal role. On this view, the 'qualia' of experience are purely *epiphenomenal*.[11] However, that is an illegitimate conclusion to draw from the inverted spectrum argument. The fact, if it is a fact, that mental states with

---

[11] One philosopher who thinks, for other reasons, that qualia are epiphenomenal is Frank Jackson: see his 'Epiphenomenal Qualia', *Philosophical Quarterly* 32 (1982), pp. 127–36, reprinted in Lycan (ed.), *Mind and Cognition*.

different qualitative characters can have exactly the same causal role does *not* imply that the qualitative characters of such states make no contribution to the causal role of those states: for the fact in question is perfectly consistent with the alternative possibility that the qualitative characters of such states make exactly *the same* contribution to the causal role of those states, which implies that they do indeed make some such contribution. Indeed, the idea that 'qualia' exist but are causally inert is difficult to sustain: for if they are causally inert, how can we even know about them? My belief that I am now undergoing an experience with a certain qualitative character must, arguably, be caused by just such an experience of mine in order to qualify as knowledge. The functionalist might grudgingly accept this, I suppose, and yet contend that functionalism still provides an *almost* completely adequate account of the nature of our mental lives: that, in particular, it gives a completely adequate account of the nature of our *non*-qualitative mental states, such as our beliefs and other attitudinal states. However, this presupposes that the qualitative character of our experiential states, such as our visual experiences, has no bearing whatever on the nature of our attitudinal states. But that presupposition can certainly be challenged: indeed, we shall see ways in which it may be challenged when we come to discuss the nature of conceptual thinking in chapter 7.[12]

THE ABSENT QUALIA ARGUMENT AND TWO NOTIONS OF CONSCIOUSNESS

Another argument against functionalism which is often mentioned in the same breath as the inverted spectrum argument is the *absent qualia argument*.[13] The objection raised here is

[12] For further discussion of how functionalism might handle the inverted spectrum case, see Sydney Shoemaker, 'Functionalism and Qualia', *Philosophical Studies* 27 (1975), pp. 291–315, reprinted in his *Identity, Cause, and Mind* (Cambridge: Cambridge University Press, 1984).
[13] For the absent qualia argument, see Ned Block, 'Troubles with Functionalism', in C. W. Savage (ed.), *Perception and Cognition: Issues in the Foundations of Psychology, Minnesota Studies in the Philosophy of Science, Volume 9* (Minneapolis: University of

that, since functionalism contends that all that is required
for certain states of an object to qualify as *mental* states of
certain types is that those states should stand in appropriate
causal relations to each other and to states of certain other
types – namely, the causal relations demanded by the causal
or functional roles of those mental state types – it seems to
follow that something could, in principle, have a mind just
like yours or mine *even though it would appear to lack 'qualia'*
altogether. The thing in question might be, for instance, the
pile of pebbles mentioned earlier, or – a much-used
example – the combined population of China. A variant on
this theme is provided by the notion of a *zombie* (not to be
confused with the 'zombies' of Haitian voodoo lore). A creature in this hypothetical condition could supposedly have
beliefs, desires and even pains functionally equivalent to
yours or mine, and yet it would never enjoy mental states
with qualitative character: there would be *nothing it was like*
for this creature to experience the tang of lemon, the whiff
of woodsmoke, the colour of ripe tomatoes, or the sting of a
nettle. And the issue raised here by the absent qualia argument is whether the existence of such zombies is really possible, as functionalism seems to imply. For if it is not – as
many opponents of functionalism would claim – then functionalism must apparently be false.

   As I have just indicated, the zombie question is reminis-
cent of the question raised earlier as to whether something
like a pile of pebbles could, in principle, possess states of
consciousness. The functionalist was envisaged as responding
to that question by contending that states of consciousness
can be accommodated by functionalism as being 'second-
order' states, involving a subject's knowledge, or awareness,
of certain 'first-order' states of itself. However, the absent
qualia objection cannot plausibly be tackled in this way,
because the presence or absence of 'qualia' in a subject's
experience does not, plausibly, have anything to do with

Minnesota Press, 1978), reprinted in Block (ed.), *Readings in Philosophy of Psycho-*
logy, Volume 1.

whether or not that subject has 'second-order' knowledge of its own 'first-order' experiential states. In fact, it seems that we have to distinguish between two quite different notions of consciousness.[14] On the one hand, there is what may be called *phenomenal* consciousness, which is what is distinctive of qualitative states of experience, such as the experience of tasting the tang of lemon. And on the other hand, there is what may be called *apperceptive* consciousness, which is the awareness which subjects sometimes possess of some of their own mental states, not only their qualitative states but also their non-qualitative states, such as their beliefs and desires. The absent qualia argument evidently concerns the possibility of there being minded creatures altogether lacking phenomenal consciousness. Functionalism seems committed to this possibility. Indeed, functionalism seems committed to the possibility of there being creatures having *apperceptive* consciousness while altogether lacking phenomenal consciousness. My own view is that this is *not* a genuine possibility, for a reason indicated earlier: namely, that to suppose that it is a possibility is to ignore the connection between being a creature capable of possessing attitudinal states with conceptual content and being a creature capable of possessing experiential states with qualitative character.[15] However, consideration of the issues which bear upon this point must be postponed until chapter 7.

ELIMINATIVE MATERIALISM AND 'FOLK PSYCHOLOGY'

Qualia-based objections to functionalism claim that functionalism at best provides only a partial account of the nature of mental states. But functionalism also has other enemies who

[14] See further Ned Block, 'On a Confusion about a Function of Consciousness', *Behavioral and Brain Sciences* 18 (1995), pp. 227–87, and Norton Nelkin, *Consciousness and the Origins of Thought* (Cambridge: Cambridge University Press, 1996).

[15] See further my 'There are No Easy Problems of Consciousness', *Journal of Consciousness Studies* 2 (1995), pp. 266–71, reprinted in Shear (ed.), *Explaining Consciousness*.

claim that it is not even partly successful in its aims, because they see its aims as being thoroughly misguided. Central to functionalism is its treatment of attitudinal states, such as beliefs, desires and intentions. Functionalism regards such states as really existing states of subjects which may properly be invoked in causal explanations of the behaviour of those subjects. In this respect, functionalism seems to be fully in keeping with common sense. Terms such as 'belief', 'desire' and 'intention' are frequently used in everyday speech: they are not part of some exclusively scientific vocabulary known only to experts. However, the common-sense and everyday character of propositional attitude vocabulary is, according to some critics, precisely what unsuits it to use in a scientifically acceptable account of the nature of psychological states. These critics, known as *eliminative materialists*, regard propositional attitude vocabulary as belonging to a pre-scientific theory of mind, disparagingly described as 'folk psychology'.[16] Folk psychology, they suggest, is no better than folk physics, being a repository of misconceptions and confusions devoid of genuine explanatory power. Just as the march of scientific progress has swept away the primitive notions of witchcraft and alchemy, so too it will in time sweep away the primitive terminology which we use to describe and explain our states of mind and behaviour. At least, even if we retain the terminology in everyday speech, we shall realise that it is mistaken to interpret it realistically.[17] On this view, there really are no such states as beliefs, desires and intentions, any more than there are such things as witches or the elixir of life.

It is important to distinguish between eliminative materialism and reductive physicalism. Reductive physicalists accept a type-type identity theory of mental and physical states, according to which every genuine type of mental state

---

[16] Perhaps the best-known exponent of eliminative materialism is Paul Churchland: see his 'Eliminative Materialism and the Propositional Attitudes', *Journal of Philosophy* 78 (1981), pp. 67–90, reprinted in Lycan (ed.), *Mind and Cognition*.

[17] What is sometimes called an 'instrumentalist' view of propositional attitude talk, which accepts its pragmatic utility, is defended by Daniel C. Dennett: see his *The Intentional Stance* (Cambridge, MA: MIT Press, 1987).

is identical with some type of physical state, such as some type of neuronal state of the brain. Reductive physicalists do not, in general, want to deny the very existence of many of the types of mental state talked about by functionalists, such as beliefs, desires and intentions. Rather, their hope is that with the advance of science we shall come to discover that mental states of these types just *are* – that is, are identical with – certain types of brain state: just as science has revealed, say, that the temperature of a heated body of gas is in fact identical with the mean kinetic energy of its constituent molecules and that the meteorological phenomenon of lightning is in fact identical with a kind of electrical discharge. By contrast, eliminative materialists hold that states of belief, desire and intention simply *do not exist*, and hence *a fortiori* that such states are not identical with physical states of any sort. Their attitude towards beliefs and desires is rather like the modern scientist's attitude towards phlogiston, the substance which was thought to be involved in processes of combustion before the role played by oxygen in those processes was discovered. The phlogiston theory is now rejected as completely false: phlogiston simply does not exist. There is no prospect of identifying phlogiston with oxygen, because the way in which phlogiston was supposed to act in processes of combustion is quite different from the way in which oxygen does in fact act in those processes. Similarly, then, eliminative materialists hold that nothing at all acts in the ways in which we fondly suppose that beliefs and desires act in the processes giving rise to human behaviour: nothing, that is to say, really has the causal roles in terms of which functionalism attempts to characterise such states as beliefs and desires. (This is a suggestion which we shall examine more closely in chapter 8, when we discuss the implications of 'connectionist' models of the mind.)

Why are eliminative materialists so sceptical about the judgements of folk psychology? To understand this, we must appreciate that they think of folk psychology as a *theory* which purports to explain and predict human behaviour, but which in fact signally fails to do so. A scientifically acceptable theory of some range of phenomena has to propose empirically testable laws which enable us to infer what changes in such phenomena will occur in specific circumstances – as, for example, the laws of mechanics enable us infer how massive bodies will move under the influence of the forces acting upon them. But, it is pointed out, folk psychology provides us with no such laws. At best it provides us with empirically unfalsifiable platitudes, such as the platitude that people generally act in such ways as to satisfy their desires in the light of their beliefs, unless they are prevented from doing so by factors beyond their control. Moreover, there are large areas of human behaviour concerning which folk psychology is quite silent, such as the behaviour of people suffering from various forms of mental illness.

Consequently, it is urged, folk psychology is hopelessly bad, by scientific standards, at explaining the range of phenomena with which it is concerned: so bad that it is beyond repair and needs to be replaced by a quite different theory. Such a replacement theory could not be one in which states such as belief and desire have any place, because they are too deeply embedded in the folk psychological theory to be extractable from it.

SOME RESPONSES TO ELIMINATIVE MATERIALISM

One may be tempted to respond to the eliminative materialist that his position is simply incoherent. For one of his contentions is that *beliefs do not exist*: and this seems to imply that he cannot rationally claim to believe in the truth of his own theory. He cannot consistently claim to *believe* the theory if the theory itself maintains that there are no beliefs. But such a response seems too glib. All that matters for the eliminative materialist is that his theory should be *true*, not that it should be true *that he believes it*. Even so, perhaps the eliminative materialist's position really is threatened by incoherence at a deeper level. For it would seem that the very notion of *truth* is inextricably bound up with the notions of belief and the other 'propositional attitudes'. The primary bearers of truth, it may be urged, are not abstract sentences or theories, but beliefs. Sentences are linguistic items and as such are only true or false inasmuch as they are capable of expressing *beliefs* which are true or false: for unless they are *interpretable* by thinking subjects, sentences are merely lifeless strings of meaningless marks or sounds. If that is so, then to abandon the category of belief is implicitly to abandon also the very notions of truth and falsehood and therewith, it seems, the very notion of rational argument which lies at the heart of the scientific approach to understanding the world.[18] It would be ironic indeed if the eliminative materialist, in his pursuit of a scientific theory of human behaviour, could be convicted of undermining the very enterprise of science itself.

Another complaint which can be made against eliminative materialism is that it mischaracterises 'folk psychology' in describing it as a would-be scientific *theory*. Very arguably, when we ascribe beliefs and desires to people and attempt to understand their behaviour in terms of their possession of such mental states, we are not doing anything at all analogous to what scientists do when they explain the movements of massive bodies by reference to the forces acting upon them. For one thing, explanations framed in terms of beliefs and desires are *rational* explanations, in which we explain why people act in the ways they do by reference to their putative reasons for so acting. Inanimate objects which act in conformity with the laws of mechanics do not act in those ways because they have *reasons* for so acting. Rational explanations are subject to *normative* constraints, unlike the explanations of physical science. Norms are standards by which we may judge an agent's reasons for acting as being good or bad. And such norms obviously have no relevance to purely physical explanations of phenomena: we do not criticise a stone for falling or praise the sun for rising each day. We shall return to these issues when we discuss the philosophy of action in

---

[18] Some radical pragmatists, it has to be said, *are* ready to abandon the notion of truth: see Stephen Stich, *The Fragmentation of Reason* (Cambridge, MA: MIT Press, 1990), ch. 5.

chapter 9. But there is, in any case, another reason for contending that 'folk psychology' is not any sort of *theory* of human behaviour. This is that – or so many philosophers and psychologists would now maintain – when we form expectations of how people will behave on the basis of the beliefs and desires which we attribute to them, we are not 'predicting' their behaviour by inferring it from lawlike generalisations which we suppose to govern their behaviour, in the way that the laws of mechanics govern the behaviour of massive bodies. Rather, what we may do is to engage in an empathetic 'simulation' of what we take to be their outlook upon the world, and imagine how we ourselves would act in their situation with the beliefs and desires that we ascribe to them.[19] It would seem, indeed, that 'folk psychological' patterns of thinking are deeply engrained in us, probably having an evolutionary basis in our hominid ancestors' need to cooperate and compete effectively with other members of a closely knit group. As such, these patterns of thinking are not to be viewed as a proto-scientific theory of human behaviour but, rather, as part of what it is to be a human being capable of engaging meaningfully with other human beings. They are not dispensable intellectual artefacts, but partially constitutive of our very humanity.[20]

CONCLUSIONS

Our aim in this chapter has been to look with a critical eye at a number of different accounts of the nature of mental states, including both propositional attitude states, such as beliefs, and sensational states, such as pains. We expect such an account to be able to tell us what is distinctive about

---

[19] See further Martin Davies and Tony Stone (eds.), *Folk Psychology: The Theory of Mind Debate* (Oxford: Blackwell, 1995).

[20] For further robust criticism of eliminative materialism, see Lynne Rudder Baker, *Saving Belief* (Princeton, NJ: Princeton University Press, 1987), chs. 6 and 7. For further discussion of the status of folk psychology, see John D. Greenwood (ed.), *The Future of Folk Psychology: Intentionality and Cognitive Science* (Cambridge: Cambridge University Press, 1991).

mental states, how they are to be classified, and what entitles us to ascribe them to ourselves and to other people. *Logical behaviourism*, we saw, attempts to provide such an account by identifying mental states with behavioural dispositions: but it is an account which is fatally flawed because it oversimplifies the relationship between a person's mental states and his or her patterns of behaviour. *Functionalism*, however, appears to overcome this difficulty, while still allowing that the evidence which licences us to ascribe mental states to people is ultimately behavioural in nature. This it does by characterising mental states in terms of their typical causal relations to environmental states, other mental states, and behavioural states – in short, in terms of their 'causal' or 'functional' roles.

Functionalism is an ontologically liberal doctrine, being consistent with various forms of physicalism and even with a thoroughgoing dualism. The underlying reason for this is that functionalism has nothing positive to say about the *intrinsic* properties of mental states, only something about their *relational* properties. However, this very fact leaves functionalism open to attack in various ways. Thus it is accused of leaving out of account the *qualitative* character of certain kinds of conscious mental state, such as those which we experience in seeing and tasting things: for the qualitative character of such a state seems indeed to be an intrinsic property of the state in question. For the same reason, functionalism seems to commit us to bizarre possibilities, such as the possible existence of 'zombies' – creatures capable of possessing beliefs, desires and even pains just like ours and yet altogether lacking any sort of 'phenomenal' consciousness. There are various ways in which functionalists may try to respond to such objections, but none so far has proved wholly convincing.

On the other hand, functionalism also faces criticism from advocates of so-called *eliminative materialism*, who reject its endorsement of the categories of 'folk psychology' and especially its commitment to the existence of propositional attitude states, such as beliefs and desires. These critics hold that the causal roles in terms of which functionalism attempts to characterise such states are not in fact occupied by anything whatever. However, eliminative materialism may be accused of incoherence, insofar as it threatens to eliminate reason and truth along with the propositional attitudes, thereby undermining the very edifice of science in the name of which it rejects the categories of folk psychology. Very arguably, folk psychology should not be seen as a proto-scientific theory of mind, to be evaluated by the kinds of empirical criteria used in testing scientific hypotheses.

So where does all this leave us? We seem to have good reasons for taking a *realist* view of mental states, as states which can quite properly be invoked in causal explanations of people's behaviour. And yet it seems that what is truly distinctive of mental states – the features in virtue of which it is 'like something' to be a subject of such states – cannot be captured in terms of their putative 'causal roles'. What seems to elude not only functionalism but also any form of physicalism are the central facts of *consciousness* and *subjectivity*. One's access to these facts, however, appears to be irremediably personal and introspective: it seems that one knows of them, primarily, from reflection upon *one's own* condition and that one can at best achieve only an empathetic understanding of how they may affect the conditions of other people. There seems, then, to be a fundamental asymmetry between 'first-person' and 'third-person' knowledge of mental states – the knowledge of such states which one has in virtue of being *a subject* of such states oneself and the knowledge of such states which one has in virtue of being *an observer* of other subjects of such states. This makes mental states quite different from any of the other kinds of state known to empirical science, all of which are studied scientifically from a purely 'third-person' point of view. Rather than see this as a problem, however, perhaps we would do better to see it part of the solution to another problem: the problem of saying what it is that is truly distinctive of mental states and sets them apart from merely physical states.

4

Mental content

We came to the conclusion, in the previous chapter, that mental states really do exist and can properly be invoked in causal explanations of people's behaviour. Thus, for example, it is perfectly legitimate to cite John's belief that it is raining amongst the probable causes of his action of opening his umbrella as he walks to work. In this respect, it seems, the commonsense judgements of 'folk' psychology and the explanatory hypotheses of 'scientific' psychology are broadly compatible with one another, whatever eliminative materialists may say to the contrary. However, when we try to understand more fully how propositional attitude states can be causally efficacious in generating bodily behaviour, some serious difficulties begin to emerge. So far, we have described propositional attitude states – 'attitudinal states', for short – as involving a subject's 'attitude' towards a proposition. The proposition in question constitutes the state's *propositional content*. And the attitude might be one of belief, desire, hope, fear, intention or whatnot. The general form of a statement ascribing an attitudinal state to a subject is simply 'S ϕs that p', where 'S' names a subject, 'ϕ' stands for any verb of propositional attitude, and 'p' represents some proposition – such as the proposition that it is raining. An example is provided by the statement that *John believes that it is raining* and another by the statement that *John fears that he will get wet*.

Now, it seems clear that the propositional content of an attitudinal state must be deemed causally relevant to whatever behaviour that state may be invoked to explain. When one cites John's belief that it is raining in causal explanation of his action of opening his umbrella, it is relevant that the cited belief is a belief *that it is raining* rather than, say, a belief *that two plus two equals four.* It is true that, as we noted in the previous chapter, one and the same action could be explained as proceeding from many *different* possible beliefs, depending upon what other attitudinal states we are prepared to ascribe to the agent. Someone who opens his umbrella while walking to work need not do so because he believes that it is raining and desires not to get wet: he might do so, for instance, because he believes that he is being spied upon and desires to hide his face. Even so, these different possible explanations of the agent's behaviour all make essential reference to the *contents* of the agent's putative attitudinal states and presume that those contents are causally relevant to the behaviour in question. However – and this is where the real difficulties begin to arise – when we consider that propositions appear to be *abstract* entities, more akin to the objects of mathematics than to anything found in the concrete realm of psychology, it seems altogether mysterious that states of mind should depend for their causal powers upon the propositions which allegedly constitute their 'contents'. For abstract entities themselves do not appear to possess any causal powers of their own.

Some of the questions which we shall need to address in this chapter are the following. How do the contents of mental states contribute to the causal explanation of behaviour? Can the contents of mental states be assigned to them independently of the environmental circumstances in which the subjects of those states are situated? And in virtue of what do mental states possess the contents that they do? But before we can address any of these questions, we need to look more closely at the nature of *propositions*.

PROPOSITIONS

It is customary in the philosophy of language and philosophical logic to distinguish carefully between *propositions*, *state-*

ments, and *sentences*.[1] *Sentences* are linguistic items – strings of words arranged in a grammatically permissible order – which may take either written or spoken form. One must differentiate between sentence-*tokens* and sentence-*types*, recalling here the type/token distinction discussed in the previous chapter. Thus, the following string of words – IT IS RAINING – constitutes a token of a certain English sentence-type, of which another token is this string of words: *it is raining*. The two tokens happen to differ in that one is written in upper case letters while the other is written in lower case letters, but this difference does not prevent them from qualifying as tokens of the same sentence-type. *Statements* are assertoric utterances of sentence-tokens by individual users of a language. Thus John may make the statement that it is raining on a given occasion by uttering, with assertoric intent, a token of the English sentence-type 'It is raining'. Not all utterances of sentences are made with assertoric intent, that is, to make assertions: we also use sentences to ask questions, issue commands, and so forth. Finally, *propositions* constitute the meaningful content of statements in the context in which they are made. Thus, when John makes the statement that it is raining at a particular time and place, his statement expresses the proposition that it is raining then and there – a proposition which could equally well be expressed by other speakers using other languages at other times and places. The proposition which an English speaker expresses in asserting 'Snow is white' is the very same proposition which a French speaker expresses in asserting 'La neige est blanche' and which a German speaker expresses in asserting 'Der Schnee ist weiss'.

But what exactly *is* a 'proposition'? That is, what *kind* of entity is it? Many philosophers would say that propositions are *abstract* entities and thus akin ontologically to the objects of mathematics, such as numbers and sets.[2] Numbers are not

---

[1] See, for example, Susan Haack, *Philosophy of Logics* (Cambridge: Cambridge University Press, 1978), ch. 6.

[2] For a general discussion of the issues involved here, see my 'The Metaphysics of Abstract Objects', *Journal of Philosophy* 92 (1995), pp. 509–24.

concrete, physical objects existing in space and time: we cannot see, hear or touch the number 3. Indeed, it does not seem that we can interact *causally* with the number 3 in any way whatever. Nor does the number 3 change its properties over time: it is apparently eternal and immutable. And yet it would seem unwarranted to deny that the number 3 exists. At least in our unphilosophical moments, we are all happy to assert that *there is* a number which is greater than 2 and less than 4: and this seems to commit us to recognising the existence of the number 3. It is true that not all philosophers are happy with this state of affairs and that some of them would like to eliminate numbers and all other abstract entities from our ontology, often on the grounds that they do not see how we could have knowledge of anything which supposedly does not exist in space and time.[3] But it is not so easy to eliminate the ontology of mathematics without undermining the very truths of mathematics, which we may be loth to do. If numbers do not exist, it is hard to see how it could be *true* to say that 2 plus 1 equals 3. So perhaps we should reconcile ourselves to the existence of abstract entities. And, certainly, propositions would appear to fall into this ontological category. The proposition that snow is white is no more something that we can see, hear or touch than is the number 3. We can touch snow and see its whiteness, because snow is a concrete, physical stuff. Equally, we can see and touch a token of the English sentence-type 'Snow is white', because it consists of a string of physical marks on a page. But the *proposition* that snow is white, it appears, is something utterly different in nature from any of these concrete, physical things. We can apprehend it intellectually – that is, understand it – but we cannot literally see or touch it, for it does not occupy any position in physical space nor does it exist at any particular time.

Perhaps, however, it will be doubted whether we have as

---

[3] For an example of this sort of view, see Hartry Field, *Science Without Numbers: A Defence of Nominalism* (Oxford: Blackwell, 1980) and *Realism, Mathematics and Modality* (Oxford: Blackwell, 1989). See also Paul Benacerraf, 'Mathematical Truth', *Journal of Philosophy* 70 (1973), pp. 661–80, reprinted in Paul Benacerraf and Hilary Putnam (eds.), *Philosophy of Mathematics: Selected Readings*, 2nd edn (Cambridge: Cambridge University Press, 1983).

much reason to believe in the existence of propositions as we do to believe in the existence of numbers. Are there undeniable truths which require the existence of propositions, in the way in which certain mathematical truths seem to require the existence of numbers? Very plausibly, there are. Consider, for instance, a claim such as the following, which could surely be true: *there is something which John believes but which Mary does not believe* – which could be true because, for example, John believes that snow is white but Mary does not. What is this 'something' if not a *proposition* – as it turns out, the proposition that snow is white? Here it may be objected that I explained what is meant by a 'proposition' earlier by saying that a proposition constitutes the meaningful content of a *statement* in the context in which it is made, but that I am now assuming without argument that the very same thing may constitute the content of a *belief*. However, the assumption that the very same entity may serve both purposes is not an unreasonable one, because people typically make statements precisely in order to express their beliefs. Thus, if John makes the statement that snow is white, we naturally take him to be expressing a belief that snow is white: and so it is reasonable to suppose that the meaningful content of his statement coincides with the content of his belief – in short, that one and the same proposition provides the content both of his statement and of his belief. That, surely, is why we use the very same that-clause – 'that snow is white' – to specify the contents of both. The fact that we assume that statements and beliefs *have* 'contents' – and in appropriate circumstances the *same* contents – shows that we assume that the entities which we have been calling 'propositions' do indeed exist and that we have some sort of grasp of their identity-conditions. If we were to deny the existence of propositions, it seems that we would disqualify ourselves from admitting a host of truths to which we are currently committed quite as strongly as we are committed to the truths of mathematics. So let us assume, at least as a working hypothesis, that propositions do exist, are abstract entities, and constitute the contents of beliefs and other so-called propositional attitude states. And let us then see whether this hypothesis gives rise to any insuperable difficulties.

THE CAUSAL RELEVANCE OF CONTENT

A problem which we raised earlier was this: given that propositions themselves are abstract entities devoid of causal power, how is it that the propositional content of an attitudinal state can be causally relevant to any behaviour which that state may be invoked to explain? When I give a causal explanation of John's action of opening his umbrella by citing his belief *that it is raining* and his desire *that he should not get wet*, the success of my explanation depends upon my assigning those particular contents to his attitudinal states – and yet the contents in question are, it appears, just certain *propositions*, which surely cannot themselves have any causal impact whatever upon John's physical behaviour. One way in which we can try to resolve this difficulty is by distinguishing carefully between causal *relevance* and causal *efficacy*. Arguably, an item can have the former even if it lacks the latter. An item has *causal relevance* if reference to that item has a non-redundant role to play in a causal explanation of some phenomenon, whereas an item has *causal efficacy* if it has a power actually to be a cause of some phenomenon. Thus, it could be maintained that propositions lack causal efficacy but nonetheless possess causal relevance inasmuch as reference to them has a non-redundant role to play in causal explanations of human behaviour. But the problem remains as to *how* it could be the case that reference to propositions has a non-redundant role to play in causal explanations of human behaviour, given that they are purely abstract entities.

In answer to this problem, an analogy between propositions and numbers might be drawn upon.[4] Very often, it seems, reference to numbers has a non-redundant role to play in causal explanations of physical phenomena. For instance, we

---

[4] Sympathy for the following sort of analogy is expressed by Robert C. Stalnaker in his *Inquiry* (Cambridge, MA: MIT Press, 1984), pp. 8–14.

frequently explain physical events in terms which refer to the
lengths, *velocities* and *masses* of certain physical objects involved
in those events – and we report the magnitudes of these
quantities by using numerical expressions. Thus, we may say
that it was because a billiard ball weighing 100 grammes and
moving at a velocity of 2 metres per second collided with a
stationary billiard ball possessing the same mass, that the
two balls subsequently moved off in such-and-such a fashion.
Here the numbers 100 and 2 are invoked in the explanation
in what appears to be a non-redundant way. Of course, if we
had chosen different units for measuring mass and velocity,
we would have invoked different numbers in the explanation,
so that reference to *these particular numbers* is not essential to
the success of the explanation – but reference to numbers
one way or another does seem unavoidable, simply because
the explanation turns on the *magnitudes* of certain physical
quantities and such magnitudes seem to require numerical
expression. But there is no suggestion, obviously, that the
numbers invoked in such an explanation are themselves
amongst the *causes* of the physical event which is being
explained. Rather, the numbers simply serve to register the
results of possible *measurements* which could be performed
upon the physical quantities which are causally responsible
for the event in question. In analogous fashion, then, perhaps
we could regard abstract propositions as 'measures' or 'indi-
ces' of beliefs and other attitudinal states, that is, as providing a way of registering concrete differences between such
states analogous to concrete differences in magnitude
between physical quantities.

But there are serious difficulties facing this proposal, even
if we can really make sense of it. First of all, the analogy
breaks down at a crucial point.[5] As we have already noticed,
the choice of units for measuring a physical quantity is an
arbitrary one, so that there is no *particular* number which

---

[5] For further elaboration of some of the difficulties about to be raised, see Tim
Crane, 'An Alleged Analogy between Numbers and Propositions', *Analysis* 50
(1990), pp. 224–30.

uniquely serves to specify the magnitude of such a quantity: the same mass may be assigned a certain number when measured in kilogrammes and a quite different number when measured in pounds. By contrast, however, it seems clear that it is not at all arbitrary which proposition we chose to specify the content of a belief. It is true that one and the same belief may be expressed by statements made in any number of different languages, so that different *sentences* may certainly be used to specify the contents of one and the same belief. But sentences are not propositions. Indeed, where sentences of two different languages are mutually translatable – as, for example, are 'Snow is white' and 'La neige est blanche' – they serve to express *one and the same* proposition: and this proposition may constitute the content of someone's belief, irrespective of which language he or she may use to express that belief. So, while it is in a sense arbitrary whether one choses to express a belief by this or that sentence, it is not at all arbitrary whether one choses this or that proposition to specify its content. Furthermore, in the case of physical quantities – such as the masses of two lumps of lead – we can make direct comparisons which reveal their relative magnitudes independently of any choice of units in which to measure those quantities. Thus, we can ascertain that one lump of lead weighs *twice as much as* another by dividing the first into two pieces, each of which can be balanced in a scale against the other lump of lead. This difference between their relative magnitudes is an objective and fixed one which obtains independently of any choice of units we may decide upon for expressing those magnitudes numerically. However, in the case of beliefs, it does not appear that we can compare them for sameness or difference of content 'directly', that is, independently of selecting particular propositions to specify their contents. This implies once again that the relation between a belief and its propositional content is not at all like the relation between a physical quantity and a number which serves to register its magnitude, so that it becomes highly doubtful whether the way in which numbers can be invoked in causal explanations of physical events can provide any real insight into the way in which propositions can be invoked in causal explanations of human behaviour. It is far from evident that there is any concrete feature of a belief of which a proposition could serve as something like a 'measure' or 'index', but which exists independently of the proposition 'measuring' or 'indicating' it: rather, beliefs seem to involve particular propositions *essentially*, as constituents which partly determine the very identities of the beliefs whose contents they are.

At this point, some philosophers may urge that there is in fact a way of conceiving of beliefs and other attitudinal states which preserves the idea that they have abstract propositional contents and yet which accounts for the explanatory relevance of those contents in terms of *concrete* features of the states in question. This is to think of attitudinal states by analogy with *sentence-tokens*. Sentence-tokens are concrete strings of physical marks with a definite spatiotemporal location and distinctive causal powers: and yet they may also be assigned abstract propositional contents to the extent that they are meaningful bits of language. The suggestion, then, would be that 'beliefs', for example, are sentence-like items which the brain utilises in a particular kind of way in the course of generating certain patterns of bodily behaviour, rather as a computer utilises messages in binary code in the course of generating certain patterns of activity in its printer or on its video screen. In calling the items in question 'sentence-like', it is not being suggested that they take the physical form of strings of words written in any recognisable natural language, such as English or French, but only that they exhibit something like a formal *grammatical* or *syntactical* structure, in much the same way that sentences of a natural language and messages in artificial computer code both do. The 'brain code' might exploit, say, certain repeatable and systematically combinable patterns of neuronal activity, rather as the machine code of a computer exploits patterns of electromagnetic activity in the computer's electronic circuits.[6] Now, if brain-code tokens could be assigned meaningful propositional contents, and if the propositional content of such a token were somehow reflected by its formal syntactical structure, we can see in principle how the propositional content of a brain-code token might derive causal relevance from its relationship to the structural features of that token, which have physical form and thus genuine causal powers. This proposal is highly speculative and a proper evaluation of it is beyond the scope of this chapter, though we shall return to it in chapters 7 and 8 when we come to discuss the relationship between language and thought and the prospects for artificial intelligence. For the time being, we may observe that brain-code tokens certainly could not acquire meaningful propositional content in anything like the way in which sentence-tokens of natural language do, since the latter are meaningful precisely because people use them to express and communicate their contentful thoughts – and it would plainly be circular to try to explain the propositional content of brain-code tokens in this way. However, later in this chapter we shall look at some naturalistic theories of representation which might be drawn upon to explain how brain-code tokens could possess meaningful propositional content.

The questions raised in this section are difficult ones, which we cannot hope to settle conclusively just now. Suffice it to say that the problem of explaining how mental states can have 'contents' which are causally relevant to the behaviour which such states are typically invoked to explain is a serious one. We seem to be strongly committed, in our commonsense or 'folk psychological' ways of thinking about people, to the idea that attitudinal states with abstract propositional content can legitimately be invoked in causal explanations of people's actions. And yet we also seem to be somewhat at a loss to explain how propositional content, thus conceived, could have any causal relevance to physical behavi-

---

[6] The idea of a brain code, or 'language of thought', modelled on the machine code of a digital computer, has been defended by Jerry A. Fodor: see his *The Language of Thought* (Hassocks: Harvester Press, 1976).

our – unless, perhaps, the 'brain code' proposal just canvassed can be made to bear fruit. Some philosophers may be tempted to say that the way out of this difficulty is to realise that the kind of 'explanation' of human action which is involved when we make appeal to an agent's beliefs and desires is not, after all, *causal* explanation but, rather, 'rational' explanation. On this view, we cite an agent's putative beliefs and desires as *reasons for*, but not as *causes of*, his or her actions. After all, the abstract nature of propositional content provides no barrier to its *rational* relevance to action, even if it does provide a barrier to its *causal* relevance. However, this approach too faces certain difficulties, as we shall see when we come to discuss action and intention in chapter 9. But even if an obvious way out of the difficulty is not yet available, I do not think that this should persuade us to abandon 'folk psychological' modes of explanation, as eliminative materialists would like us to. For, as we saw in the previous chapter, it is doubtful whether this is a coherent option for us.

THE INDIVIDUATION OF CONTENT

We have been taking it that contentful attitudinal states, such as beliefs and desires, have their abstract propositional content *essentially*, an implication of this being that the very identity of a particular belief or desire depends upon the identity of the proposition which constitutes its content. Thus, just as *John's* belief that snow is white is numerically distinct from *Mary's* belief that snow is white, in virtue of the fact that John is a different person from Mary, so also John's belief *that snow is white* is numerically distinct from John's belief *that grass is green*, in virtue of the fact that the proposition that snow is white is different from the proposition that grass is green. But *how*, exactly, do we individuate the propositional content of a belief or other attitudinal state? In practice, of course, we try to do this by citing a *sentence* which we take to express the same propositional content as belongs to the attitudinal state in question. But now certain complications arise, because tokens of one and the same sentence-type may serve to express different propositions in different contexts of utterance. For example, suppose I say that John believes that it is raining. Here I use the sentence 'It is raining' to specify the propositional content of John's belief. But tokens of the sentence-type 'It is raining' express different propositions when uttered in different contexts. What I assert to be the case when I assert 'It is raining' *in Durham* is not what John asserts to be the case if he asserts 'It is raining' *in New York*. So, when I in Durham say that John in New York believes that it is raining, which proposition I am identifying as the content of his belief? Most probably, the proposition that John would express if *he* were to assert 'It is raining', rather than the proposition that *I* would express by asserting 'It is raining'. One might endeavour to make this clear by saying that what John believes is that it is raining *in New York*, or that it is raining *where he is*. However, in saying this one must be careful not to imply that John's belief would be more aptly expressed *by him* as 'It is raining in New York' or 'It is raining where I am'. Indeed, John could possess the belief that it is raining where he is without having the slightest idea that he is in New York and even in complete ignorance as to his whereabouts.

These complications have arisen in the case of John's belief that it is raining because the content of that belief is implicitly *indexical*. Indexicality is commonly exhibited in language through the medium of expressions such as 'here', 'now' and 'this', whose reference is determined partly by their context of use. Thus, 'here' and 'now' are standardly used by speakers to refer, respectively, to the *place* and the *time* at which they are speaking, while 'this' is standardly used by a speaker to refer to some object at which he or she is pointing (often with his or her 'index' finger). It may superficially seem that indexicality is a relatively unimportant feature of human thought and language, but in reality that is far from being the case. Indeed, it may be argued that virtually all of our thought is implicitly indexical, in one way or another. Take, for instance, John's belief *that snow is white*. One might imagine that this, at least, contains no element of indexicality. The case seems quite unlike that of John's belief *that it is raining*, where the propositional content of his belief is partly determined by contextual factors, namely, the time and place at which John has the belief in question. How could contextual factors have any bearing upon the propositional content of John's belief that snow is white? Well, it certainly seems that they do, as the following considerations serve to show.[7]

Snow, as practically everyone knows, is just frozen water – and water is now known by scientists to be nothing other than H_2O, that is, a stuff composed of molecules containing two hydrogen atoms bonded to a single oxygen atom. However, not everybody who is acquainted with water knows that it is H_2O and, indeed, more than 200 years ago no one at all knew this. Clearly, then, John can possess the belief that snow is white without being aware that water is H_2O. Even so, it seems that inasmuch as John's belief that snow is white is a belief concerning the properties of *water*, it is a belief about the kind of stuff which is in fact H_2O. If John were to be miraculously transported to some distant planet whose seas were composed of a different kind of liquid, but one which looked and tasted just like water and which turned white upon freezing, he might *think* that the white, fluffy stuff descending from that planet's skies on a cold day was snow – but he would be mistaken. But now suppose that, by some strange coincidence, the inhabitants of this planet speak a language which sounds just like English and that *they* use the word 'snow' for the stuff descending from their skies. An inhabitant of the planet who believed, correctly, that this stuff is white would naturally express that belief by asserting 'Snow is white'. But, it seems, the propositional content of such a belief would be different from the propositional

---

[7] Considerations of this sort were first articulated by Hilary Putnam in his influential paper, 'The Meaning of "Meaning" ', in K. Gunderson (ed.), *Language, Mind and Knowledge: Minnesota Studies in the Philosophy of Science, Volume 7* (Minneapolis: University of Minnesota Press, 1975), reprinted in Hilary Putnam, *Mind, Language and Reality: Philosophical Papers, Volume 2* (Cambridge: Cambridge University Press, 1975).

content of *John's* belief that snow is white. It would be wrong for *us* – and wrong for *John* – to say that the inhabitants of the distant planet believe *that snow is white*, even though they themselves would correctly describe their own state of belief by saying 'We believe that snow is white'. The best that *we* can do to describe the inhabitants' state of belief is to say that they believe that 'their' snow is white, or something like that. The implication of these considerations is that even beliefs about the properties of kinds of stuff are implicitly indexical, or context-dependent, in character. The propositional content of such a belief is partly determined by the believer's physical relationship to the kind of stuff in question. Although John and one of the inhabitants of the distant planet would both be prepared to assert the sentence 'Snow is white', they would thereby be expressing beliefs with different propositional contents, simply because 'snow' denotes different kinds of stuff for them, whether they are aware of this fact or not. It denotes different kinds of stuff for them because, whether they know it or not, different kinds of fluffy, white stuff descend from their respective home skies on a cold day.

EXTERNALISM IN THE PHILOSOPHY OF MIND

If contextual factors have a bearing upon the propositional content even of so general a belief as the belief that snow is white, then it seems that they will have a bearing upon practically all of our beliefs – certainly upon all those beliefs which we express using so-called *natural kind terms*, such as 'water', 'gold', 'cat', 'elm', 'dolphin', and the like. In the case of such beliefs, their propositional content will depend upon what kinds of stuff or things *in fact* populate the physical environment of the believer and serve as the referents of the natural kind terms which the believer uses in expressing his or her beliefs. This conclusion has surprisingly far-reaching implications both for the philosophy of mind and for epistemology. Consider, for instance, Descartes's famous attempt to call into doubt all of his commonsense beliefs about what exists.[8] Descartes thought it made sense to suppose that his beliefs about all manner of natural kinds of things and stuffs were simply *false*, because they could conceivably have been induced in him by a malicious demon. Thus, he supposes, the demon might have induced him to believe that snow is white, even though in reality no such stuff as snow exists at all because the entire physical world is illusory. But is it right to assume that the belief which Descartes would express by asserting 'Snow is white' in the hypothetical circumstances of a demon-induced illusion would have *the very same propositional content* as the belief which Descartes in fact expresses by asserting 'Snow is white' in a world in which snow really does exist? Not if our earlier considerations are correct. Those considerations seem to imply that only someone whose world really does contain *water* – that is, H_2O – can have the belief *that snow is white*. But if Descartes were the victim of a demonic illusion, he would *not* be someone living in such a world and thus would not be able to have a belief with that very propositional content: consequently, the demon would not be able to deceive Descartes into believing, falsely, *that snow is white*. If, in the hypothetical circumstances of a demon-induced illusion, Descartes were to assert 'Snow is white', he would not be expressing *the very same belief* upon which he is trying to cast doubt, namely, his belief that snow is white. Indeed, it is not clear that, in those hypothetical circumstances, Descartes could express any determinate belief at all by asserting 'Snow is white', any more than it is clear that we can express any determinate belief at all by asserting 'Unicorns are white'. The trouble with the latter assertion is that 'unicorn' purports to be a natural kind term and yet there is no natural kind which it actually serves to denote.[9]

It seems, then, that a subject's state of mind – at least

---

[8] See René Descartes, *Meditations on First Philosophy*, in *The Philosophical Writings of Descartes*, ed. J. Cottingham *et al.* (Cambridge: Cambridge University Press, 1984).

[9] See further Saul A. Kripke, *Naming and Necessity* (Oxford: Blackwell, 1980), p. 24 and pp. 156–8.

to the extent that it involves the possession of contentful attitudinal states – is not what it is independently of that subject's relations to his or her physical environment. Contrary to what appears to be the Cartesian assumption, our minds are not self-contained and hermetically sealed vessels of thought: rather, they 'reach out', as it were, into our physical environment, since our thoughts depend for their content and thus for their very identity upon what things that environment contains. It is important to appreciate, however, that this is not an objection to Descartes's *dualism* of mind and body, even if such dualism is objectionable for other reasons. Rather, it is an objection to his *individualistic* or *internalist* conception of the mind, whereby mental states depend for their *content* upon nothing external to the person whose states they are. Even a thoroughgoing physicalist could espouse internalism of this sort and even a thoroughgoing dualist could reject it in favour of its opposite, *externalism*.[10]

BROAD VERSUS NARROW CONTENT

The line of argument which we have just been pursuing and which has led us to a rejection of an 'individualistic' or 'internalist' conception of the mind is not one which all contemporary philosophers would look upon with favour. Many philosophers feel strongly committed to the view that contentful attitudinal states can quite properly be invoked in causal explanations of people's behaviour, but at the same time consider that this explanatory role cannot easily be attributed to attitudinal states if their content is individuated

---

[10] For an influential defence of externalism, see Tyler Burge, 'Individualism and the Mental', *Midwest Studies in Philosophy* 4 (1979), pp. 73–121. See also his 'Individualism and Psychology', *Philosophical Review* 95 (1986), pp. 3–45. Burge argues that mental content depends on *social* as well as merely physical environmental circumstances. For an extended discussion and critique of internalism, see Robert A. Wilson, *Cartesian Psychology and Physical Minds: Individualism and the Sciences of the Mind* (Cambridge: Cambridge University Press, 1995). For a defence of internalism from a physicalist perspective, see Norton Nelkin, *Consciousness and the Origins of Thought* (Cambridge: Cambridge University Press, 1996), Part 3.

in an externalist way.[11] Consider the following case. Suppose that John is seen to pick up and drink from a glass of water which is standing on a table in front of him. Part of a plausible explanation of John's action would be that he felt thirsty, saw the glass and judged that it contained water, a liquid which he believes to be drinkable. Here we are invoking John's putative beliefs *that the glass contains water* and *that water is drinkable* in explanation of his action of drinking from the glass. Now, externalism contends that John could not even possess these beliefs but for the fact that his physical environment contains water, that is, H_2O. But recall the distant planet of our earlier discussion, whose oceans contain a clear, tasteless liquid which *its* inhabitants call 'water', but which is *not* H_2O. Imagine an exact counterpart, or 'Doppelgänger', of John living on that planet who drinks from a glass of that liquid in circumstances exactly similar to John's – and consider how one might explain *his* action. We may suppose, if we like, that John and his counterpart are exactly similar not only in appearance and character, but right down to the level of neurological organisation and activity. According to externalism, we cannot explain the action of John's counterpart by saying that he believes that the glass in front of him contains *water* and that *water* is drinkable, because according to that view John's counterpart does not possess such beliefs. And yet John and his counterpart appear to behave in exactly the same way in exactly similar circumstances, so that it seems reasonable to *explain* their behaviour in exactly the same way, by assigning to them exactly similar states of mind – that is to say, states of mind with exactly the same contents. This is simply to apply the well-tried explanatory principle, 'Same effect, same causes'. But externalism, it

[11] This kind of concern has been influentially voiced by Jerry A. Fodor in several important papers, including 'Methodological Solipsism Considered as a Research Strategy in Cognitive Psychology', *Behavioral and Brain Sciences* 3 (1980), pp. 63–109, reprinted in his *Representations: Philosophical Essays on the Foundations of Cognitive Science* (Brighton: Harvester Press, 1981), and 'A Modal Argument for Narrow Content', *Journal of Philosophy* 88 (1991), pp. 5–26. More recently, Fodor has retreated somewhat from this position: see his *The Elm and the Expert: Mentalese and its Semantics* (Cambridge, MA: MIT Press, 1994).

seems, does not permit us to do this. (Of course, we *do* sometimes discover that the same effect can proceed from different causes – for instance, that a skin burn can be caused either by acid or by fire: so the principle 'Same effect, same causes' is certainly not infallible. But when we abandon the principle we should only do so for good empirical reasons, whereas in the case at issue externalism apparently compels us to abandon it on non-empirical grounds.)

What appears to be called for, then, is a notion of mental content which allows us to say, as externalism does not, that John and his counterpart have beliefs with exactly the same propositional contents. Content of the desired kind is standardly called *narrow* content, in contrast with the so-called *broad* (or *wide*) content associated with the externalist account.[12] The idea is that whereas broad content is determined in part by a thinker's relations to his or her wider physical environment, narrow content is identifiable independently of any such relations. But is such a notion of narrow content really available? In support of a positive answer to this question, it may be urged that there clearly *is* something in common between John and his counterpart in respect of their beliefs concerning the things and stuffs confronting them: *both of them* believe that they are confronted by a glass containing a clear, tasteless liquid which composes the oceans of their planets and which rains down from their skies and *both of them* believe that that liquid is drinkable. The chemical differences between these stuffs may well be quite unknown to John and his counterpart and, certainly, the processes of thought and reasoning which lead them to act as they do need make no appeal to the chemical constitutions of those stuffs. Perhaps, indeed, it would be mistaken to say that both John and his counterpart believe that the glass in front of them contains *water*, for the reasons which the externalist gives. But maybe this only goes to show that our

---

[12] For a wide-ranging discussion of rival conceptions of mental content, see Colin McGinn, *Mental Content* (Oxford: Blackwell, 1989). McGinn defends a version of externalism in this book.

commonsense or 'folk-psychological' assignments of mental content implicitly assume a 'broad' notion of content, not that such a notion is the only one available. Ordinary English may not contain a general term which enables us to specify the hypothesised content which the beliefs of John and his counterpart allegedly have in common, but nothing seems to prevent us from *inventing* one – say, 'schwater'. Then, it seems, we could say that both John and his counterpart believe that the glass in front of them contains *schwater* and that both of them believe that *schwater* is drinkable. The fact that neither John nor his counterpart has the word 'schwater' in their respective vocabularies – and thus cannot *express* the beliefs which they supposedly have in common by means of simple sentences – need not be seen as an embarrassment for this approach. For there are obvious reasons why ordinary language, which has evolved to serve the communicative purposes of people who inhabit much the same physical environment, should not contain general terms which function in the way in which we have stipulated that 'schwater' does.

However, the argument which motivated us to introduce the notion of 'narrow' content may itself be queried. The crucial premise of that argument was that John and his counterpart *behave in the same way*, whence we concluded that it is reasonable to *explain* their behaviour in the same way – appealing to the principle 'Same effect, same causes'. But the claim that John and his counterpart behave in the same way may itself be challenged.[13] After all, it may be pointed out, what *John* does is to drink a glass of *water*, whereas John's counterpart does not do this – instead, he drinks a glass of the different kind of stuff found in the oceans of his planet. Given this difference between their actions, it seems altogether reasonable to explain those actions as proceeding from beliefs with *different* contents – in John's case, the beliefs that the glass in front of him contains *water* and that *water* is

---

[13] A useful discussion of some of the points raised here may be found in Gregory McCulloch, *The Mind and its World* (London: Routledge, 1995), pp. 211–16.

drinkable and, in his counterpart's case, the beliefs that the glass in front of him contains what *he* calls 'water' and that what *he* calls 'water' is drinkable. In short, it now looks as though the notion of 'narrow' content, even if it makes sense, is superfluous, because there is no special difficulty after all in supposing that 'broad' content is relevant to the causal explanation of behaviour. (This is not to deny that, as we discovered earlier, there is a *general* difficulty concerning the causal relevance of content: it is just to deny that the notion of 'broad' content is somehow more problematic than the notion of 'narrow' content in this respect.)

Now, the advocates of narrow content have a possible response to this objection. They can urge that the actions of John and his counterpart only differ on a *broad* construal of their respective behaviours. Behaviour itself, then, as well as the contents of its mental causes, might be characterised in both a 'broad' and a 'narrow' way. Thus, both John and his counterpart might be described as drinking a glass of *schwater*, in which case it seems reasonable, once more, to explain this sameness of behaviour in terms of the two agents having beliefs with the same contents. However, this reply does not really undermine the point of the objection, which was that there is no special difficulty in supposing that 'broad' content is relevant to the causal explanation of behaviour. The fact that we have not shown that the notions of 'narrow' content and 'narrow' behaviour are untenable is beside the point. Given that our intuitive notion of content seems to be the 'broad' notion and that it suffices for explanatory purposes at least as well as the far less intuitive 'narrow' notion, our conclusion that the latter notion is superfluous would appear to stand. Of course, physicalists who hold that the mental state types exemplified by a person at any given time *supervene* upon the neurological state types exemplified by that person at that time – see chapter 3 for this idea – will want to insist that, inasmuch as John and his counterpart are neurological duplicates, they must exemplify the same mental state types and thus possess beliefs with the same contents (on the assumption, at least, that we type beliefs by reference to their contents). Such philosophers will accordingly be committed, it seems, to the notion of 'narrow' content, for better or worse. But we should not suppose that an externalist is prevented from espousing physicalism, even of the relatively weak non-reductive variety: for the externalist may contend that, while a person's mental state types at any given time do not supervene upon that person's concurrent neurological state types *alone*, they do supervene upon the latter *in conjunction with* certain types of physical state exemplified by the person's environment at that time.

CONTENT, REPRESENTATION AND CAUSALITY

What is it that confers upon attitudinal states the particular propositional contents that they possess? When John has the belief that snow is white, what gives his belief the content *that snow is white* – as opposed, say, to the content *that grass is green*? Most contemporary philosophers would prefer, if possible, to find a perfectly naturalistic answer to this sort of question – that is, an answer which does not appeal to divine creation and which does not assume that the phenomenon in question is so fundamental as to be inexplicable save in its own terms. Thus, they would not be satisfied with any sort of answer which only explains how one subject's attitudinal states get their content by reference to the contentful states of *another* subject. They would like an explanation of the origin of content which shows how it can derive from *non*-contentful states of naturally existing objects. This is a tall order: it is far from clear that an explanation of this sort really is available, even in principle. But it is worthwhile looking for one, if only in order to see why such an explanation is so difficult to achieve.

Now, attitudinal states are contentful because they are *representational* states. Thus, for example, John's belief that snow is white represents the world as *being* a certain way. Desires, equally, are representational states, although they do not represent the world as *being* a certain way but, rather, represent how their subject would *like* the world to be. This difference between beliefs and desires is often described as a difference in their 'direction of fit' with the world.[14] We aim to make the contents of our beliefs fit the way the world is – that is, we aim at *true* beliefs – whereas, by contrast, we aim to make the way the world is fit the contents of our desires: we aim to *satisfy* our desires. However, in order to simplify matters, let us concentrate on the case of beliefs and their contents. And let us then ask: in virtue of what does a particular belief represent the world as being a particular way? Perhaps we can make some headway with this question by seeing how other kinds of states of natural objects can be representational states.

The following looks as if it may be a promising example of such a state. Consider the way in which the pattern of rings in a cross-section of a tree-trunk serves to represent the age of the tree in years. We know why it serves to do this: it does so because there is a causal relationship between seasonal climatic variations and variations in the organic growth of the tree, which has the consequence that a new ring is laid down during each year of growth. It seems, then, that the tree's ring-pattern represents the fact that the tree is a certain number of years old because the tree's being that many years old is the *cause* of its having that ring-pattern. We might try to extend a causal account of representation of this sort to the case of beliefs. Thus, we might venture to say something like the following:

(1) A belief B represents the world as including a state of affairs S just in case S is the cause of B.

However, it is immediately apparent that some serious problems beset this suggestion, two of which I shall now describe.

First of all, it will never be the case that there is just a *single* state of affairs, S, which is 'the' cause of a given belief B. For, in virtue of the transitivity of causation, if a state of affairs, S_1, causes another state of affairs, S_2, and S_2 in turn

[14] See further John R. Searle, *Intentionality* (Cambridge: Cambridge University Press, 1983), pp. 7–9.

causes the belief B, then S_1 *as well as* S_2 is a cause of B. This sort of complication already arises in the case of the tree-ring example. For it is certainly not the case that the *only* state of affairs which can be said to be causally responsible for the tree's having its particular ring-pattern is the fact that the tree has lived for a certain number of years, that is, through a certain number of revolutions of the earth around the sun. After all, the mere passage of time does not cause the tree's cyclical pattern of growth: rather, that pattern of growth is caused by variations in climatic conditions which are themselves caused by variations in the earth's distance from and orientation towards the sun as the earth revolves in its orbit. So why should we say that the ring-pattern represents the fact that the tree *is a certain number of years old*, as opposed to the quite distinct fact that the tree *has lived through a certain number of climatic cycles*? It seems that we have no good reason at all to say this, other than that we may be more interested in the ring-pattern for what it tells us about the age of the tree than we are for what it tells us about the number of climatic cycles the tree has lived through. Viewed objectively, the ring-pattern carries information about the *entire* causal chain of processes which gave rise to it, not just about a particular stage in that causal chain. This creates no problem for what we say about tree-ring patterns, but it does create a problem for a causal theory of belief-content. For the fact is that a belief B will represent the world as including a quite specific state of affairs, S, not *every* state of affairs which, perhaps along with S, may be causally responsible for the generation of B. We might call this problem *the problem of the specificity of content*.

Another problem for a causal theory of belief-content is that, even if it could successfully account for a belief's *correctly* representing the world as being a certain way, it is not clear that it could successfully account for a belief's *mis*representing the world as being a certain way. It goes without saying that not all of our beliefs are true. A belief, B, is false if B represents the world as including a certain state of affairs, S, when in fact the world does *not* include S. But the

trouble is that if the world does not include *S*, then *S* cannot
be a *cause* of *B*. Rather, *B* will have certain other, actually
existing states of affairs as its causes: and it looks as though
the causal theory is committed to judging that *B* represents –
truly – the world as including some or all of *these* states of
affairs, rather than as including *S*. In short, the causal theory
seems condemned to treat all beliefs as *true* beliefs, which is
absurd. Consider again the tree-ring example. If we were to
discover a tree which had a pattern of twenty-five rings, say,
when we knew that the tree had in fact lived for twenty-six
years, what would we say? Would we say that the ring-pattern
misrepresents the tree's age? Arguably we should not. Tree-ring
patterns do not literally err or lie, even though we may be
misled by them. What we would probably surmise, in such a
case, is that the climatic conditions through which this particular tree had lived must have been such that one of its
rings took two years rather than one to be laid down. Surely,
the tree's ring-pattern does not carry 'false' information
about its causal history, because it seems that the notion of
'false' information does not even make sense in such a context. Yet truth and falsehood are certainly properties of our
beliefs: properties which any adequate theory of mental representation must be able to account for. The causal theory of
content seems ill-equipped to do that, however. We may call
this second problem *the problem of misrepresentation*.

MISREPRESENTATION AND NORMALITY

Perhaps, though, the two problems which we have raised for
a causal theory of belief-content only threaten an oversim-
plified version of that approach, as exemplifed by (1) above.[15]
It may be suggested, for instance, that the problem of misrepresentation can be overcome by referring to the *normal*
causes of a given *type* of belief rather than simply to the *actual*

---

[15] For a sophisticated version of the causal theory of representation, see Jerry A.
Fodor, *Psychosemantics: The Problem of Meaning in the Philosophy of Mind*, (Cambridge,
MA: MIT Press, 1987), ch. 4.

causes of this or that *particular* or *token* belief. This distinction could even be invoked in the case of tree-ring patterns. Thus, while a pattern of twenty-five rings in a particular tree could conceivably be laid down as a result of climatic changes spanning twenty-six years, we have reason to believe that this would be highly unusual. As a general rule, a twenty-five ring pattern in a tree is a highly reliable indication that the tree's age is twenty-five years. So perhaps we could, after all, say that a freak pattern of twenty-five rings laid down in twenty-six years would 'misrepresent' the real age of the tree in question. We could say this if we held that the reason why a pattern of twenty-five rings in a particular tree 'represents' the age of that tree as being twenty-five years is not that *this particular pattern* has been caused by twenty-five years' growth, but rather that this particular pattern is one of a *type* that is *normally* caused by twenty-five years' growth. By extension, we could similarly alter our earlier proposal concerning belief-content, (1), to something like this:

(2) A belief B represents the world as including a state of affairs S of a certain type just in case a state of affairs of S's type is normally the cause of a belief of B's type.

Then we could say that a belief B *mis*represents the world as including a state of affairs S of a certain type just in case a state of affairs of S's type is normally the cause of a belief of B's type but B was *not* in fact caused by a state of affairs of S's type.

However, we need to look very carefully at the notion of 'normality' that is in play here. In the case of tree-ring patterns, it would appear that we can only appeal to a *statistical* notion of normality: in this sense, to say that a twenty-five ring pattern is *normally* caused by twenty-five years' growth is just to say that there is a very high probability that any such pattern will have such a cause. But the sense in which it is 'normal' for *beliefs* to represent correctly or truly is not a statistical but a *teleological* one, in that truth is the *aim* or *goal* of belief and beliefs which fall short of it are criticised on that account. It can be quite 'normal', in the *statistical* sense, for beliefs to be caused by states of affairs which are contrary to how those beliefs represent the world as being. This, after all, is the basis of many perceptual illusions. For example, when people see an object lying at the bottom of a tank of water, it is very common for them to believe that the object is closer to the surface than it really is: and yet its being at its actual depth in the water is causally responsible for their mistaken belief – for if it had been where they believe it to be, they would have believed it to be closer still. Again, it is very common for people to exhibit unwarranted optimism, or wishful thinking, believing that some desirable state of affairs obtains when in reality it does not. We may criticise them for holding such false beliefs because they fall short of the norm of truth: but if we had to say that what a belief represents as being the case is merely a matter of what is *likely* to cause such a belief, we could not even make sense of the notion of there being types of belief which are commonly false. However, the problem now is that although the *statistical* notion of normality is undeniably a naturalistic one, which in no way relies upon a prior notion of mental content, it is far from clear that the same can be said about the *teleological* notion of normality. Talk about 'aims' or 'goals' seems to be unescapably mentalistic in character. Surely, only minded beings – subjects of experience – can *literally* have aims or goals: and they have them, moreover, precisely in virtue of having contentful mental states, such as beliefs and desires. If that is so, and if the statistical notion of normality will not help the causal theory of content to solve the problem of misrepresentation, then it begins to look as though the causal theory is doomed to failure. Nor should we forget that the theory is also beset by other problems. The problem of the specificity of content is one of these, which afflicts proposal (2) quite as much as proposal (1). (Another problem is posed by beliefs whose content concerns *the future* – for example, a belief that it will rain tomorrow – for we do not want to say that tomorrow's rain can be the cause of today's belief, as this would involve backward causation.)

THE TELEOLOGICAL APPROACH TO REPRESENTATION

Despite suspicions of the kind just raised, some philosophers consider that a wholly naturalistic account of certain teleological notions can in fact be provided and that these notions can then be used, without circularity, as the basis of a naturalistic account of the origin of mental content.[16] The key idea here is to appeal to the biological theory of evolution by natural selection – the underlying supposition being that mental states are essentially states of biological organisms. It is relatively uncontroversial that many biological structures have quite specific *functions*: for instance, that the function of the heart is to pump blood around the body.[17] We might even say that the heart beats as it does *in order to* pump blood around the body. This is to ascribe to the heart a certain *aim* or *goal*: indeed, it is to describe it as acting in the way it does as a *means* to a certain *end*. And such terminology is quite explicitly teleological in character. Of course, most of us no longer think that the heart was literally *designed* to act in this way – not, at least, in any sense which implies that it was the product of an intelligent designer. We think, rather, that hearts are so ubiquitous in the animal kingdom because creatures possessing such organs are well adapted to their environment and consequently survive to pass on to their offspring genes which cause them also to have hearts. In short, hearts have been *selected* for their blood-pumping capacity because that trait is *adaptive* – and *that* is why we can describe the heart

[16] Two important developments of this idea are to be found in Ruth Garrett Millikan, *Language, Thought and Other Biological Categories: New Foundations for Realism* (Cambridge, MA: MIT Press, 1984) and David Papineau, *Reality and Representation* (Oxford: Blackwell, 1987), ch. 4. See also David Papineau, *Philosophical Naturalism* (Oxford: Blackwell, 1993), ch. 3.

[17] 'Function', in this sense, should not be conflated with the notion of 'function' that is associated with the doctrine of 'functionalism', discussed in the previous chapter. For more on functions in this sense – or 'proper functions', as Millikan calls them – see Millikan, *Language, Thought and Other Biological Categories*, ch. 1.

in seemingly teleological terms as having the 'function' of pumping blood around the body.[18] There are many other things which the heart does which it is not its *function* to do, because hearts were *not* selected for these other traits. For example, when it beats, the heart makes a certain noise, which can be heard with the help of a stethoscope. But it is not the *function* of the heart to make this noise, because it was not in virtue of the heart's making this noise that possession of a heart enhanced our ancestors' chances of survival.

Now, just as there has been selection for certain of the physiological traits of animals in the course of evolution, so also, very plausibly, has there been selection for certain of their *mental* and *behavioural* traits. Consider, for instance, the various different alarm-calls used by vervet monkeys to alert other monkeys to the presence of various kinds of predator.[19] One type of call appears to represent the presence of eagles, another the presence of snakes, and yet another the presence of leopards. Notice that we are already talking here about a system of *representation* – one which we can reasonably suppose to have an evolutionary origin. What entitles us to say, though, that a certain type of call has the function of alerting the monkeys to the presence of a specific kind of predator – *eagles*, say? An evolutionary answer to this question might proceed as follows. First, we should appreciate that different types of behaviour will enable monkeys to evade attack by different kinds of predator. Thus, in the presence of eagles, protection will be afforded by running into the bushes, but such behaviour will not afford protection against snakes. Monkeys which are genetically predisposed both to make a

---

[18] On the notion of selection 'for' a trait and its significance for the teleological approach to representation, see Daniel C. Dennett, *Darwin's Dangerous Idea* (London: Penguin Books, 1995), pp. 407–8. See also his *The Intentional Stance* (Cambridge, MA: MIT Press, 1987), ch. 7.

[19] For further background to this example, see Dorothy L. Cheney and Robert M. Seyfarth, *How Monkeys See the World: Inside the Mind of Another Species* (Chicago: University of Chicago Press, 1990), ch. 4. For discussion of the philosophical implications, see Daniel C. Dennett, 'Intentional Systems in Cognitive Ethology: The "Panglossian Paradigm" Defended', *Behavioral and Brain Sciences* 6 (1983), pp. 343–90, reprinted in his *The Intentional Stance*, ch. 7.

certain type of call in the presence of eagles and to respond
to that type of call by running into the bushes will accordingly
have a greater chance of surviving attacks by eagles – and
passing on this predisposition to their offspring – than will
monkeys which are not predisposed to behave in these ways.
So, it would seem, the reason why we can say that this type
of call has the function of alerting the monkeys to the presence of eagles is that there has been selection for this predisposition because it helps the monkeys to evade attack by
eagles.

Notice how this approach to representation differs from
the causal account illustrated earlier by the example of tree-
ring patterns. For one thing, the present approach attempts
to explain why a certain type of call represents what it does
for the monkeys which make this type of call, whereas there was no
suggestion, in the tree-ring example, that a given pattern of
rings represents anything *for the tree exhibiting it*. This immediately makes the teleological approach more appealing as a
potential explanation of the basis of mental representation,
for such representation, too, is 'for' the subjects of the representational states in question. Notice, next, that on the teleological approach, it is not being suggested – as the causal
account would imply – that a certain type of call made by the
monkeys represents the presence of eagles simply because
the presence of eagles *normally causes* the monkeys to make
calls of this type. Here we should once again recall the problem of the specificity of content. When the presence of an
eagle causes a monkey to make one of these calls, it presumably does so because a soaring or swooping eagle presents a
certain characteristic silhouette against the sky, which is the
visual cue for a monkey to make the call. Evidence for this
would be that if one were to simulate the presence of an
eagle by flying a kite with an eagle-like silhouette, one could
thereby cause a monkey to make such a call even in the
absence of a real eagle. And yet we want to say that what
this type of call represents for the monkeys who use it is the
presence of *eagles*, not the presence of a certain kind of *silhouette*. The causal theory does not explain what entitles us to

say this, however, because it is just as true to say that the presence of that kind of silhouette normally causes a monkey to make that type of call as it is to say that the presence of an eagle normally causes a monkey to make that type of call. In normal circumstances, the presence of an eagle causes the presence of the characteristic silhouette, which in turn causes the monkey to make the call: and yet we want to say that what the call represents is only one of these causes – the presence of an eagle. A teleological theory of representation can explain why we are entitled to do so. For its advocates can point out that the monkeys' calling-and-hiding behaviour is adaptive because it helps them to evade attack by *eagles*: it is the eagles, not their silhouettes, which present a threat to the monkeys' survival, even though their silhouettes provide the monkeys' visual cue for the presence of eagles. Indeed, if all the eagles in the monkeys' environment were to be replaced by numerous kite-flying children who constantly triggered the monkeys' calling-and-hiding behaviour, that behaviour would soon cease to be adaptive because the monkeys would waste time and energy in needless activity.

So, it seems, a teleological theory of representation can, at least in principle, overcome the problem of the specificity of content. Equally, it seems that it can, in principle, overcome the problem of misrepresentation. For where we can ascribe a *function* to a biological structure, in the evolutionary sense explained above, we can also talk about that structure *mal*-functioning – as when a heart fails to pump blood in the way that it should. If a monkey were to make an eagle-call in the presence of a child's kite rather than a real eagle, we would say that the call was a 'false alarm' – and rightly so, according to the teleological theory, because the call would not be serving the purpose for which evolution had 'designed' it. This is a better solution to the problem of misrepresentation than the one canvassed earlier, which appealed – in the context of a causal theory of representation – to a merely statistical notion of 'normality'. We observed that that solution could not accommodate the fact that, in certain circumstances, false representations could be more common than true ones.

The teleological theory can cope with this fact, however. For example, in circumstances in which most of the eagles in the monkeys' environment have been replaced by kite-flying children, *most* of the monkeys' eagle-calls will be false alarms: but their calls will still serve to represent the presence of *eagles* – albeit falsely – since that is what evolution designed them for, even though there is now a high probability that a call of this kind is not triggered by the presence of an eagle.

OBJECTIONS TO A TELEOLOGICAL ACCOUNT OF
MENTAL CONTENT

These advantages of the teleological theory of representation over the causal theory may encourage us to try to extend it to the case of *mental* representation, that is, to the attitudinal states of subjects of experience. However, we should not underestimate the difficulties of doing so. There is a very big gap between the simple alarm-calls of monkeys and the thought-processes of human beings. We shall return to such issues in chapter 7, when we discuss the relationship between language and thought. Furthermore, there are some major problems of principle which lie in the way of applying the teleological approach to the phenomenon of mental content. One is that the teleological approach has a *biological* basis, whereas it is not at all clear that mental states with content can only be possessed by biological organisms: indeed, it is not even clear that such states can properly be ascribed to *organisms* at all, since – as we saw in chapter 2 – it is arguable that a subject of experience is never to be *identified* with its organic body or any part of it, such as its brain, even if it has such a body. (I shall return to this issue in chapter 10.) Moreover, many philosophers think it perfectly intelligible to suppose that a subject of experience could have a wholly *in*organic, *non*-biological body: a possibility to which we shall return in chapter 8, when we discuss the prospects for artificial intelligence.

Another major problem for the teleological approach to mental content is that, according to this approach, whether or not a state has a given content, or any content at all, is a matter which is largely determined by the *evolutionary history* of creatures possessing states of that type. This seems to imply, however, that it is impossible in principle for a being to possess mental states with content – such as beliefs and desires – unless that being is the product of evolution by natural selection. And yet this is highly counterintuitive. For suppose that – by whatever natural or artificial means, other than the normal process of sexual reproduction – a molecule-for-molecule duplicate of a certain human being were to be created, replicating in exact detail the neuronal structures of that human being's brain. We would not be surprised if the replica were to behave in a very similar way to the original person and, if it did so, we would be strongly inclined to attribute to the replica beliefs and desires very similar to those that we would attribute to the original person. But, it seems, according to the teleological approach, we would be wrong to do so – indeed, we would be wrong to attribute to the replica *any beliefs and desires at all*, because the replica would not be the product of evolution by natural selection. This seems absurd, however. Surely, whether or not a creature possesses mental states with content is entirely a matter of what non-historical properties that particular creature has here and now, not at all a matter of what properties its ancestors may have had in the past.[20]

CONCLUSIONS

In this chapter, we have looked at three different but overlapping issues to do with mental content: the causal relevance of mental content, the individuation of mental content, and the origin of mental content. With regard to the first issue, we found no easy way to explain how mental content could be causally relevant, given that the propositions which consti-

---

[20] For a criticism of the teleological theory along these lines, see Robert Cummins, *Meaning and Mental Representation* (Cambridge, MA: MIT Press, 1989), ch. 7. For further discussion, see Papineau, *Philosophical Naturalism*, pp. 91–4.

tute such content are abstract entities. But we were not persuaded that this problem should make us give up our commonsense or 'folk psychological' conception of the nature of attitudinal states or our intuitive conviction that they may legitimately be invoked to explain human behaviour. As for the question of how mental content is to be individuated, we found reason to favour a 'broad' conception of content, according to which the contents of a person's attitudinal states are, very often, at least partly determined by that person's relations to his or her physical environment. We saw no reason to rule out a 'narrow' conception of content as incoherent, but we were not persuaded that only such a conception is consistent with the explanatory role that we wish to assign to attitudinal states. Finally, with regard to the question of what it is that confers a specific content upon a given attitudinal state, we did not find either of the leading naturalistic approaches – the causal theory and the teleological theory – free from serious difficulties. Both theories provide quite plausible accounts of certain types of naturally occurring representational states, but neither seems straightforwardly applicable to the kind of mental representation involved in the attitudinal states of intelligent subjects of experience. Clearly, *if* we could extend a thoroughly naturalistic theory of representation, either causal or teleological, to the case of contentful mental states, then we might hope to make some headway with the problem of the causal relevance of mental content: but as yet this looks to be at best a very distant prospect. All three of the issues discussed in this chapter continue to present serious challenges, then – which should not surprise us, given their inherent difficulty. But this is not the last that we shall see of them, for they will all crop up again, in one form or another, in later chapters of this book.

5

Sensation and appearance

In the preceding two chapters, we have had a good deal to say about various kinds of mental state. Although we have focused chiefly on *propositional attitude* states, such as beliefs, we have also had occasion to mention *sensational* states, such as pain and nausea. States of the latter sort lack 'propositional content'. When one feels a pain, one may feel it 'in' a certain part of one's body, such as one's left big toe, and consequently have a belief that one's left big toe is hurting. But we must distinguish that belief – which does of course have propositional content – from the pain which gives rise to it, which does not. We do, it is true, say such things as 'I *feel* that my left big toe is hurting', but such a statement is more like the expression of a perceptual judgement than a report that one is experiencing a certain kind of sensation. In the latter kind of report, a term denoting a kind of sensation figures as the direct grammatical object of a verb such as 'feel', as in 'I feel a pain in my left big toe'.

An example of a sentence clearly expressing a perceptual judgement would be 'I see that the tree is in front of the house', in which the verb takes a that-clause as its object. Now, *perceptual* states, such as an experience of seeing a tree to be in front of a house, are curious in that they seem partly like propositional attitude states and partly like sensational states. They are like the latter inasmuch as they involve qualitative characteristics – the notorious 'qualia' of experience discussed in chapter 3 – but they are like the former in having some sort of *conceptual* content. It may be that someone – a young infant, for example – can see a tree to be in

102

front of a house without possessing the concepts of a *tree* or a *house*, but it does seem that one must be able to bring the objects in question under concepts of some sort if one is to have such a perceptual experience, since such an experience seems to involve a recognition of those objects *as* objects of certain kinds. We shall have to postpone consideration of some of the complex issues involved here until the next chapter, however, when we shall discuss theories of perception in more depth.

What we are going to concentrate on in the current chapter are those qualitative features of experience which seem to be present both in purely sensational states, such as pains, and in perceptual states, such as visual experiences. One of the things that we shall need to do is to see what motivates our talk of experiences having such qualitative features. Another will be to examine the ontological implications of such talk: should we or should we not *reify* the 'qualia' of experience, by regarding them as 'inner' *objects* of experiential awareness, in the way that so-called 'sense-datum' theorists do? Finally, we shall need to examine what implications these qualitative features of experience have for our conception of the properties that we ascribe to the 'external' objects of perception – things such as trees and houses. For many of those properties, such as colour-properties, may seem to have more to do with how we experience the objects in question than they do with how those objects are in themselves.

APPEARANCE AND REALITY

It is a commonplace that things are not always really as they seem to be: appearances can deceive. There is a danger, however, of magnifying this truism into a doctrine of cosmic significance by talking of 'Appearance' and 'Reality' as if they were realms separated by an impassable gulf. Sceptics over the ages have always tempted us to do this. A more sober, if less exciting, view to take is that talk about how things appear to be is an integral part of talk about how things really are. It is just as much an objective fact about a coin that it 'appears' elliptical when seen at an oblique angle as that it is 'really' round in shape. It is true that we commonly judge a thing's overall shape by observing how it appears from different directions, and that sometimes such a judgement can be mistaken. But we should be wary of concluding from this and similar examples that we can only ever observe the 'appearances' of things and are compelled to rely on doubtful inferences from these in order to judge what their 'real' properties are. The questionable step here is the *reification* of 'appearances' – the supposition that 'appearances' are themselves objects of observation and, indeed, the 'immediate' objects of observation from which our knowledge of so-called 'external' objects, such as coins, must be inferred. In ordinary speech, it is harmless enough to paraphrase the sentence 'The coin appears elliptical' by means of the sentence 'The appearance of the coin is elliptical'. Harm is threatened only when a philosopher unwarrantedly assumes that the latter sentence implies that there is something – the 'appearance of the coin' – that *is* elliptical.

What is called for at this point is closer attention to how we use the verb 'appear' and certain closely related verbs, such as 'look' and 'feel'. It would seem that these verbs have at least two distinct kinds of use, an *epistemic* use and a *phenomenal* use.[1] Consider first the following case. I am at the seaside and spot a distant figure in the water moving his arm about in the air, and I say 'That swimmer appears to be waving'. What I am doing here is expressing a cautious judgement that the swimmer is waving, recognising that I might be mistaken – for perhaps the swimmer is really not waving, but drowning. This is the epistemic use of 'appear' – 'epistemic' because it is used to qualify or hedge an implicit claim to knowledge made by the speaker. But now compare this case with the example of the coin discussed earlier,

---

[1] For more on the uses of 'look' or 'appear', see Frank Jackson, *Perception: A Representative Theory* (Cambridge: Cambridge University Press, 1977), ch. 2. See also my *Subjects of Experience* (Cambridge: Cambridge University Press, 1996), pp. 97–100, 110–12.

where the speaker says 'The coin appears elliptical from this angle'. Here the speaker is clearly not expressing a cautious judgement that the coin *is* elliptical (much less that it is elliptical 'from this angle', which scarcely makes any sense). So what *is* the speaker trying to express in such a case? Before we venture to answer this question, let us consider a few more examples of the same sort. When viewing a red ball under a blue light, one may say 'The ball looks black in this light'. When dipping one's cold hand into a basin of luke-warm water, one may say 'This water feels hot to my hand'. When drinking a dry wine just after having eaten something very sweet, one may say 'This wine tastes sour to me'. In each case, it seems, one is trying to express something about *what it is like* to perceive an object in certain somewhat unusual conditions. In other words, one is trying to convey something about the *qualititative* or *phenomenal* character of one's perceptual experience, rather than just something about the object that one is perceiving (the coin, the ball, the water, or the wine).

So what, exactly, does a statement such as 'The coin appears elliptical from this angle' *mean*, when 'appear' is used in what I shall call the 'phenomenal' sense? Perhaps it means something roughly like this: 'Seeing the coin from this angle is very like seeing an elliptical object face-on'. Here one is comparing one kind of perceptual experience with another in order to draw attention to a qualititative feature which both kinds of experience have in common, and thereby convey to one's audience some idea of what that qualitative feature is. And notice what kind of perceptual experience one chooses for the sake of comparison here: one chooses an experience which is in some sense 'standard', 'normal', or 'optimal' for the purpose of forming a reliable judgement with regard to the relevant property of the object perceived. Thus, in order to form a reliable judgement concerning the shape of a thin, flat object such as a coin, one does best to look at it face-on. (Here, of course, I am speaking of its 'shape' in the two dimensions in which it is spread out thinly; if one wants to see how thin it is, one should look at it edgewise-on.) Similarly, in order to form a reliable judgement concerning the surface colour of an object, one does best to look at it in ordinary daylight. Ordinary daylight constitutes 'standard' or 'normal' conditions for viewing the surface colours of objects.[2] Generalising, then, perhaps we can say that a sentence of the form 'Object O appears F in conditions C' – where 'appear' has its *phenomenal* sense – means something like this: 'Perceiving object O in conditions C is very like perceiving an object which is F in normal conditions for perceiving objects which are F'.

If the purpose of the phenomenal use of 'appear' is to convey something about the qualitative features of our experiences, why do we have recourse to such a roundabout procedure? Why don't we simply describe those features 'directly'? But how could we have generated the necessary vocabulary? It is no accident that ordinary language contains few resources for directly describing the qualitative features of our experiences. As children we necessarily learn, first of all, words to describe objects that we and other speakers of our language can perceive in common – objects such as coins, balls, and basins of water. As part of this process, we learn under what conditions we are best situated to form reliable judgements, based on observation, as to what properties those objects possess, and thus how best to describe them. It is a relatively sophisticated intellectual achievement to realise that, in being perceivers of objects, we are also subjects of perceptual experience, and that our perceptual experiences are themselves capable of description in various ways. But we need not (and possibly could not) learn a wholly new vocabulary in order to describe those experiences. Instead, we can simply exploit the descriptive vocabulary which we have already learnt to apply to the familiar objects of perception, with the aid of verbs like 'appear' and 'look' used in the phenomenal sense. But, of course, this procedure harbours

---

[2] A word of caution is in place here, as the notion of 'standard' or 'normal' conditions has been challenged by some philosophers: see, for example, C. L. Hardin, *Color for Philosophers* (Indianapolis: Hackett, 1988), pp. 67ff.

snares for unwary philosophers. For we may be tempted to suppose that the descriptive vocabulary which we originally learnt to apply to the familiar, 'external' objects of perception quite literally *also* applies – or perhaps really *only* applies – to qualititative features of our experiences. Thus, we may be tempted to suppose that qualitative features of our experiences may themselves be 'elliptical' or 'black' or 'hot' or 'sour', when, perhaps, these adjectives are properly only applicable to the familiar objects that we perceive rather than to our perceptual experiences of them. Where the truth lies in this difficult matter is something we shall look into later in this chapter.

SENSE-DATUM THEORIES AND THE ARGUMENT FROM ILLUSION

I have already spoken of the dangers of reifying appearances and of supposing that familiar descriptive terms, such as 'elliptical' and 'black', apply quite literally to the qualitative features of our perceptual experiences. But some philosophers have effectively combined these two contentious lines of thought by treating the 'qualia' of experience as 'inner' objects of awareness in their own right, describable as *really* possessing the properties which 'external' objects *appear* to possess. Historically, one argument above all others has been invoked in support of this doctrine: the notorious *argument from illusion*.[3] The argument proceeds in four stages. (1) First, it is noted that in certain circumstances an object can appear other than the way it really is. To use again our well-worn example, a round coin appears elliptical when it is seen at an oblique angle. (2) Next, it is contended that in these circumstances we are aware of something that really *does* have the property which the object in question merely appears to have: thus, for example, it is contended that we are aware of something that really *is* elliptical. (3) Then it is pointed out

---

[3] For a particularly well-known presentation of the argument from illusion, see A. J. Ayer, *The Foundations of Empirical Knowledge* (London: Macmillan, 1940), ch. 1.

that this 'something' cannot be identical with the object which merely appears to have the property in question, because these things have different properties. Thus, the elliptical object of awareness cannot be *the coin*, since the latter is round rather than elliptical. (4) Finally, it is urged that even in circumstances in which an 'external' object appears no different from the way it really is – for instance, when a round coin is seen face-on and thus *appears* round – there is still an 'inner' object of awareness, distinct from that 'external' object, which possesses the property in question (in this case, roundness). The reasoning behind this last stage of the argument is that there is no relevant difference between this special case and other cases which differ from it only marginally. Thus, it is urged, if the existence of an inner object of awareness must be acknowledged in the coin case for all angles of observation under which the coin appears elliptical, no matter how slightly so, it would be extravagant to suppose that such an inner object does not also exist in the limiting case when the coin appears round, since this case is continuous with the previous ones. These supposed inner objects of awareness have been variously dubbed, but are most commonly called 'sense-data' or 'sensa' (the singular forms of these nouns being 'sense-datum' and 'sensum').[4]

It seems fairly clear that the argument from illusion, conceived as above as an argument for the existence of sense-data, is implicitly question-begging – that is, it assumes, at least in part, what it is supposed to prove. What it is supposed to prove is that, whenever we perceive an 'external' object (if, indeed, we ever do), what we are 'directly' aware of is some 'inner' object, which really possesses the properties which that external object appears to possess. However, in stage (2) of the argument it is simply asserted, without proof, that in certain circumstances we

---

[4] For a sophisticated modern defence of the sense-datum theory, see Jackson, *Perception: A Representative Theory*, ch. 4. At one time, I favoured the theory myself: see my 'Indirect Perception and Sense Data', *Philosophical Quarterly* 31 (1981), pp. 330–42. More recently, sense-data have been vigorously championed by Howard Robinson, in his *Perception* (London: Routledge, 1994).

are aware of something which really does possess a property which some external object merely appears to possess. Why should we accept that? It must be conceded that in some cases, at least, the impulse to believe something like this is very strong. Try, for example, the following experiment. Focus your eyes on some distant object, such as a clock on the other side of the room, and hold your index finger up a few inches in front of your nose. You will seem to see two semi-transparent fingers a little way apart from each other, one to either side of the distant object. It is difficult to resist the temptation to say that in these circumstances you see two elongated, semi-transparent *objects* of some sort. If that is correct, then at least one of these objects cannot be *your finger*, since two different things cannot both be identical with one thing. Moreover, since the two objects are very similar to one another, it would seem to be unjustifiable to identify one rather than the other of them with your finger, so we should apparently conclude that *neither* of them is your finger and thus that what you are directly aware of is not your finger but two 'inner' objects or sense-data. One possible response to this line of reasoning is to say that it involves a confusion between the number of objects seen and the number of acts of seeing performed. Thus, it may be said, you really see only *one* elongated, fingerlike object in the circumstances described – namely, *your finger* – but you see it *twice*, once with each eye. As seen with one eye, the finger appears slightly displaced to the left, while as seen with the other eye, it appears slightly displaced to the right. However, the sense-datum theorist can accept the latter description of the situation as correct, as far as it goes, without conceding that he is making a mistake in claiming that two distinct 'inner' objects of awareness are present in these circumstances. Indeed, he will no doubt urge that he is in a position to explain *why* the finger appears to be in two different places at once, namely, because two spatially separated 'appearances' or sense-data of the finger are present. From this example, I think it is clear that the dispute between sense-datum theorists and their opponents is not one which is going to be resolved by any sort of simple knock-down argument.

OTHER ARGUMENTS FOR SENSE-DATA

Besides appealing to illusions, sense-datum theorists also appeal to other evidence in support of their position. Thus they also appeal to the existence of *hallucinations*. Illusions and hallucinations differ in the following way. In the case of an illusion, one perceives a certain 'external' object but it appears, in some respect, other than the way it really is – for instance, one sees one's finger, but it appears to be in two different places at once. In the case of an hallucination, however, one does not perceive any 'external' object at all, of the sort that one seems to perceive. For example – perhaps under the influence of some drug – one may seem to see a snake wriggling across the floor, when in fact there is nothing but a plain carpet on the floor. Here the sense-datum theorist will urge that, in this particular case, one really is aware of *some* snakelike object, which evidently cannot be identical with any external object which one sees, since no appropriate external object is present – not even something which might *appear* snakelike, such as a stick which happens to be lying on the carpet. Then the theorist will go on to urge that, since this hallucinatory experience of seeming to see a snake is so like an experience of seeing a real snake, it is reasonable to suppose that even in the latter case what one is *directly* aware of is some 'inner' snakelike object, since this is all that one can be directly aware of in the hallucinatory case. But, as with the argument from illusion, opponents of the sense-datum theory may simply refuse to accept the sense-datum theorist's crucial claim that, in the hallucinatory case, one is at least aware of *some* snakelike object. They may insist that the most that can safely be said about the hallucinatory case is that in it one *seems* to see some snakelike object – and seeming to see a snakelike object cannot necessarily be equated with seeing (or being aware of) a seemingly snakelike object.

However, this is not the only possible response which opponents of the sense-datum theory may make to the argument from hallucination. Some of them challenge the sense-datum theorist's claim that having a hallucinatory experience can be exactly like having a veridical perceptual experience – that, to use our example, having a hallucination of a snake wriggling across the floor can be exactly like actually *seeing* a snake wriggling across the floor. Others challenge the sense-datum theorist's argument at the point at which it is urged that, since (allegedly) a hallucinatory experience can be exactly like a veridical perceptual experience and in the case of the former one is (allegedly) aware of some 'inner' object, it is reasonable to suppose that in the case of a veridical perceptual experience, too, what one is directly aware of is some 'inner' object or sense-datum. I shall consider this last sort of challenge more fully in the next chapter, in the course of discussing objections to causal theories of perception.

Talk of causal theories of perception prompts me to mention, if only briefly, one other kind of consideration which sense-datum theorists have often adduced in support of their position. This is the fact that there is always a delay – sometimes a very long one – between our perceiving some event and the event itself. Thus, if one is watching a man hammering a stake into the ground several hundred yards away, one will hear each strike of the hammer a fraction of a second after one sees it, simply because sound travels much more slowly than light. But even light travels at a finite velocity, so that an astronomer observing a distant supernova today may be seeing a star which, by the time he sees it, no longer exists. Sense-datum theorists are apt to urge at this point that what the astronomer is directly aware of in this case cannot be the star itself, since that no longer exists, and consequently that the astronomer must be directly aware of some 'inner' object or sense-datum. But opponents of the sense-datum theory can respond simply by challenging the implicit assumption that one can only be 'directly' aware of objects which exist at the time at which one is aware of them. If that assumption is rejected, it is open to us to say what the astronomer is directly aware of is indeed the star itself, even though it no longer exists.

OBJECTIONS TO SENSE-DATUM THEORIES

Why should it matter to us, as philosophers, whether or not sense-data exist? Opponents of sense-data object to them on various grounds, both epistemological and ontological.[5] On the epistemological side, they urge that sense-datum theories promote scepticism, by interposing a 'veil' of sense-data between us and the 'external' objects which we ordinarily take ourselves to be able to perceive. If all that we are directly aware of in perception are sense-data, how can we be sure that external objects are anything like the way we think they are – indeed, how can we be sure that they really exist at all? However, setting aside the rhetorical talk of a 'veil', is there really any reason to suppose that sense-datum theories give more succour to scepticism than so-called 'direct realist' theories do? The direct realist maintains that there are no 'inner' objects of perceptual awareness and consequently that the only objects that we can be aware of when we have perceptual experiences are *external* objects, such as coins and fingers. But, surely, the direct realist is in no better position than the sense-datum theorist to give us a guarantee against the sceptic that at least some of our perceptual experiences are veridical. It is little comfort to be told that *if* there are any objects of which we have direct awareness in perception, then those objects are 'external' objects rather than 'inner' ones, when the sceptic raises his general doubts about trust-

---

[5] One of the most influential critics of sense-datum theories was J. L. Austin: see his posthumously published lectures, *Sense and Sensibilia*, ed. G. J. Warnock (Oxford: Clarendon Press, 1962), which are especially critical of Ayer's account in *The Foundations of Empirical Knowledge*. For more recent criticism, see David M. Armstrong, 'Perception, Sense Data and Causality', in G. F. Macdonald (ed.), *Perception and Identity* (London: Macmillan, 1979).

worthiness of our perceptual experiences. For the sceptic can challenge the direct realist to prove that we do at least sometimes have direct awareness of really existing objects. It will not do for the direct realist to reply that we simply *know*, for sure, that at least sometimes when we have a perceptual experience we are directly aware of some really existing object. After all, the sense-datum theorist made just this sort of claim concerning hallucinatory experiences and yet was seen to be open to challenge. The mere fact that one *seems* to be aware of some object does not imply that, in reality, there must be some object of which one is aware.

On the ontological side, opponents of sense-datum theories object that sense-data are queer entities which are difficult to accommodate within a naturalistic view of the world. They do not appear to be physical objects, nor do they seem to be located in physical space, even though some of them appear to have spatial characteristics. Consider, for instance, the two fingerlike sense-data allegedly present in the double-vision illusion described earlier. It is natural to describe these sense-data as having shape and position and as being capable of moving – and yet it is difficult to see how the space in which they are located could be the very same space in which one's physical finger is located. If they were in the same space, it would make sense to ask how far away from one's finger they are, but it doesn't seem to make sense to ask this. However, if the space in which these sense-data are located is not physical space, what kind of space is it and how is it related to physical space? And how many such non-physical spaces are there? Again, in what kinds of *causal* relationship, if any, can sense-data stand to physical objects? Are they purely 'epiphenomenal' – that is, caused by physical states of affairs but having no effect upon physical things themselves? It may be that a careful sense-datum theorist can answer all of these questions satisfactorily, but one is bound to wonder whether the effort to do so is well-spent. If it can plausibly be maintained that sense-data simply do not exist, we can be spared the trouble of endeavouring to answer such awkward questions. Thus, one can readily understand why some philosophers have thought it well worthwhile trying to find alternative accounts of the phenomena which sense-datum theorists adduce in support of their theory. We shall turn, next, to one such alternative, the *adverbial* theory of sensation.[6]

THE ADVERBIAL THEORY OF SENSATION

For ease of exposition, I shall introduce the adverbial theory by presenting first of all its account of purely sensational states, such as pain states, and only then go on to explain how it deals with the qualitative features of perceptual experiences, which sense-datum theories treat as 'inner' objects of awareness. Consider, then, a sentence reporting the occurrence of a certain kind of sensation, such as 'I feel a sharp pain in my back'. Purely in terms of its grammatical structure, this sentence resembles one such as 'I keep a wooden ladder in my shed', reporting a relationship between me and another object located in a certain place. Just as the adjective 'wooden' serves to describe this object, so the adjective 'sharp' apparently serves to describe the pain that I feel. And, indeed, a sense-datum theorist would be happy to take this analogy between the two sentences pretty much at its face-value. Such a theorist adopts a so-called *act-object* analysis of sensation-reports, according to which such a report announces the fact that a certain subject of experience – that is, a person, such as myself – is in the act of being aware of a certain kind of mental object. However, we should sometimes be wary about taking the grammatical structure of a sentence too literally. Consider, for instance, a sentence such as 'John is wearing a broad grin all over his face'. Do we really want to regard this as being analogous to 'John is wearing a broad hat on his head'? Are 'grins' *objects* which stand in certain relations to people and possess certain loca-

---

[6] An important early version of the adverbial theory is to be found in Roderick M. Chisholm, *Perceiving: A Philosophical Study* (Ithaca, NY: Cornell University Press, 1957), ch. 8. For a more recent account, see Michael Tye, *The Metaphysics of Mind* (Cambridge: Cambridge University Press, 1989), ch. 5.

tions, in the way that hats do? Plausibly not. And, indeed, we reveal the fact that we do not seriously regard 'grins' as being objects by our readiness to paraphrase the sentence 'John is wearing a broad grin all over his face' by the sentence 'John is grinning broadly all over his face'. What this paraphrase suggests is that the verb-phrase 'is wearing a broad grin', with its apparent act-object structure, is really just equivalent to one of the form 'is grinning broadly', in which no apparent reference to an 'object' of any kind is present. And notice that in the course of this grammatical transformation, the adjective 'broad' has been transmuted into an *adverb*, 'broadly', describing the manner of an action rather than a property of some object.

The adverbial theory – whose name we can now understand – proposes that we treat sensation-reports in much the same way as we treat reports about 'grins'. Thus, it may be urged, a more perspicuous way of saying 'I feel a sharp pain in my back' is to say something like 'My back pains me sharply', so that the noun 'pain' is transmuted into a verb and the adjective 'sharp' into an adverb. If we do this, we shall be under less temptation to think that 'pains' are mental *objects* which are, or seem to be, located in certain parts of our bodies and which we detect by means of a special kind of mental act, somewhat in the way in which we detect 'external' objects by seeing or otherwise perceiving them. Thus, the adverbial theorist is trying to discourage us from discerning any analogy between 'feeling a pain' and, for example, 'seeing a tree'. To see a tree is to stand in some genuine relationship to a genuine object, but – according the adverbial theorist – to feel a pain is nothing of the sort. We are misled – if indeed we are misled – by the fact that the noun-phrase 'a pain' is the *grammatical* object of a transitive verb, 'feel'. But not every grammatical object denotes a 'real' object, that is, some *thing* to which other things can stand in genuine relations.

One immediate advantage of the adverbial theorist's way of thinking about pains and other bodily sensations is that it helps us to avoid certain awkward questions about *where* such sensations are located. We speak as if pains were located 'in' various parts of our bodies, such as our backs or our toes. And yet it is difficult to interpret this manner of speaking literally, especially when we consider the so-called 'phantom limb' phenomena experienced by some amputees. Sometimes, a person who has had a leg amputated continues feeling pains and other sensations 'in' the amputated leg, but it is difficult to suppose that what such a person is aware of is anything literally *located* where his or her leg would have been, since that part of space may apparently contain nothing but thin air. Of course, we might still want to say that an act of sensing, like any other event, has a spatial location, and thus that the amputee's feeling of pain has a spatial location. But perhaps the proper thing to say here is that the amputee's feeling of pain is located *where the amputee is*, just as my act of running is surely located *where I am*. We might want to narrow down the location of the feeling still further – indeed, if we are physicalists we might want to locate it in the amputee's central nervous system, because we might want to identify the feeling with some neural event. But, if the adverbial theorist is right, there is no contradiction at all between saying 'I feel a pain in my leg' and 'My feeling of pain is located in my head', because the first sentence should not be construed as reporting where some sensation is *located*, but merely what bodily part is paining me. To this it may be objected that, in the amputee's case, there is no leg to do the paining. That is so, but in this case it is still true that it *seems* to the amputee that his leg is paining him, and we may take his sensation-report to convey this fact.

THE ADVERBIAL THEORY AND SENSE-DATA

Having seen how the adverbial theory deals with sensation-reports, it is now time to see how it deals with the more difficult case of statements about the qualitative features of perceptual experiences. Recall that the sense-datum theorist maintains that, whenever it is true to say that some 'external' object appears to have a certain property,

F – where 'appear' is used in what I have called the 'phenomenal' sense – it is also true to say that some 'inner' object of awareness, or sense-datum, really *does* have the property *F*. Thus, in the case in which the coin appears elliptical, the sense-datum theorist says that what one is directly aware of is a sense-datum which really is elliptical. The adverbial theorist, of course, refuses to recognise the existence of any such 'inner' objects of awareness. However, he need not reject completely what the sense-datum theorist says in this regard, for he can paraphrase the latter's sense-datum reports in much the same way as he paraphrases reports about pains and other bodily sensations. Consider, thus, the sense-datum theorist's statement 'I am aware of an elliptical sense-datum' and compare this with the statement 'I feel a sharp pain in my back'. Just as the latter may be paraphrased as 'My back pains me sharply', so the former may arguably be paraphrased as something like 'I am appeared to elliptically', or 'I sense elliptically'. Of course, the latter sentences are not examples of ordinary colloquial English – but neither is the sense-datum sentence which they purport to paraphrase. However, an apparent advantage which the adverbial theorist's paraphrases have over the original sense-datum sentences is that the descriptive vocabulary which they employ is not simply identical with that employed to describe 'external' objects. The sense-datum theorist has to address the awkward question of whether adjectives like 'sharp' and 'elliptical' can have the same meaning when applied to pains and visual sense-data as when they are applied to such things as knives and tables, but the adverbial theorist can happily say, for instance, that 'I am appeared to elliptically' just means something like 'I am appeared to in a manner in which I would be appeared to by an elliptical object viewed in normal conditions'. This suggestion fits in comfortably with our earlier proposal concerning the meaning of a statement such as 'The coin appears elliptical from this angle', in which 'appear' has its phenomenal sense. (However, later on, when we come to discuss the distinction between primary and secondary qualities, we shall see that the adverbial theorist may have reason to think again about the foregoing suggestion.)

But what, it may be asked, is the point of trying to save what the sense-datum theorist says by paraphrasing it in such a fashion? Just this. The adverbial theorist acknowledges that there is an important germ of truth in the sense-datum theory, namely, that whenever some 'external' object appears to have a certain property, this is because the person perceiving it is sensorily affected by that object in a certain way. In denying the existence of sense-data, we must – so the adverbial theorist believes – be careful not to throw the baby out with the bathwater. So-called 'direct' or 'naïve' realists are apt to do just this. By rejecting sense-data without offering anything in their place, they deny themselves the resources with which to accommodate the subjective aspects of perception. For the fact is that we perceive objects at least partly in virtue of the sensory effects which they have on us, and these effects can vary according to environmental circumstances and the conditions of our sense-organs. This is why perceptual experiences, unlike such propositional attitude states as beliefs, have qualitative characteristics. What both the sense-datum theorist and the adverbial theorist are trying to do, in their own ways, is to provide an account of this aspect of perceptual experience. The adverbial theorist has the advantage of offering an account which is ontologically more economical and free of certain perplexing questions which beset the sense-datum theory. But the direct realist who simply rejects the sense-datum theory lock, stock and barrel may fairly be accused of having nothing to say about this seemingly undeniable aspect of perceptual experience.

I should not conclude this discussion of the adverbial theory without mentioning any objections which have been raised against it. Perhaps the most important charge that sense-datum theorists have brought against the adverbial theory is that it is incapable of providing satisfactory paraphrases of certain complex sense-datum sentences.[7] Consider, for instance, a sense-datum report such as 'I am aware of a red square sense-datum to the right of a blue round sense-datum'. How could one hope to paraphrase this in an adverbial way? It plainly will not do to paraphrase it as 'I am appeared to redly and squarely and bluely and roundly', not only because that leaves out of account the spatial relation between the two sense-data but also because it fails to preserve the connection between redness and squareness on the one hand and blueness and roundness on the other – that is, it fails to distinguish between the original sense-datum report and the quite different sense-datum report 'I am aware of a blue square sense-datum to the right of a red round sense-datum'. I shall not attempt to resolve this dispute here, though an obvious suggestion – in view of my earlier remark about how one might interpret the adverbial theorist's sentence 'I am appeared to elliptically' – is that the original sense-datum report should ultimately be paraphrased as 'I am appeared to in a manner in which I would be appeared to by a red square object to the right of a blue round object viewed in normal conditions'. But, in any case, it is perhaps worth remarking that the adverbial theorist need not feel committed to finding a satisfactory paraphrase for *every* sense-datum report which a sense-datum theorist might feel inclined to make. That would be to concede too much to the sense-datum theory and suggest that the adverbial theory differs from it merely verbally.

PRIMARY AND SECONDARY QUALITIES

I remarked a moment ago that we perceive objects at least partly in virtue of the sensory effects which they have on us. But sometimes it is difficult to disentangle those effects from

---

[7] For a detailed development of this objection, see Jackson, *Perception: A Representative Theory*, ch. 3. For a response on behalf of the adverbial theory, see Tye, *The Metaphysics of Mind*, ch. 5.

the properties of the perceived objects which give rise to them. What exactly does it mean to ascribe a colour-property, such as redness, to an 'external' object, such as a rubber ball? Do such colour-properties really exist and if so, are they really properties of external objects or are they, rather, properties of our perceptual experiences which we somehow 'project' upon external objects? Throughout history, many philosophers have argued for a fundamental distinction between two kinds of properties or qualities – *primary* qualities, such as shape and mass, and *secondary* qualities, such as colour and taste.[8] Some say that only the primary qualities are really 'in' external objects and that the secondary qualities are, if anything, only 'in' us. Others say that, although the secondary qualities are really 'in' external objects, they are not 'in' them in the way that they appear to be, or that they are 'in' them only insofar as those objects have an ability to affect us sensorily in certain ways. Of course, this talk of qualities being 'in' objects or 'in' us is hardly very perspicuous. An object either has a certain quality or it does not, though we can certainly ask why, or in virtue of what, the object has the quality if it does have it. And it may indeed be the case, for example, that objects have *shapes* quite independently of any relation they may stand in to the people who perceive them whereas they have *colours* at least partly in virtue of their ability to affect those who perceive them in certain ways.

But why should we think that shapes and colours are different in this sort of way? One reason for thinking so which is often advanced is that our judgements of colour seem to be much more subjective and variable than our judgements of shape. People often disagree about the exact colour of a piece of cloth, even if they are both looking at it in ordinary daylight. Of course, people can also disagree about the exact

---

[8] Historically, one of the most important advocates of the distinction between primary and secondary qualities was John Locke: see his *Essay Concerning Human Understanding*, ed. P. H. Nidditch (Oxford: Clarendon Press, 1975), Book II, ch. 8. For further discussion of Locke's views about this distinction and more generally about perception, see my *Locke on Human Understanding* (London: Routledge, 1995), ch. 3.

shape of an object even when viewing it at a reasonable distance and in good light. But in the latter sort of case we can resort to procedures of measurement which will almost always settle the issue as to the object's exact shape. For instance, if one person judges the object to be square and another judges it to be oblong, we can use a tape measure to determine whether or not all of the object's sides are equal in length. It is less clear what we can do to resolve a disagreement as to whether a piece of cloth is green or blue in colour. We can ask other people to offer their opinion on the matter, but they too might disagree amongst themselves. We could even use some scientific instrument to measure the wavelengths of light reflected by the cloth: but whereas there is an indisputable relationship between an object's having four sides of equal length and its being square, there is no indisputable relationship between an object's reflecting light of certain wavelengths and its being green. Another point that is often made is that the apparent colours of things vary a great deal according to their environmental conditions, especially according to the kind of light source that is illuminating them. Objects appear to have very different surface colours under a sodium lamp from those that they appear to have in daylight. And, after all, it is just an accident of history that our planet is orbiting a yellow star rather than a red or a white one. Eventually, indeed, the sun will turn into a giant red star; and if human beings are still around to view things in what will then be 'normal' lighting conditions, objects will appear to have somewhat different colours from the ones they appear to have now. Nothing closely analogous to this applies, it seems, in the case of the *shapes* of objects.

SENSE-DATUM THEORIES AND THE PRIMARY/SECONDARY DISTINCTION

Some philosophers who have advocated sense-datum theories of perception have been tempted to draw the distinction between primary and secondary qualities in the following way. They have suggested that the primary qualities of 'external' objects *resemble* the qualities of the sense-data of which we are directly aware when we perceive those objects, whereas this is not the case with secondary qualities.[9] So, consider once more our example of the coin which appears elliptical when viewed at an oblique angle. The coin itself is round, but what one is directly aware of, according to the sense-datum theorist, is an elliptical sense-datum. However, being round and being elliptical are both *shape* properties and, moreover, closely resembling ones. But now consider the *colour* of the coin. Perhaps the coin is silvery and, indeed, *appears* silvery. Then the sense-datum theorist will say that the elliptical sense-datum of which one is directly aware is itself silvery in colour. However, he may well deny that this quality of the sense-datum *resembles* any quality possessed by the coin. He may concede that the coin possesses some quality which is causally responsible for the fact that the sense-datum of which one is aware is silvery in colour, but he may deny that that quality is anything like this quality of the sense-datum. He may even allow that that quality of the coin may be called 'silveriness', but he may none the less insist that the predicate 'is silvery' has a different meaning as applied to the coin from its meaning as applied to the sense-datum. He may suggest, for instance, that, as applied to the coin, 'is silvery' means something like 'is disposed to cause silvery sense-data in normal viewing conditions' – which, of course, cannot be what 'is silvery' means as applied to *sense-data*.

One question which we could raise with such a sense-datum theorist is this. Why should it be supposed that the predicate 'is elliptical' is not similarly ambiguous as applied to 'external' objects and sense-data? Does it even make sense to suppose that items as different from one another as external objects and sense-data could literally share properties such as shape? Suppose, however, that the sense-datum theorist acknowledges this apparent difficulty and ventures

---

[9] Locke himself suggests this and was roundly criticised for doing so by his near-contemporary, George Berkeley. For discussion of the issue between them, see my *Locke on Human Understanding*, pp. 55–8.

to say that, strictly speaking, the predicate 'is elliptical', as applied to an external object such as a coin or a plate, really just means something like 'is disposed to cause elliptical sense-data in normal viewing conditions'. Then, in the first place, this would undermine his account of the distinction between primary and secondary qualities, since he would be treating shape and colour qualities alike. More seriously, however, it would imply that the only predicates which we can literally apply to external objects are *dispositional* ones, attributing to them an ability to cause sense-data with various qualities of shape, colour and so forth. By this account, it seems, the only qualities with which we are acquainted are the qualities of sense-data. But such an account is entirely the reverse of common-sense thinking. Before our exposure to the sense-datum theory, we thought that qualities of shape and colour and so forth were properties of familiar 'external' objects, such as coins and rubber balls. Now we are told that nothing could be further from the truth and that these qualities really belong to 'inner' objects of our direct awareness. But how, then, have we managed to learn names for these qualities from other people, given that no two people can be directly aware of the same 'inner' objects? Clearly, something has gone wrong.

Many opponents of sense-data will regard the foregoing considerations as confirming their doubts about the sense-datum theory and reinforcing their allegiance to so-called direct or naïve realism. But such a reaction would be too hasty. Suppose the sense-datum theorist is persuaded to agree that predicates such as 'is elliptical' and 'is silvery' must have their primary application to *external* objects, such as coins. He could do so and yet still venture to account for the distinction between primary and secondary qualities in the following way. First, he could continue to say that the meaning of a secondary-quality predicate, such as 'is silvery', is dispositional in character. Thus he could say that the predicate 'is silvery', as applied to things such as coins, means something like 'is disposed to cause silvery* sense-data in normal viewing conditions', where the new predicate 'is silvery*' is one that exclusively applies to sense-data and picks out that property of sense-data which they are typically caused to have by silvery things in normal viewing conditions. There need be no circularity here, provided that the sense-datum theorist does not contend that 'is silvery*' simply *means* something like 'has that property which sense-data are typically caused to have by silvery things in normal viewing conditions'. Instead, he could insist that the meaning of 'is silvery*' is primitive and undefinable, but none the worse for that (since some terms in any language must be primitive and undefinable). Secondly, he can contend that, although there is similarly a predicate 'is elliptical*', which is exclusively applicable to sense-data and picks out that property of sense-data which they are typically caused to have by elliptical things in normal viewing conditions, it is *not* similarly the case that the predicate 'is elliptical', as applied to things such as coins, means 'is disposed to cause elliptical* sense-data in normal viewing conditions'. He may agree that it is *true*, at least in the world which we actually inhabit, that elliptical things are disposed to cause elliptical* sense-data in normal viewing conditions, but deny that having such a disposition is what we do or should *mean* by describing something as being elliptical. By contrast, in describing something as being silvery, he may say, we *do* (or, at least, *should*) mean to ascribe to it a disposition to cause silvery* sense-data in normal viewing conditions, and this is why silveriness is properly regarded as being a 'secondary' rather than a 'primary' quality: it is so because it is a quality which things have only in virtue of their ability to affect us sensorily in a certain way.

Of course, in contending that the predicate 'is silvery', as applied to things such as coins, means 'is disposed to cause silvery* sense-data in normal viewing conditions', the sense-datum theorist cannot seriously be suggesting every ordinary speaker of English explicitly understands 'is silvery' to have this meaning. Rather, he is advancing this thesis as a *philosophical analysis* of the concept of being silvery, and hence as revealing the implicit meaning of the predicate in the light of a reflective understanding of our use of it. Indeed, the sense-datum theorist may urge that the error of the direct or naïve realist is to defer too readily to a philosophically untutored understanding of colour-predicates. The naïve speaker may simply be confused, failing to distinguish between the concept of being *silvery* and the concept of being *silvery**, and incoherently imagining the latter to be applicable to external objects.[10]

AN ADVERBIAL VERSION OF THE PRIMARY/SECONDARY DISTINCTION

Now, I have formulated the foregoing account of the distinction between primary and secondary qualities on behalf of a sense-datum theorist. But, it would seem, a similar sort of account should equally be available to an adverbial theorist who is prepared to paraphrase the relevant sense-datum sentences in an appropriate way. Thus, where the sense-datum theorist says that 'is silvery' means 'is disposed to cause silvery* sense-data in normal viewing conditions', the adverbial theorist should presumably say that it means something like 'is disposed to cause people to be appeared to silverily* in normal viewing conditions'. However, if so, such a theorist can no longer endorse our earlier proposal and interpret the sentence 'I am appeared to silverily*' as meaning 'I am appeared to in a manner in which I would be appeared to by a silvery* object viewed in normal conditions', because 'is silvery*' is not a predicate applicable to external objects. Instead, however, he could say that the adverb 'silverily*', although having a primitive and undefinable meaning, denotes a mode of being appeared to (a mode of sensing) which, as a matter of contingent fact, is typically caused in people when they look at silvery things in normal viewing conditions. And

---

[10] For further interesting discussion of the distinction between primary and secondary qualities and dispositional analyses of colour-predicates, see Colin McGinn, *The Subjective View: Secondary Qualities and Indexical Thoughts* (Oxford: Clarendon Press, 1983), ch. 8, and Christopher Peacocke, *Sense and Content: Experience, Thought, and their Relations* (Oxford: Clarendon Press, 1983), ch. 2.

maybe this is, after all, the right approach for the adverbial theorist to take. That is to say, it may be that he should treat the adverbs which he uses to describe modes of being appeared to as having primitive and undefinable meanings, rather than as deriving their meanings from the meanings of adjectives applicable to 'external' objects. For it would seem to be a purely contingent fact that those modes of being appeared to are typically caused by objects describable by those adjectives (after all, they might instead have been caused solely by certain disturbances in people's central nervous systems).

DO COLOUR-PROPERTIES REALLY EXIST?

We have not quite yet done with our discussion of secondary qualities. I have suggested, albeit only tentatively, that colour-predicates may be interpreted as having a dispositional meaning: that 'is red', for example, may mean something like 'is disposed to cause red* sense-data in normal viewing conditions', or 'is disposed to cause people to be appeared to redly* in normal viewing conditions'. But we should not assume that every meaningful predicate denotes a genuine *property* of the things it applies to. Why not? Well, we know that as a matter of pure logic this cannot be so, on pain of contradiction. Consider, thus, the predicate 'is non-self-exemplifying'. This is certainly meaningful, because there are many things which do not exemplify themselves. Thus the property of being divisible by two, although it is exemplified by many things, such as the number 128, is clearly not exemplified by itself: the property of being divisible by two is not itself divisible by two. However, if the predicate 'is non-self-exemplifying' denotes a property – the property of being non-self-exemplifying – then we can ask whether or not that property exemplifies itself. But however we try to answer this question, we arrive at a contradiction: for if it does exemplify itself, then it doesn't, and if it doesn't, then it does. Hence we must conclude that no such property exists and thus that not every meaningful predicate denotes a property.[11]

Now let us inquire whether a predicate such as 'is disposed to cause people to be appeared to redly* in normal viewing conditions' should be construed as denoting a *property* of objects. The first thing to observe here is that objects of many very different kinds are disposed to act in this way. For example, red stars are, as are red roses and sheets of translucent red glass. But it would appear that the properties in virtue of which these different kinds of objects are disposed to act in this way are quite *different* from one another. Red stars are disposed to act in this way because they *emit* light of certain wavelengths, but red roses are disposed to do so because they *reflect* light of certain wavelengths, while sheets of red glass do so because they *transmit* light of certain wavelengths. If the properties in virtue of which things are disposed to act in this way are quite different from one another, then we certainly cannot say that the property of being red, if it exists, is any *one* of those properties. But what else could we say? We might venture to say that the property of being red is a *disjunctive* property – for instance, that it is the property which a thing has just in case it *either* emits light of certain wavelengths, *or* reflects light of those wavelengths, *or* transmits light of those wavelengths. (This is not, of course, to say that the meaning of the predicate 'is red' is definable in terms of such a disjunctive predicate; plainly it is not.) But philosophers are wary, and I think rightly so, about countenancing the existence of disjunctive properties.[12] Another alternative would be to regard the property of being red as a 'second-order' property, such as the property of possessing some property in virtue of which its possessor is disposed to cause people to be appeared to redly* in normal viewing

---

[11] For further elaboration of the point that not every predicate can denote a property, see Michael J. Loux, *Metaphysics: A Contemporary Introduction* (London: Routledge, 1998), pp. 34–5.

[12] For more on doubts about disjunctive properties, see David M. Armstrong, *Universals: An Opinionated Introduction* (Boulder, CO: Westview Press, 1989), pp. 82–3.

conditions.[13] But, again, I think we should be wary of including such second-order properties in our ontology, because it is not clear that they have any real work to do. It may be, then, that we should conclude that there is no such thing as the property of being red, or redness. We should not be too alarmed by such a conclusion. It doesn't imply that nothing is really red. It only implies that the things which are red are not all red in virtue of possessing some *one* property. By contrast, it would appear that there really is some one property in virtue of which all square things are square. And this in itself seems to be an important difference between being red and being square, confirming the intuitions of those philosophers who contend that there is an ontological distinction of some significance between colours and shapes.[14]

CONCLUSIONS

In this chapter, we have been concerned to understand how our talk about the way things appear is related, on the one hand, to the qualitative or phenomenal aspects of our experiences and, on the other, to the properties that things themselves possess. We distinguished between an epistemic and a phenomenal sense of the verb 'appear' and saw that the latter is used to convey, in an oblique way, information about the qualitative aspects of our experiences. Then we looked at two rival theories which attempt to explain how it is that our experiences have these qualitative aspects, the sense-datum theory and the adverbial theory. The former maintains that experiencing involves being 'directly' aware of 'inner', mental objects, while the latter maintains that it merely involves distinctive modes of sensory awareness, or ways of sensing. We saw that the adverbial theory is ontologically more economical than the sense-datum theory and is able to avoid

---

[13] The possibility of treating colours as second-order properties is mentioned by David Braddon-Mitchell and Frank Jackson in their *Philosophy of Mind and Cognition* (Oxford: Blackwell, 1996), p. 264.

[14] A much more radical colour scepticism than anything suggested here is advanced by C. L. Hardin: see his *Color for Philosophers*, pp. 59–112.

certain awkward questions which beset the latter, but that neither is better equipped than the other to deflect the sort of doubts which sceptics raise about the reliability of the senses. Finally, we examined the distinction between primary and secondary qualities and concluded, albeit only tentatively, that it is defensible both according to the sense-datum theory and according to the adverbial theory. The suggestion was that predicates expressing secondary qualities, such as colour-predicates, are distinctive in that they can be given a dispositional analysis in terms of the kinds of sensory effects which objects describable by those predicates characteristically give rise to in people who perceive those objects. However, we also saw that we should be cautious about assuming that colour-predicates denote genuine *properties* of the objects they apply to – that, for instance, there is such a property as the property of being red, or redness. But it is important to appreciate that to deny the existence of redness is not necessarily to deny that things can *really be red*, in the sense that the predicate 'is red', appropriately understood, can truly be applicable to them.[15]

---

[15] The point that realism regarding the application of a predicate is consistent with a denial that the predicate denotes a property is well made by John Heil in his *Philosophy of Mind: A Contemporary Introduction* (London: Routledge, 1998), pp. 194–7.

6

Perception

At the beginning of the previous chapter, I remarked that *perceptual* states, such as an experience of seeing a tree to be in front of a house, are partly like sensational states and partly like propositional attitude states. They are like the former in that they have qualitative or phenomenal features and they are like the latter in that they have conceptual content. I had a good deal to say in that chapter about the qualitative aspects of perceptual experiences, but not much about their conceptual content. In the present chapter I shall try to redress the balance and say more about the latter. But one of the things that we shall need to discuss is how the conceptual content of a perceptual experience is related to its qualitative features – for it can scarcely be supposed that these two dimensions of perceptual experience are quite unconnected.

However, we should acknowledge that an account of the nature of perceptual experiences is only part of what is demanded of a philosophical analysis of the concept of *perception*, which is another chief concern of this chapter. According to most contemporary philosophers, perceiving certainly involves having perceptual experiences, but is more than just that. The question is: *what* more? One plausible suggestion is that perceiving additionally involves some sort of *causal* relationship between the perceiver's perceptual experiences and those objects which, in virtue of that relationship, the perceiver may be said to perceive. Causal theories of perception are currently quite popular, but are also subject to certain objections which we shall have to look into carefully. In the light of those objections, some philosophers have advanced rival theories of perception, of which the so-called *disjunctive* theory of perception is perhaps the most important. Later in this chapter, I shall try to adjudicate between these two approaches.

Part of the problem which confronts us here is to determine what properly belongs to a philosophical analysis of the concept of perception and what properly belongs to an empirical theory of perception of the sort that is more appropriately advanced and evaluated by scientific psychologists than by philosophers. But we should not assume that these two domains are quite unrelated: indeed, they cannot be. Consequently, we shall find it useful to look at some of the approaches to perception currently favoured by empirical psychologists and see how they are related to philosophical treatments of the topic. Two such approaches, in particular, deserve our attention – the *computational* approach and the *ecological* approach – as the differences between them echo, to some extent, disagreements amongst contemporary philosophers of perception. We should also recognise that many of the empirical findings of psychologists working in the field of perception provide interesting subject-matter for philosophical reflection, which is apt to be one-sided if restricted to everyday and familiar examples. One recently investigated phenomenon is especially worth mentioning in this connection – the phenomenon of so-called 'blindsight', a condition in which subjects claim not to be able to see certain objects despite clearly possessing visually-based information concerning them. First, however, we must return to the topic of perceptual experience.

PERCEPTUAL EXPERIENCE AND PERCEPTUAL CONTENT

I have already given a familiar example of a perceptual experience: the experience of seeing a tree to be in front of a house. This, of course, is a *visual* experience. Every type of perceptual experience belongs to a distinctive sensory modality, depending on which of our sense-organs are characteristically involved in generating experiences of that type. Thus, as well as enjoying visual experiences, we enjoy auditory, gustatory, olfactory and haptic experiences (relating, respectively, to the senses of hearing, taste, smell and touch). The sensory modality of a perceptual experience determines what kind of qualitative features it can possess. A sense-datum theorist would make this point by saying that perceptual experiences of different sensory modalities are accompanied by, or involve, their own distinctive kinds of sense-data – visual, auditory, gustatory, olfactory, or haptic sense-data. An adverbial theorist would say, correspondingly, that perceptual experiences of different sensory modalities are characterised by different modes of sensing, or ways of 'being appeared to'. Whichever approach we favour, though, we must acknowledge that, for example, *seeing* a table to be rectangular is qualitatively quite unlike *feeling* a table to be rectangular. This is despite the fact that the *conceptual* content of the two experiences could be exactly the same.

But what exactly might one mean by attributing 'conceptual' content to perceptual experiences – and why should we suppose that they have such content? We have already discussed the topic of mental content in the course of examining the nature of propositional attitude states, in chapters 3 and 4. There, of course, we were solely concerned with *propositional* content. The propositional content of a state such as a belief is given by a 'that'-clause: we may say, for instance, that John believes *that it is raining* or *that the table is rectangular*. Now, we also attribute to people what could be called *perceptual judgements*. Thus, John expresses such a judgement if he says that he *feels* that it is raining, or *sees* that the table is rectangular.[1] But we must be careful to distinguish such a

---

[1] Some philosophers distinguish between simply 'seeing' and 'seeing *that*' – for instance, between simply seeing a green apple and seeing that the apple is green – as though these were different kinds of seeing. See, for example, Fred I. Dretske, *Seeing and Knowing* (London: Routledge and Kegan Paul, 1969), pp. 78ff. However, it is questionable whether 'seeing that' is a kind of *seeing*. 'I see that *p*' appears to express a visually based judgement that *p*, rather than a report that one is seeing something.

perceptual judgement from a perceptual experience. A person may have a perceptual experience of seeing a table to be rectangular without necessarily being willing, or even able, to form the perceptual judgement that he sees that a certain table is rectangular. On the one hand, the person may be *able* to form that judgement but be *unwilling* to do so, because he suspects that his perceptual experience is deceptive – he may consider, for instance, that he is the victim of a visual hallucination. On the other hand, the person may be *unable* to form the perceptual judgement in question, because he lacks the requisite concepts. Thus, for example, one might be prepared to attribute to a young child a perceptual experience of seeing a table to be rectangular and yet doubt whether the child is capable of forming the perceptual judgement that *it sees that* a certain table is rectangular, because one doubts whether it possesses the concept of a *table* or the concept of something's being *rectangular* (that is, the concept of something's having four rectilinear sides set at right angles to one another). Even more fundamentally, one may doubt whether the child possesses the concept of *seeing* or the concept of *itself* as a subject of experience. At the same time, however, it seems that one must attribute to the child at least *some* concepts if one is to attribute to it a perceptual experience of seeing a table to be rectangular, because an ability to enjoy such an experience seems to require an ability to recognise tables as objects of some kind (even if not as *tables*) and likewise an ability to distinguish between rectangularity and other shapes that objects can possess. In short, the child must apparently be able to bring objects and their properties under concepts in order to enjoy such an experience; and the concepts which it exercises in any given case will constitute the conceptual content of its experience. (That ordinary language may lack words expressing the concepts in question is of no consequence.)

There is a further important difference between perceptual experiences and perceptual judgements. When a person forms a perceptual judgement that, for example, he sees *that a tree is in front of a house*, the 'that'-clause provides an exhaustive specification of the propositional content of his perceptual judgement and thus an exhaustive inventory of the concepts involved in that judgement. By contrast, when a person has a perceptual experience of seeing a tree to be in front of a house, the conceptual content of his experience will typically be far richer and more complex than that of the foregoing perceptual judgement (even though, for reasons just explained, it may not in fact include the concept of a *tree* or a *house*). This is because, in seeing a tree to be in front of a house, one must ordinarily have a visual experience of many things other than just a tree and a house and their position relative to one another – things such as the colour and shape of the tree and of the house, the intervening ground between them, the sky behind them, and other objects in their vicinity (together with their colours and shapes). And these other ingredients of the perceived scene – or many of them, at any rate – must, it would seem, also be brought under concepts of some sort. In forming a perceptual judgement, then, we typically abstract away from many ingredients of the perceived scene and focus on a limited sub-set of them.

But a question which we could raise at this point is this. Could it be right to suppose that, when a person has a perceptual experience, *every* ingredient of the perceived scene must be brought under some concept by that person, or can there (indeed, must there) be ingredients which he or she fails to bring under concepts? As we may put it, do perceptual experiences typically have *non*-conceptual content in addition to conceptual content?[2] One reason for thinking that this might be the case is that the perceived scene is often of such richness and complexity that it is hard to suppose that anyone could in fact bring all of its ingredients under concepts, even if he or she possesses the requisite concepts to do

---

[2] For fuller discussion of the notion of non-conceptual content, see Tim Crane, 'The Nonconceptual Content of Experience' and Christopher Peacocke, 'Scenarios, Concepts and Perception', both in Tim Crane (ed.), *The Contents of Experience: Essays on Perception* (Cambridge: Cambridge University Press, 1992). This collection of essays contains many other useful contributions on the topic of perceptual content.

so. Consider, for instance, the sort of visual experience that one might enjoy upon suddenly entering a cluttered workshop or a highly variegated region of jungle for the first time. The perceived scene may be immensely complex and rich in detail – and yet one is seemingly able to take it all in at a single glance, without having time to recognise every one of its ingredients individually as something of this or that kind. However, even if we accept for this sort of reason that perceptual experiences must generally have non-conceptual content, it seems incoherent to suppose that *all* of the content of *all* of a person's perceptual experiences could be non-conceptual. This is because perceptual experiences characteristically form the basis of our perceptual judgements and many of our beliefs – and mental states of the latter kinds undoubtedly *do* possess conceptual content, which is evidently related to the conceptual content of the perceptual experiences upon which they are based.

Some philosophers speak of perceptual experiences as having *representational* or *informational* content, in a way which prescinds from any distinction between conceptual and non-conceptual content. Roughly speaking, the representational content of a perceptual experience is a matter of how that experience represents objects in the perceiver's environment as being. Thus, a partial description of the representational content of a perceptual experience might be that it represents the perceiver's environment as containing a tree in front of a house. This would only be a partial description because, of course, a perceptual experience would normally represent much more than just that. However, precisely because it ignores the distinction between conceptual and non-conceptual content, talk of representational content in this context, although perfectly legitimate, is too indiscriminate. A satisfactory philosophical treatment of perception needs to be sensitive to that distinction.

PERCEPTUAL CONTENT, APPEARANCE AND QUALIA

How, exactly, is the perceptual content of an experience related to its qualitative character? This is an extremely difficult question to answer. We can, however, begin to get a grip on it by drawing on some of the findings of the previous chapter. We noted there that our talk of how things 'appear' or 'look' to us when we perceive them – where 'appear' and 'look' have their *phenomenal* senses – serves to convey, in an oblique fashion, various qualitative aspects of the perceptual experiences that we are undergoing. Suppose, once more, that I am having a visual experience of seeing a table to be rectangular. Then it will seem to me that the table *appears* a certain way and, indeed, it is in virtue of *how* it appears to me that I will experience it *as* an object of a certain kind and *as* having a certain distinctive kind of shape. The concepts under which I bring objects and their properties in my perceptual experiences of them are concepts which are intimately related to my accumulated knowledge of how those objects and properties characteristically *appear* to me in various circumstances. Consider, thus, the concept of a *table*. Typically, we expect a table to consist of a flat rigid surface supported by four upright legs of equal length. But a bare knowledge that tables have this form will not enable one to *recognise* a table visually, or see something as *being* a table, unless one also knows how something with such a form typically *appears* or *looks* from a variety of different angles. Thus, the sort of concepts under which one brings objects in one's perceptual experiences of them are concepts the possession of which embodies an implicit knowledge of how such objects characteristically *appear* to the senses – whether visually, or haptically, or via some other sensory modality. We could perhaps call such concepts 'observational' concepts. By no means all of the objects we are capable of thinking of fall under such observational concepts: for example, subatomic particles, such as electrons, do not, for we do not (and could not coherently) think of electrons as *appearing* or *looking* some way to the senses in any circumstances whatever.

So, in answer to our question of how the perceptual content of an experience is related to its qualitative character, we can perhaps say that, in general, the qualitative features or 'qualia' present in a perceptual experience will belong to a range of such features associated with the observational concepts involved in that content. Roughly speaking, the qualia of a perceptual experience must be such as to make it seem to the perceiver that he or she is perceiving objects which appear or look how objects *should* appear or look if they are to fall under the observational concepts which that person exercises in respect of the experience in question.[3] (This answer does not, of course, address the question of how the *non*-conceptual content, if any, of a perceptual experience is related to its qualitative character, but perhaps that is of less immediate concern to us just now.)

PERCEPTION AND CAUSATION

In certain of their central uses, verbs of perception, such as 'see' and 'hear', are clearly *transitive* verbs, taking noun-phrases as their grammatical objects, as in the sentences 'John sees the table' and 'Mary hears the bell'. Such sentences report cases of *object*-perception. In such cases, it is a plausible suggestion, as I remarked earlier, that perception involves some sort of *causal* relationship between the perceiver's perceptual experiences and those objects which, in virtue of that relationship, the perceiver may be said to perceive. We shall look into this sort of proposal in a moment. But before doing so, it is worth remarking that we also employ other types of grammatical construction in reporting cases of perception. One such construction is the so-called 'naked infinitive construction', exemplified by the sentence 'John sees the men enter the room', in which the verb 'to enter' appears in its infinitive form but stripped of the particle 'to'. Another kind of construction very close to this, which we have already met, is illustrated by the sentence 'Mary sees the tree to be in front of the house'. Such sentences appear to report the perception of *situations* or *states of*

---

[3] I say more about the relationship between perceptual content and the qualitative features of experience in my *Subjects of Experience* (Cambridge: Cambridge University Press, 1996), ch. 4.

affairs.[4] Clearly, most cases of what we may call *situation-perception* are also cases of object-perception – though apparently not all of them, since one may, for example, see it to be dark or foggy without necessarily seeing any *object*. Equally, we normally perceive objects only in the context of perceiving some situation involving them. But despite this close interdependency between object-perception and situation-perception, it none the less seems that the concept of object-perception is the more central or basic one, so that a philosophical analysis of perception should deal with this first. That is why I shall concentrate on object-perception in what follows. (However, much of what I have to say about it could be adapted quite straightforwardly to apply equally to situation-perception.)

Causal analyses of object-perception maintain that it is a conceptual truth that the perception of an object involves some sort of causal transaction between that object and the perceiver.[5] It is important to emphasise that what is at issue here is whether the concept of object-perception involves the concept of causation. Few people would dispute that, as a matter of scientific fact, whenever somebody sees or hears an object, some causal process involving both that person and the object in question enables him or her to perceive it – a process such as the transmission of light-waves or sound-waves from the object to the person's sense organs. But, of course, truths of this kind are a matter of empirical discovery rather than conceptual in character. Why should we think that causation is involved in the very concept of object-perception? For the following kind of reason.

Suppose that John has a visual experience of seeing a green apple sitting on a table in front of him and suppose that, as

[4] For more on the naked infinitive construction and seeing situations, see Jon Barwise and John Perry, 'Scenes and Other Situations', *Journal of Philosophy* 78 (1981), pp. 369–97 and *Situations and Attitudes* (Cambridge, MA: MIT Press, 1983), ch. 8.
[5] The classic presentation of the causal theory of perception in modern times is by H. P. Grice: see his 'The Causal Theory of Perception', *Proceedings of the Aristotelian Society*, Supp. Vol. 35 (1961), pp. 121–52, reprinted in his *Studies in the Way of Words* (Cambridge, MA: Harvard University Press, 1989) and also in Jonathan Dancy (ed.), *Perceptual Knowledge* (Oxford: Oxford University Press, 1988).

a matter of fact, just such a green apple *is* sitting on a table in front of him. Should we therefore say that John *sees* that apple? Not necessarily, for it could be that John's visual experience is a hallucination induced in him by some drug, or by some neuroscientist activating electrodes implanted in John's visual cortex, in which case it is a pure coincidence that his experience 'matches' the scene in front of him. This sort of case is customarily described as one of 'veridical hallucination'.[6] What such cases suggest is that it is part of the very concept of object-perception that there should be some sort of causal relationship between a person's perceptual experiences and the objects which, in virtue of having those experiences, he or she may be said to perceive. To a first approximation, we might attempt to capture this idea by the following principle:

(P) A subject *S* perceives an object *O* if and only if *S* has a perceptual experience whose content suitably matches *O*'s situation and which is appropriately caused by *O*'s situation.

Thus, to continue with our current example, principle (P) implies that in order for John to see the green apple sitting on the table in front of him, it is not enough that he should have a visual experience of seeing just such a green apple sitting on a table in front of him, since it should also be the case that this experience is *caused* by the presence of the green apple sitting on the table in front of him. In this example, of course, we are supposing that the content of John's visual experience *perfectly* matches the scene in front of him, but it would plainly be wrong to insist on such a perfect match in order for perception to be said to occur. We have to allow for the possibility of illusion, that is, for cases

---

[6] The notion of veridical hallucination and its implications for the causal theory of perception are illuminatingly discussed by David Lewis in his 'Veridical Hallucination and Prosthetic Vision', *Australasian Journal of Philosophy* 58 (1980), pp. 239–49, reprinted in his *Philosophical Papers, Volume II* (New York: Oxford University Press, 1986) and in Dancy (ed.), *Perceptual Knowledge*. See also Martin Davies, 'Function in Perception', *Australasian Journal of Philosophy* 61 (1983), pp. 409–26.

in which a person does perceive an object, but he or she seems to perceive something which differs in some respect from the object which is actually perceived. A classic example is the Müller-Lyer illusion, in which one sees two lines which are in fact of equal length and yet they seem to be of different lengths, because they terminate in arrow-heads pointing in opposite directions:

This is why, as I have stated principle (P), it speaks only of a 'suitable' match rather than of a perfect match. But we should not be too liberal in our interpretation of what is 'suitable' in this context. Clearly, John cannot be said to be seeing the green apple in front of him if his visual experience is one of seeing a red double-decker bus.

More problematic than the matter of 'matching', however, is the matter of what constitutes an 'appropriate' causal relation between perceptual experience and object perceived. This problem may be brought out by the following thought-experiment. Suppose, as before, that John has a visual experience of seeing a green apple sitting on a table in front of him and again suppose that, as a matter of fact, just such a green apple *is* sitting on a table in front of him. Now suppose in addition that the presence of the green apple sitting on the table in front of John is causally responsible for John's visual experience, but in the following unusual or 'deviant' way. A neuroscientist has rigged up some apparatus incorporating electrodes implanted in John's visual cortex which, when activated, induce in John a visual experience of seeing a green apple sitting on a table in front of him. Furthermore, the apparatus is wired up to electronic sensors attached to the table in front of John which are so designed that the electrodes will only be activated if something is placed on the table. Finally, the neuroscientist has placed a green apple on the table, thereby activating the electrodes and inducing John's visual experience of seeing just such a green apple sitting on a table in front of him. In this case it is true to say, as principle (P) requires, that John's visual experience not only has a content matching the presence of the green apple in front of him but is also *caused* by the presence of the green apple in front of him – and yet I think we would rightly be reluctant to say that John *sees* that apple, because *this* sort of causal relationship seems somehow inappropriate. But what, exactly, is 'inappropriate' about it? The problem we confront here is generally known as the problem of 'deviant causal chains' – and the problem is to specify what sort of causal relation qualifies as 'deviant' and hence 'inappropriate' for the purpose of providing a philosophical analysis of the concept of object-perception.

We might be tempted to say that an 'appropriate' causal relation in this context is the sort of causal relation that is *normally* involved in cases of veridical perception. But, in the first place, this would threaten to introduce a fatal circularity into our philosophical analysis of the concept of object-perception, since we would be appealing to the notion of what normally happens in cases of veridical *perception* in order to analyse that very concept. Secondly, such a suggestion would be too restrictive, in that it would wrongly disqualify certain possible cases from counting as genuine cases of perception. What I have in mind here are cases in which a person is enabled to perceive by means of an artificial prosthetic device. In human beings, vision is normally made possible by means of light-waves being reflected from the surfaces of objects and entering people's eyes. In the example discussed above, John's visual experience is certainly not caused in this normal way; indeed, his eyes could well be closed or the room be dark. But we should be wary of saying that *this* is why he cannot be said to see the apple in front of him. For, conceivably, someone who has completely lost the natural use of his eyes might be fitted with some electronic device implanted in his visual cortex and wired up to electromagnetic sensors attached to the top of his head, functioning in such a way as to restore, to all intents and purposes, his lost sense of sight.

How, then, does the case involving John differ significantly from such a case of 'prosthetic vision'? One important difference would appear to be this. As I described John's case, it was implied that the apparatus connected to his visual cortex was designed to induce in him a quite specific type of visual experience when the electrodes were activated, namely, an experience of seeing a green apple sitting on a table in front of him. Moreover, it was implied that if the neuroscientist had placed something quite different from a green apple on the table, such as a red vase, the sensors attached to the table would still have activated the electrodes and have induced in John an experience of seeing a green apple sitting on the table, rather than an experience of seeing a red vase sitting there. Thus it still seems to be a mere coincidence that John happens to have a visual experience matching the scene in front of him. Perhaps, then, what is required for John to see the apple is that his visual experience should be generated by some sort of mechanism – whether natural or artificial – which reliably brings about a suitable match between his visual experiences and the scene in front of him, whatever (within reasonable limits) that scene may be. However, this requirement may be too strong. For suppose that John is indeed equipped with such a mechanism but it begins to malfunction. Suppose, for instance, that the mechanism only works when a green apple is placed in front of John. Are we then to say that John does *not* see the apple, simply because if any other kind of thing were placed in front of him, he would not be able to see that? Surely not. Perhaps, then, all that is really required for John to see the apple is the following: not only must the presence of the green apple in front of John cause John to have a visual experience of seeing a green apple in front of him (or, at least, a sufficiently closely matching visual experience), but it must also be true that if there had been something quite different from a green apple in front of John, he would *not* have had such a visual experience. The latter condition is not satisfied in John's case as originally described, because in that case he would still have had such a visual experience even if a red vase, or any other kind of object, had been placed on the table in front of him.

And there we must leave the issue, even though it invites a good deal more debate. At least we have discovered that it is by no means a simple matter to determine what kind of causal relation is 'appropriate' as far as an analysis of the concept of object-perception is concerned.

OBJECTIONS TO CAUSAL THEORIES OF PERCEPTION

What we have been exploring, in the form of principle (P) of the previous section, is a causal theory (or, more properly, analysis) of perception. But such theories have many critics, some of whose objections we must now look at. One objection, unsurprisingly, is that the problem of 'deviant causal chains' has no satisfactory solution; however, I think that this verdict is unduly pessimistic. Another and more influential line of objection is epistemological and closely resembles the sort of epistemological objection which, as we saw in the previous chapter, is often raised against sense-datum theories. Indeed, some critics carelessly identify causal theories of perception with sense-datum theories, when in fact they are quite independent of each other. The criticism, then, is that causal theories of perception promote a form of scepticism which can only be avoided by some kind of 'direct' or 'naïve' realism. The thinking here is as follows.

As is implicit in principle (P), a causal theorist assumes that veridical perception involves the occurrence of perceptual experiences which, although *in fact* caused by 'external' objects, logically *could have been* caused in some quite different manner – in which case those experiences would instead have been hallucinatory. This is implicit in principle (P) because, quite generally, whenever one event, c, causes another event, e, it is true to say that it is logically possible for e to have occurred without c occurring – and vice versa – since causal relations between events are purely contingent relations.[7] (A contingent relation between two items

---

[7] The view that causal relations are contingent is one that we owe to David Hume, who famously contended that 'There is no object, which implies the existence of any other if we consider these objects in themselves': see *A Treatise of Human*

is one in which those items do in fact stand but quite possibly might not have stood.) Now, if the causal theorist is committed to saying that all of our perceptual experiences which we suppose to be veridical *could*, logically, be hallucinatory, it seems that he is committed to the logical possibility of global perceptual scepticism, that is, to the possibility that we never really perceive 'external' objects at all and, indeed, that no such objects really exist. For the causal theory seems to imply that we could have all the perceptual experiences which we in fact have even in the complete absence of any 'external world' whatsoever.

One very blunt response to this sort of objection would be to say 'So what?'. We can hardly suppose that philosophical scepticism is going to go away if we abandon a causal theory of perception. It is better, perhaps, to confront such scepticism head-on. Moreover, even if it is true that the causal theorist is committed to the *logical* possibility that all of our perceptual experiences are hallucinatory, how worrying should this be to him? All sorts of things are logically possible which it would be utterly unreasonable to believe actually to be true. For instance, it seems logically possible that the whole world sprang into existence just five minutes ago, with the fossil record and our 'memories' misleadingly suggesting that it had been in existence for much longer than this.[8] In any case, we very arguably shouldn't conflate the philosophical task of providing an analysis of the concept of perception with the quite different philosophical task of attempting to answer the sceptic. If we do conflate the two, we may end up failing to perform either task satisfactorily.

However, even if, for the reasons just given, we are not convinced by the foregoing line of objection against causal theories of perception, we might be well advised to consider the merits of alternative theories whose advocates are motiv-

---

Nature, ed. L. A. Selby-Bigge and P. H. Nidditch (Oxford: Clarendon Press, 1978), p. 86.

[8] On the sceptical hypothesis that the world came into being five minutes ago, see Bertrand Russell, *The Analysis of Mind* (London: George Allen and Unwin, 1921), pp. 159–60.

ated by that sort of objection. One such theory is the so-called
disjunctive theory, to which we shall now turn.

THE DISJUNCTIVE THEORY OF PERCEPTION

Disjunctive theorists reject the assumption which I have just
attributed to the causal theorist, namely, the assumption
that veridical perception involves the occurrence of perceptual experiences which, although in fact caused by
'external' objects, logically could have been caused in some
quite different manner, in which case those experiences
would instead have been hallucinatory.[9] They urge that there
is nothing literally in common between, on the one hand,
a case of veridical perception and, on the other, a case of
hallucination which its subject might *mistake* for being just
such a case of veridical perception. The causal theorist, of
course, assumes that what two such cases have in common is
the occurrence of a certain kind of perceptual experience and
that they differ only in respect of what causes the perceptual
experience in each case. (We are now in a position to understand the disjunctive theory's somewhat obscure name: it is
called 'disjunctive' because it holds that when a subject takes
him or herself to be perceiving something, then *either* this is
a case of veridical perception *or else* it is a case of hallucination, but there is no common element in the form of a 'perceptual experience' which would be present in either case
and merely be caused in two different ways.)

The first thing to be said about the disjunctive theory is
that it is not at all clear that it is any less vulnerable to the
doubts of the sceptic than is the causal theory. For the sceptic
can still urge that whenever we take ourselves to be perceiving something, it is logically possible that we are victims of

[9] Versions of the disjunctive theory of perception are to be found in J. M. Hinton,
Experiences: An Inquiry into some Ambiguities (Oxford: Clarendon Press, 1973), Paul
Snowdon, 'Perception, Vision, and Causation', *Proceedings of the Aristotelian Society*
81 (1980–1), pp. 175–92, and John McDowell, 'Criteria, Defeasibility, and Knowledge', *Proceedings of the British Academy* 68 (1982), pp. 455–79. The latter two
papers are reprinted in Dancy (ed.), *Perceptual Knowledge*.

hallucination and thus that we never in fact really perceive any 'external' object. Against this it might be urged that it simply doesn't make sense to suppose that we might be hallucinating all of the time, because we understand what a hallucination is only by contrasting it with the case of veridical perception. Having a hallucination, it may be said, is *seeming* to perceive something when in fact one fails to do so – and this account of what it is to have a hallucination evidently presupposes a prior understanding of what it is to *perceive* something. By contrast, the causal theorist does not explain the notion of a hallucination in this way: rather, he says that having a hallucination is having a perceptual experience which is not caused by an 'external' object. However, it is hard to see how this difference between the two kinds of theorist implies that the disjunctive theorist is better equipped to counter the sceptic. For even if it were true that we can only understand the notion of a hallucination in terms of a prior understanding of what it is to perceive something, why should we need actually to *perceive* anything in order to possess that prior understanding? There are many concepts which we understand even though we have never come across actual instances of them, such as the concept of a golden mountain. It might be contended, perhaps, that all such concepts are analysable in terms of concepts instances of which we *have* actually come across, such as the concept of being golden and the concept of a mountain. But, first of all, this is a contestable claim and, secondly, its application in the present context would seem to require the equally contestable claim that the concept of *perceiving* is primitive and unanalysable. For if that concept were conceded to be analysable, the sceptic could again urge that the concept of perceiving is one that we can understand even though we have actually come across no instances of it.

Are there any other considerations, however, which might tell in favour of the disjunctive theory? One such consideration could be this. It may be felt that the disjunctive theory respects our common-sense intuition that when one really is perceiving an object (and is not, thus, the victim of a hallucination), one is in 'direct contact' with that object. The causal theory, by contrast, implies that one's perceptual contact with the object is 'indirect', at least in the sense that such contact is mediated by the occurrence of a perceptual experience which is merely an *effect* of that object, rather than being the object itself. This is not to suggest that the causal theorist must hold that perceptual experiences are themselves objects of perception which are somehow more 'directly' perceived than 'external' objects are (though some philosophers have confusedly held this view). Clearly, a causal theorist can be a 'direct realist' in the sense that he can hold that the only objects of perception are external objects. Even so, it does appear that the causal theory clashes with common-sense intuition to this extent: when we take ourselves to be perceiving an external object, it does not *seem* to us that this is a matter of our being affected causally in some way by that object. Thus it may be said that the disjunctive theory is more faithful to the *phenomenology* of perception than the causal theory is, that is, that it more accurately reflects what it *seems like* to be perceiving something.

However, why should we suppose that the phenomenology of perception provides a good guide to understanding what perception *is*? Why should perception be as it seems to be? Certainly, if the causal theory implies that perception is not as it seems to be, then it is incumbent upon the causal theorist to explain *why* perception is not as it seems to be. But perhaps he has the resources with which to do this perfectly satisfactorily. To start with, he could point out that even when our perception of things is manifestly 'indirect', it can *seem* 'direct'. For example, when one is absorbed in watching a film, one becomes oblivious of the fact that what one really has before one's eyes are merely images which are remote effects of the objects that one seems to see. One cannot maintain this attitude of absorption while simultaneously becoming conscious of the images on the screen *as* images, because this would require one to divide one's attention in a way which seems to be psychologically impossible. From the point of view of the causal theory, then, it is easy enough to understand why perception should always *seem* 'direct' when we are absorbed in attending to the objects that we take ourselves to be perceiving, for such attention is incompatible with a consciousness of the effects which those objects are having upon us. Moreover, since evolution has, for obvious reasons, designed us to attend to external objects rather than to their perceptual effects on us, we can understand why the phenomenology of perception should so compellingly favour 'direct' realism. But precisely because the causal theorist can explain why this should be so, that it is so does not count against him and in favour of the disjunctive theorist.

All things considered, then, it does not seem that the disjunctive theory has any advantage over the causal theory. Yet it does appear to have some disadvantages of its own. For instance, if it really is committed to regarding the concept of (veridical) perception as being primitive and unanalysable, that would surely be a major disadvantage. If the concept of perception is primitive and unanalysable, how is one to decide, in a principled way, what to say about some of the thought-experiments we considered earlier involving John and the green apple sitting on the table in front of him? It must also be said that the disjunctive theory has a certain air of mystery or even magic about it, with its suggestion that perception puts us in 'direct contact' with external objects. To be fair, the disjunctive theorist can do quite a lot to dispel this air of mystery. In the first place, he can emphasise that he is not in the business of formulating a *scientific* theory of perception and can happily accept what physicists, physiologists and psychologists tell us concerning the causal processes that go on in our environment and in our brains when we perceive things. Secondly, he can try to forge a connection between the idea that we perceive objects 'directly' and the kind of *externalism* in the philosophy of mind which we discussed in chapter 4. It may be recalled that we described externalism there as maintaining that our minds 'reach out' into our physical environment, at least in the sense that our states of mind can depend for their very existence and identity upon what things that environment contains. Thus the disjunctive theorist may maintain that a person's mental state of perceiving some external object is dependent for its existence and identity upon the object in question, so that if that object had not existed or if another object had been in its place, the person would not have been in that very state of mind. However, it is not clear that a causal theorist cannot equally espouse an externalist position, in which case such considerations cannot play a decisive role in the debate between him and the disjunctive theorist. But there, for present purposes, we must leave this debate.

THE COMPUTATIONAL AND ECOLOGICAL APPROACHES TO PERCEPTION

Although philosophers and empirical psychologists have somewhat different concerns in their attempts to understand the nature of perception, it is difficult and unhelpful to try to draw a perfectly clear dividing line between those concerns, as though conceptual analysis and scientific theory were utterly unrelated to one another. Unsurprisingly, then, we find echoes of the philosophical debate between 'direct' and 'indirect' realists in disagreements between empirical psychologists as to the proper theoretical framework for investigating perceptual systems and processes. Most contemporary psychologists assume that the chief function of perceptual systems in living organisms is to enable those organisms to extract useful information from their physical environment and thereby facilitate adaptive behaviour, that is, behaviour which favours their survival. But there are deep disagreements both as to what is involved in perceptual processes and as to how those processes can best be investigated experimentally. Here we may distinguish, in particular, between the 'computational' approach and the 'ecological' approach.

According to the computational approach, a perceptual system – such as the human visual system – can be thought of as an information-processing system which functions somewhat analogously to the way in which an electronic digital

computer does and which, accordingly, can usefully be modelled by means of such a device. On this view – whose best-
known proponent was the psychologist David Marr – one can
gain insight into how the human visual system works by
thinking about how one might design and programme a robot
to negotiate its way around its environment with the aid of
electronic sensors.[10] The task which faces the designer of
such a robot – and so which, it is assumed, also faced biological evolution in its role as our 'designer' – can be described
at various different levels of abstraction, of which (following
Marr) we can distinguish three. At the highest level, we may
describe the task in terms of what the system is supposed to
achieve. Thus, in the case of the visual system, what it is
supposed to achieve is to provide relevant information for
the robot or organism concerning the physical lay-out of its
immediate environment – notably, information concerning
the shapes, sizes and relative positions of objects situated in
that environment. Moreover, it is assumed that this information has to be gleaned, somehow, from the state of the system's sensors, which in the case of the human visual system
are the retinal surfaces of our eyes. At this level of abstraction, then, we may describe the task in terms of what sorts
of computational processes are required to transform
information concerning the state of the system's sensors into
information concerning the robot's or organism's environment. The underlying presupposition here is that an information-processing system can only process information which is
represented in the system through some method of encoding –
such as the digital machine code of an electronic computer –
and that computational processes operate on such representations. Lower than this level of abstraction, however, is
the level at which a quite specific computer programme or set
of algorithms might be devised to achieve the computational

[10] David Marr's computational theory of vision is explained in his *Vision: A Computational Investigation into the Human Representation and Processing of Visual Information*
(New York: W. H. Freeman and Company, 1982). A good introduction to Marr's
theory is to be found in Vicki Bruce and Patrick Green, *Visual Perception: Physiology,
Psychology and Ecology* (London: Lawrence Erlbaum Associates, 1985), Part II.

objectives described at the preceding level. Finally, at the lowest level of abstraction, we may describe the task in terms of what kinds of physical structures, whether electronic or neuronal, are required in order to implement or run the programme devised for the system.

From the point of view of the computational approach to perception, the first two levels of abstraction are obviously of most interest – which is not to deny that questions of physical implementation are important in their own right, though these are seen as being chiefly matters for the electronic engineer or the neurophysiologist. Let us then consider, in barest outline, what is involved at these first two levels. The human retina might loosely be compared to an array of light-sensitive electronic cells, each one capable of registering degrees of light-intensity on, say, a twenty-point scale. A very simple array of this sort might contain a few hundred such cells arranged adjacent to one another to form a rectangular grid. When light reflected from objects in the environment is focused on to this grid, an optical image is formed there and the cells register the varying degrees of light-intensity over the grid's surface. Thus information about the two-dimensional pattern of light-intensities at the grid's surface is encoded in the output of the light-sensitive cells. This encoded information then has to be transformed, somehow, into information concerning the shapes, sizes and relative positions of objects in the environment. That is a difficult task, which is complicated by many environmental factors, such as the fact that some objects are partly hidden by or in the shadow of others. However, an important part of the solution lies in the application of formal principles of projective geometry, which can help the system to compute the three-dimensional shapes of objects from their two-dimensional optical images as registered from various different angles – rather as one may work out the three-dimensional shape of an object from the way it is depicted in a series of photographs taken from different points of view. Various assumptions have to be made if this sort of solution is to be workable in practice – for instance, that objects in the environment are fairly stable and that they are illuminated from a fairly constant direction. However, in the sort of environment in which the human visual system has evolved, such assumptions as these are in fact justified.

The foregoing is only a very rudimentary outline of how adherents of the computational approach think we should try to understand perceptual systems, but it will serve to highlight the differences between that approach and the rival 'ecological' approach. A key feature of the computational approach, which makes it comparable with 'indirect' realism as we have characterised it hitherto, is that it assumes that perception involves the construction of *representations* of objects in the environment. This process of construction is assumed to be a complex one, in which lower-level representations of information about the state of the system's sensors are transformed, through the application of mathematical algorithms, into higher-level representations of information about the state of objects in the environment. Of course, it is not suggested that we are aware of these computational processes supposedly going on in our heads. Rather, we are at most only aware of the end-products, the representations of the state of objects in our environment. Perceptual systems, such as the human visual system, are described as being *modular* or *informationally encapsulated*, the implication being that our higher-level conscious thought-processes are incapable of influencing the information-processing which goes on in such systems.[11] This, it is said, is why we find that we cannot dispel a visual illusion simply by realising that it *is* an illusion. Thus, even when we *know* that the two lines in the Müller-Lyer illusion are really equal in length, we can't help *seeing* them as being unequal, because our visual system delivers to us the (mis)information that they are unequal and we are unable to 'correct' it by altering the way in which it processes visual information. Why the

---

[11] For the notion that perceptual systems are 'modular', see Jerry A. Fodor, *The Modularity of Mind* (Cambridge, MA: MIT Press, 1983), pp. 47ff. I raise some doubts about this in my *Subjects of Experience*, pp. 128ff.

visual system should mislead us in this case is a matter for debate, but the presumption is that having a system incorporating this 'error' confers compensating advantages on us in our natural visual environment.

Adherents of the *ecological* approach to perception, whose leading proponent was the American psychologist J. J. Gibson, are hostile to the idea that perception is a matter of representation and explicitly describe their position as being one which maintains that perception is 'direct'.[12] They agree that the function of perceptual systems is to provide organisms with action-guiding information about their natural environment, but don't see why this should require complex computational operations on representations. Their idea is that the natural environment itself is rich in information – for instance, that the structure of reflected light in such an environment embodies rich information about the spatial properties of reflective surfaces in it – and that the human visual system is well-attuned to picking up that information and using it to guide our actions. Indeed, such psychologists stress the mutual dependency of perception and action, with perception guiding action and action enabling perceptual systems to exploit to the full the information available in the natural environment. For this reason they are doubtful about the value of laboratory-based experiments intended to reveal the workings of the human visual system by studying cases of visual illusion. They point out that such illusions almost always occur in unnatural environments in which subjects are prevented from exploiting the natural interplay between perception and action – because, for instance, they are made to sit still and stare at images on a fixed screen. Ecological psychologists, then, are resistant to the idea that, in normal circumstances, our brains have to *construct* information about our environment by inferring it from information about the states of our sensory receptors, because they believe that the

---

[12] J. J. Gibson's 'ecological' approach to perception is presented in his *The Ecological Approach to Visual Perception* (Hillsdale, NJ: Lawrence Erlbaum Associates, 1986). A good introduction to it is provided in Bruce and Green, *Visual Perception*, Part III.

requisite information about our environment is already present in the environment itself and is available for us to pick up directly, provided that our senses are properly attuned to it.

Computational psychologists are apt to object to the foregoing picture that it leaves us entirely in the dark as to *how* our senses 'pick up' information about the environment. A properly attuned radio set will pick up information from radiowaves, but it requires a lot of complicated machinery in order to do this. Computational psychologists may say that what they are doing is explaining, in the perceptual case, how the machinery does its job – though not, of course, at a purely physiological level (the level of 'implementation'). However, the ecological psychologist may retort that he doesn't deny that some sort of machinery is required, but only denies that there is a significant level of description of what this machinery does that requires expression in terms of computations and representations. And, indeed, it seems perfectly fair to raise this sort of doubt about the computational approach.[13] We shouldn't assume, just because human designers might profitably adopt the computational approach in order to construct a robot, that nature has adopted this approach in 'designing' *us*. Very often, tasks which can be accomplished with the aid of computational techniques can also be accomplished in other and sometimes simpler ways. Consider, for instance, the task of ensuring that the water-levels in two tanks are equal. This *could* be achieved by installing an elaborate system of electronic sensors governing the inlet and outlet pipes to the two tanks, so that when the water-level in one tank goes up or down by a certain measured amount, information about this is passed to the other tank and the same amount of water is let into or out of it. But a much easier solution is to place the two tanks on the same level and join them by an interconnecting pipe, thus letting gravity do the work.

---

[13] For such doubts about the computational approach to mind in general, see Tim van Gelder, 'What Might Cognition Be, If Not Computation?', *Journal of Philosophy* 92 (1995), pp. 345–81.

I shall not attempt to adjudicate here between the ecological and computational approaches. It interesting that the debate between them resembles, in a fashion, the debate amongst philosophers between 'direct' and 'indirect' realists, but I don't think that either approach clearly stands or falls with its philosophical counterpart. It may also be suggested that the computational approach is implicitly 'internalist' whereas the ecological approach is implicitly 'externalist', in the senses of those terms explained in chapter 4 – though some philosophers of psychology have disputed this description of the computational approach.[14] But whatever the truth may be about this, I cannot help remarking that the two approaches have one striking feature in common: neither of them assigns any significant role in perception to the qualitative or phenomenal characteristics of perceptual experience. Indeed, neither of them really has any use for the notion of *perceptual experience* at all. Perhaps that will be a point in their favour as far as adherents of the disjunctive theory of perception are concerned (though their sympathies could surely lie only with the ecological approach). But to other philosophers of perception the neglect shown to the notion of perceptual experience will seem a serious omission. To them it will seem that the most important and central feature of perception has simply been ignored by both of these empirical approaches.

CONSCIOUSNESS, EXPERIENCE AND 'BLINDSIGHT'

In response to the last complaint, some psychologists may urge that, in point of fact, empirical evidence suggests that the phenomenal aspects of perceptual experience are far less important than common-sense thinking takes them to be. They could cite here recent studies of cases of so-called

[14] The view that Marr's theory of vision has an 'externalist' orientation has been defended by Tyler Burge: see his 'Marr's Theory of Vision', in Jay L. Garfield (ed.), *Modularity in Knowledge Representation and Natural-Language Understanding* (Cambridge, MA: MIT Press, 1989). For an opposing view, see Gabriel Segal, 'Seeing What is Not There', *Philosophical Review* 98 (1989), pp. 189–214.

'blindsight', in which subjects suffering from certain kinds of lesion in their visual cortex declare themselves to be unable to see anything in some region of their visual field and yet are manifestly in possession of visually-based information about items in that region.[15] Their possession of such information can be elicited by instructing them to make 'guesses' about the presence or absence of certain stimuli in the 'blind' regions of their visual field, for it turns out that their 'guesses' are correct far more frequently than chance could explain. The implication seems to be that such subjects are *seeing* the stimuli, even though – judging by their own introspective reports – they are not enjoying any kind of conscious perceptual experience of them. Of course, one might surmise that these subjects *are* undergoing conscious perceptual experiences and that it is their introspective judgement that is at fault, but that seems highly implausible. But if we don't *need* to have conscious perceptual experiences in order to see things, perhaps we overestimate the extent to which such experiences are involved in the visual processes even of normally sighted individuals. Certainly, if we don't need to have perceptual experiences in order to see things, the causal theory of perception sketched earlier in this chapter cannot be correct.

One question which we could raise here is this. Why should we say that the blindsight subjects are indeed *seeing* things in the 'blind' regions of their visual fields? After all, they themselves strongly *deny* that they can see anything there. If the answer is given that they must be seeing something since they are evidently receiving information via their eyes about items in the 'blind' regions of their visual fields, then this clearly presupposes a certain conception of what it is to see something – namely, that to see something is to receive

---

[15] For full experimental details concerning the phenomenon of 'blindsight', see Lawrence Weiskrantz, *Blindsight: A Case Study and Implications* (Oxford: Clarendon Press, 1986). Some interesting questions concerning the implications of blindsight for our understanding of the nature of consciousness are raised by Ned Block in 'On a Confusion About a Function of Consciousness', *Behavioral and Brain Sciences* 18 (1995), pp. 227–87.

information about it via the eyes. (One would have to qualify this so as to avoid having to say that one *sees* something when one reads about it in a book, but let us ignore this complication here.) But such a conception of what seeing is can certainly be challenged. For one thing, if 'prosthetic' vision of the kind discussed earlier is possible, as it certainly seems to be, one does not need eyes in order to be able to see, if by 'eye' one understands the sort of biological organ we typically find located in people's heads. On the other hand, if by 'eye' one means any kind of device, whether natural or artificial, which enables one to *see*, it will clearly be circular to define seeing in terms of acquiring information via the eyes. It is very arguable, in fact, that what is distinctive of *seeing*, as opposed to any other sensory modality, is the kind of perceptual experiences that are characteristically involved in it – and, more specifically, the kind of phenomenal or qualitative features which those experiences typically have. This, surely, explains why blindsight subjects so strongly *deny* that they can see, namely, because they believe that they lack the requisite kind of perceptual experience. And note, here, that such subjects *continue* to deny that they can see even after they have been informed about the high success-rate of their 'guesses'.

Of course, it would be idle to enter into a purely verbal dispute about what we should or shouldn't mean by the verb 'to see'. Perhaps we should even distinguish two different senses of 'see' and say that blindsight subjects 'see' in one sense but not in the other. That, indeed, would be in line with the thinking of some physiologists who maintain that the human brain is equipped with two different visual systems, an older one and a more recently evolved one, only the first of which is intact in blindsight subjects. (It is worth noting here that the sorts of stimuli about which blindsight subjects can make correct 'guesses' are fairly crude ones, such as points of light or simple shapes.) But if conscious perceptual experience is only associated with the more recently evolved system, we need to ask what biological advantage such experience confers upon creatures capable of it. This is part of a much broader question that can be raised about the function of consciousness from an evolutionary point of view. Some philosophers and psychologists suggest that consciousness – if it really exists at all – is epiphenomenal, an accidental by-product of other evolutionary developments. This suggestion is hard to believe, but difficult to dismiss unless it can be shown that a creature possessing consciousness can achieve certain things which a creature lacking it could not achieve. On the other hand, perhaps we should say that if evolutionary theory cannot explain the existence of so striking and undeniable a phenomenon as consciousness, this is indicative of the inadequacy of the theory.

CONCLUSIONS

In this chapter, the notion of a *perceptual experience* has been a central concern. Perceptual experiences are conceived of as having both qualitative features and conceptual content (though they may in addition have some kind of non-conceptual content). Their conceptual content is clearly related to, or constrained by, their qualitative features, but in a fashion which is not easy to spell out in detail. We examined a version of the causal theory of perception, which maintains that it is a conceptual truth that perception involves a causal relationship between a subject's perceptual experiences and the objects which he or she thereby perceives. We saw that such a theory has to deal with the problem of 'deviant causal chains', but tentatively concluded that this problem can be solved. Then we looked at objections to the causal theory, concentrating on the claim that it promotes scepticism – a charge which we argued to be unfounded. We also looked at a major rival to the causal theory – the disjunctive theory – but concluded that it does not have any significant advantages over the causal theory and has, besides, certain disadvantages. Then we went on to discuss the division amongst empirical psychologists between adherents of the ecological and computational approaches to perception, noting its resemblance to the division amongst philosophers between 'direct' and 'indirect' realists, but also noting the neglect by both approaches of the notion of conscious perceptual experience. Finally, we discussed whether this neglect could be justified by appeal to the existence of such phenomena as 'blindsight', but concluded that no simple argument to that effect could be sustained. The contention that perceptual experiences as we have characterised them are centrally involved in processes of perception appears, then, to survive attack both on philosophical and on empirical grounds.

7

Thought and language

So far in this book, we have discussed various different kinds of mental state, including sensations, perceptions (that is, perceptual experiences) and beliefs. We discussed beliefs (and other propositional attitude states) in quite some detail in chapters 3 and 4, before going on to talk about sensations and perceptions in chapters 5 and 6. This order of discussion – although consistent with the overall plan of the book – might strike some readers as being an inversion of the natural one, because it is natural to assume that sensations and perceptions are, in more than one sense, 'prior' to beliefs. They seem prior to beliefs, first of all, in the sense that many of our beliefs are *based on*, or *derived from*, our sensations and perceptions, whereas the reverse never seems to be the case (except, perhaps, in certain species of delusion). Secondly, sensations and perceptions seem prior to beliefs in the sense that, whereas we might be willing to attribute sensations and perhaps even perceptions to a creature which we deemed incapable of possessing beliefs, I think we would – or, at least, *should* – be less willing, and perhaps altogether unwilling, to attribute beliefs to a creature which we deemed incapable of possessing sensations and perceptions.

Part of what is implied here is that beliefs are mental states of *a higher cognitive level* than are either sensations or perceptions. One might wish to deny, indeed, that sensations are 'cognitive' states at all – although against this one could urge that sensations provide a creature with information about the physical condition of various parts of its body and its immediate environment (for example, that sensations of pain inform it about damage to certain of its body-parts and that sensations of smell inform it about the presence of food or other animals). *Perceptions*, on the other hand, clearly qualify as 'cognitive' states, if – as was urged in chapter 6 – we should think of them as necessarily possessing conceptual content: for an ability to exercise concepts is undoubtedly a cognitive ability. The adjective 'cognitive' derives from the Latin verb *cognoscere*, meaning 'to know', and knowledge properly so-called is inextricably bound up with an ability to exercise concepts. However, this very connection between cognition and concept-possession should make us reconsider whether the kind of information made available to a creature by its sensations suffices to justify our describing sensations as 'cognitive' states. Arguably, it does *not* suffice, since no exercise of concepts on the part of the creature need be involved. A dog which licks its wounded leg, upon feeling a sensation of pain there, is clearly in some sense responding to information made available to it about the physical condition of its leg. But in order to respond appropriately in this way, the dog does not apparently need to exercise *concepts* of any sort. It need, in particular, possess no concept of a *leg*, nor of *damage*, nor of *itself*, nor indeed of *pain*.

Having made this connection between cognition and concept-possession, however, we may begin to feel dissatisfied with some aspects of the discussion about beliefs and their 'propositional content' in chapter 4. In particular, we may feel that beliefs were there treated merely as 'representational' or 'informational' states, in a way which was quite insensitive to the distinction between those mental states which do, and those which do not, presuppose an ability to exercise concepts on the part of creatures possessing the states in question. That is one very important reason why we must now return to the topic of belief and, more broadly, to the topic of *thought*. Our preliminary investigations into this area in chapters 3 and 4 were not in vain, inconclusive though they were. Now we are in a position to carry them further forward in the light of what we have learnt about sensation and perception. For one thing which we must try to understand is how sensation and perception are related to thought and belief. Another is how thought and belief are related to their expression in *language*.

Some of the questions that we shall address in this chapter are the following. Is all thought symbolic and quasi-linguistic in character? Is there a 'brain code' or 'language of thought'? What is the role of mental imagery in our thinking processes? How far is a capacity for thought dependent upon an ability to communicate in a public language? Does the language which we speak shape or constrain the thoughts that we are capable of entertaining? And to what extent are our capacities for language innate?

MODES OF MENTAL REPRESENTATION

Let us begin with the seemingly innocuous proposition that cognitive states, including thoughts and beliefs, are at once *mental* states and *representational* states. Now, I have already suggested that talk of 'representation' in this context is somewhat indiscriminate, in that it is insensitive to the distinction between conceptual and non-conceptual content (recall our discussion of this point in the previous chapter). However, precisely for this reason, such talk carries with it a smaller burden of assumptions than would more specific ways of talking, which gives it certain advantages. The questions we need to think about now are (1) *how* mental states could be representational states and (2) what *modes* of representation they must involve in order to qualify as cognitive states. It is in addressing the latter question that we can impose the constraint that cognitive states must be seen as possessing some kind of conceptual content.

We have already given the first question a good deal of consideration in chapter 4, where we explored various naturalistic accounts of mental representation (although, to be sure, we found reason to be less than fully satisfied with these). So let us now concentrate on the second question. Here we may be helped by reflecting on the many different modes of *non*-mental representation with which we are all familiar. The wide variety of these modes is illustrated by the very different ways in which items of the following kinds serve to *represent* things or states of affairs: pictures, photographs, diagrams, maps, symbols, and sentences. All of these familiar items are, of course, human artefacts, which people have designed quite specifically in order to represent something or other. Indeed, it is arguable that every such artefact succeeds in representing something only insofar as someone – either its creator or its user – *interprets* it as representing something. If that is so, we might seem to be faced with a difficulty if we tried to use such items as models for understanding modes of *mental* representation. For – quite apart from its inherent implausibility – it would surely involve either a vicious circle or a vicious infinite regress to say that *mental* representations succeed in representing something only insofar as someone interprets them as representing something. For *interpreting* is itself a representational mental state (in fact, a kind of cognitive state). One way of putting this point is to say that human artefactual representations, such as pictures and maps, have only 'derived', not 'original', *intentionality* – intentionality being that property which a thing has if it represents, and thus is 'about', something else (in the way in which a map can be 'about' a piece of terrain or a diagram can be 'about' the structure of a machine).[1]

We may respond to the foregoing difficulty in the following way. First of all, the fact (if it is a fact) that artefactual representations have only derived intentionality, while it might prevent us from appealing to them in order to explain *how* mental representations can be representational states – which was question (1) above – would not prevent us from appealing to them for the purposes of answering question (2), that is, as providing models of various different possible

---

[1] For discussion of the distinction between 'original' (or 'intrinsic') intentionality and 'derived' intentionality, see John R. Searle, *The Rediscovery of the Mind* (Cambridge, MA: MIT Press, 1992), pp. 78–82. For more about the notion of intentionality quite generally, see his *Intentionality: An Essay in the Philosophy of Mind* (Cambridge: Cambridge University Press, 1983).

modes of mental representation. It could be, for example, that certain modes of mental representation are profitably thought of as being analogous to *sentences*, as far as their form or structure is concerned. Certainly, it would be unpromising to maintain that such a mental 'sentence' serves to represent something – some state of affairs – for the same sort of reason that a written sentence of English does, since it seems clear that sentences of English only manage to represent anything in virtue of the fact that English speakers *interpret* them as doing so. Hence, we must look elsewhere for an account of *how* a mental 'sentence' could manage to represent anything (appealing, perhaps, to one of the naturalistic accounts sketched in chapter 4). However, it might still be the case that there is something about the *structure* of natural language sentences which makes them a promising model for certain modes of mental representation. This is the issue that we shall look into next.

THE 'LANGUAGE OF THOUGHT' HYPOTHESIS

The following line of argument provides one reason for supposing that cognitive states, including thoughts and beliefs, must be conceived of as involving some sort of quasi-linguistic mode of representation. We have already made the point that cognitive states have *conceptual* content. But, more than that, they have conceptual *structure*. Compare the following beliefs: the belief that horses like apples, the belief that horses like carrots, the belief that squirrels like carrots and the belief that squirrels like nuts. Each of these beliefs shares one or more conceptual components with the others, but they all have the same overall conceptual structure – they are all beliefs of the form: *F*s like *G*s. Now, sentences of a language are admirably suited to capturing such structure, because they are formed from words which can be recombined in various ways to generate new sentences with the same or different structure. The grammatical or syntactical rules of a language determine what forms of combination are admissible. A competent speaker, who has an implicit knowledge of those rules together with a large enough vocabulary – which may, however, comprise only a few thousand words – can construct a vast number of different sentences, many of which he may never have encountered before, in order to express any of a vast range of thoughts that may come into his head. The *productivity* of language, then – its capacity to generate an indefinitely large number of sentences from a limited vocabulary – seems to match the productivity of thought, which suggests a close connection between the two. A plausible hypothesis is that the productivity of thought is explicable in the same way as that of language, namely, that it arises from the fact that thought involves a structural or compositional mode of representation analogous to that of language. Unsurprisingly, the existence of just such a mode of mental representation has indeed been postulated, going under the title of 'the language of thought' or 'Mentalese'.[2]

In describing the putative language of thought as being a *language*, we must be wary not to assimilate it too closely to familiar natural languages, such as English or Swahili. The only relevant similarity is structural – the possession of 'syntactical' organisation. Mentalese, if it exists, is a language in which we *think*, but not one in which we *speak* or *communicate* publicly. Moreover, if we do think in Mentalese, we are clearly not consciously aware of doing so: sentences of Mentalese are not disclosed to us when we reflect, or 'introspect', upon our own thought processes. Thus, sentences of Mentalese are not to be confused with 'inner speech' or 'silent soliloquy' – the kind of imaginary dialogue that we often hold with ourselves as we work out the solution to some problem or ponder over a decision we have to make. For we conduct this kind of imaginary dialogue in our native tongue or, at

[2] The most fully developed defence of the language of thought hypothesis, drawing on arguments of the kind sketched in this section, is to be found in Jerry A. Fodor, *The Language of Thought* (Hassocks: Harvester Press, 1976). 'Mentalese' is Wilfrid Sellars' name for the language of thought: see his 'The Structure of Knowledge II', in H. N. Castañeda (ed.), *Action, Knowledge, and Reality: Critical Studies in Honor of Wilfrid Sellars* (Indianapolis: Bobbs-Merrill, 1975). See also Hartry Field, 'Mental Representation', *Erkenntnis* 13 (1978), pp. 9–61, reprinted in Ned Block (ed.), *Readings in Philosophy of Psychology, Volume* 2 (London: Methuen, 1981).

least, in some natural language known to us, be it English or German or some other human tongue.

But why, apart from the foregoing considerations about the productivity of thought, should we suppose that Mentalese exists? Various additional reasons have been offered. One is this. It may be urged that the only way in which one can learn a language is by learning to translate it into a language which one already knows. This, after all, is how a native English speaker learns a foreign language, such as French, namely, by learning to translate it into English (unless, of course, he picks it up 'directly', in which case he presumably learns it in much the same way as he learnt English). But if that is so, then we can only have learnt our *mother* tongue (our first natural language) by learning to translate it into a language our knowledge of which is *innate* (and thus unlearned) – in short, by learning to translate it into Mentalese, or the 'language of thought'. However, although learning a language by learning to translate it certainly is *one* way of learning a language, it may be questioned whether it is the *only* way. Someone hostile to Mentalese could easily turn the foregoing argument around and maintain that, since (in his view) there is no such thing as Mentalese, it follows that there must be a way to learn a language which does not involve translating it into a language which one already knows. But then, of course, it would be incumbent upon such a person to explain what this other way could be, which might not be at all easy. We shall return to this issue later, when we come to consider to what extent our knowledge of language is innate.

Another consideration ostensibly favouring the language of thought hypothesis is that postulating the existence of such a language would enable us to model human thought-processes on the way in which a digital electronic computer operates. Such a device provides, it may be said, our best hope of understanding how a wholly physical system can *process information*. In the case of the computer, this is achieved by representing information in a quasi-linguistic way, utilising a binary 'machine code'. Strings of this code consist of sequences of the symbols 'o' and '1', which can be realised physically by, say, the 'off' and 'on' states of electronic switches in the machine. If the human brain is an information-processing device, albeit a naturally evolved one rather than the product of intelligent design, then it may be reasonable to hypothesise that it operates in much the same way as an electronic computer does, at least to the extent of utilising some sort of quasi-linguistic method of encoding information. Mentalese might be seen, then, as a naturally evolved 'brain code', analogous to the machine code of a computer. On the other hand, doubts have been raised by many philosophers and psychologists about the computational approach to the mind, some of which we aired in the previous chapter. We shall look into this question more fully in the next chapter, when we discuss the prospects for the development of artificial intelligence. In the meantime, we would do well not to put too much weight on purported analogies between brains and computers. Moreover, as we shall see in the next chapter, there are styles of computer architecture – notably, so-called 'connectionist' ones – which do not sustain the kind of analogy which has just been advanced on behalf of the language of thought hypothesis.[3]

ANALOGUE VERSUS DIGITAL REPRESENTATION

Sentences of a language, as we have just seen, provide one possible model for the mode of mental representation involved in human thought processes. But earlier on we listed many other kinds of artificial representation besides sentences – items such as pictures, photographs, diagrams and

---

[3] For evaluation of Fodor's arguments in *The Language of Thought*, see Daniel C. Dennett's critical notice of the book in *Mind* 86 (1977), pp. 265–80, reprinted as 'A Cure for the Common Code?', in Dennett's *Brainstorms: Philosophical Essays on Mind and Psychology* (Hassocks: Harvester Press, 1979) and also in Block (ed.), *Readings in Philosophy of Psychology, Volume 2*. For other criticisms of the language of thought hypothesis and an alternative perspective, see Robert C. Stalnaker, *Inquiry* (Cambridge, MA: MIT Press, 1984), ch. 1 and ch. 2. Fodor further defends the hypothesis in the Appendix to his *Psychosemantics: The Problem of Meaning in the Philosophy of Mind* (Cambridge, MA: MIT Press, 1987).

maps. All of these items involve some element of *analogue* – as opposed to *digital* – representation. The analogue/digital distinction can be illustrated by comparing an analogue clock-face with a digital clock-face. Both types of clock-face represent *times*, but do so in quite different ways. A digital clock-face represents time by means of a sequence of numerals, such as '10.59'. An analogue clock-face represents that same time by the positions of the hour hand and the minute hand of the clock. More particularly, an analogue clock-face represents differences between hours by means of differences between positions of the hour hand, in such a way that the smaller the difference is between two hours, the smaller is the difference between the positions representing those hours (and the same applies to the minute hand). Thus the analogue clock-face represents by drawing upon an analogy, or formal resemblance, between the passage of time and the distances traversed by the clock's hands.[4]

The analogue representation involved in an analogue clock-face is highly abstract or formal. Maps and diagrams are less formal than this, since they bear some genuine *resemblance*, however slight or stylised, to the things which they represent. Thus a map representing some piece of terrain is spatially extended, just as the terrain is, and represents nearby parts of the terrain by nearby parts of the map. Other aspects of map-representation may be more formal, however. For example, if the map is a contour map, it represents the *steepness* of part of the terrain by the *closeness* of the contour lines in the part of the map representing that part of the terrain. A map may also include elements of purely symbolic representation, which qualify as 'digital' rather than 'analogue' – such as a cross to represent the presence of a church (though, even here, the *location* of the cross represents the *location* of the church in an analogue fashion). Pictures and photographs represent by way of even more substantial

---

[4] For further discussion of the analogue/digital distinction, see Zenon W. Pylyshyn, *Computation and Cognition: Toward a Foundation for Cognitive Science* (Cambridge, MA: MIT Press, 1984), ch. 7.

degrees of resemblance between them and the things which they represent: thus, in a colour photograph which is, as we say, a 'good likeness' of a certain person, the colour of that person's hair resembles the colour of the region of the photograph which represents that person's hair. In this case, the resemblance needs to be of such an order that the experience of looking at the photograph is (somewhat) similar to the experience of looking at the person. But, of course, looking at a photograph of a person isn't *exactly* like looking at a person – and seeing a photograph as representing a person requires *interpretation* quite as much as does seeing a map as representing a piece of terrain.

IMAGINATION AND MENTAL IMAGERY

An obvious question to ask at this point is this. Do any of our cognitive states involve *analogue* modes of representation? How, though, should we attempt to find the answer to this question? Perhaps we could just ask people for their opinion about this, relying on their powers of introspection. But if we ask people whether, for instance, they think 'in words' or 'in images', we find that we get a surprisingly varied range of answers. Some people assert that their thinking is frequently accompanied by vivid mental imagery, while others emphatically deny that they ever experience such imagery and even profess not to understand what is meant by talk of it. Some of the latter people, however, happily assert that they think 'in words' – by which they mean words of some natural language, such as English. But then it appears that their thinking *is* accompanied by mental imagery after all, but just by *auditory* imagery rather than by *visual* imagery.

What, though, is the connection between mental imagery and modes of mental representation? It is dangerously easy to slip into arguing in the following fashion. Mental imagery, whether visual or auditory, manifestly accompanies much or all of our conscious thinking. But mental images are *images* and thus involve analogue representation. Hence, much of our thinking involves analogue modes of representation. One questionable assumption in this line of reasoning is the assumption that mental imagery literally involves *images* of some sort, where by an 'image' is meant something akin to a picture or a photograph. It is difficult to dispute that we all engage, at times, in processes of *imagination*. Thus, if someone instructs me, say, to imagine a white horse galloping across a green field, I know how to carry out that instruction – I 'visualise' a scene corresponding to the given description. But we shouldn't assume, just because the term 'imagination' is derived from the same root as the term 'image', that imagination must therefore involve the production or inspection of *images* of any kind. It may be that imagination has acquired this name because people in the past *believed* that it involved images of some kind. However, we shouldn't assume that that belief is correct. But – it may be asked – isn't it just obvious that when you visualise something you *see* something 'in your mind's eye' – a 'mental picture'? No, it isn't at all obvious that this is so. The most that can safely be said is that the experience of visually imagining something is somewhat like the experience of seeing something. But since it is far from obvious that the experience of seeing something involves any kind of 'mental picture', why should it be supposed that the experience of visually imagining something does? It won't do to answer here that because, when you visually imagine something, the thing you imagine needn't exist, there must therefore be *something else* that really *does* exist and which you 'see in your mind's eye' – a 'mental picture' of the thing which you are imagining. For why should you have to see *something else* in order to visualise something which doesn't exist?

The question that we need to address at this point is the following. Granted that much of our conscious thinking involves the exercise of our powers of imagination, what reason is there to suppose that processes of imagination involve *analogue* modes of representation? One way of trying to approach this question is to ask whether imagining a situation is more akin to *depicting* it or to *describing* it. Thus, consider again what you do when you are instructed to imagine a white horse galloping across a green field – and compare this with what you do when you are instructed to *paint a picture* of a white horse galloping across a green field. Suppose I ask you, concerning your imagined scene, whether the sky was blue or whether there were any trees nearby. In all probability, you will say that you just didn't think about those matters one way or the other. But your painting could not easily be so non-committal. You may have decided not to include the sky in your picture, but if you did include it, you will have to have given it some colour. Likewise, you will have to have made a decision about whether or not to include any other objects in the picture besides the horse, such as some trees. In this respect, imagining seems to be rather more like describing than depicting, because a description is similarly non-committal about items not explicitly included in the description. Two famous examples often cited in illustration of this point are those of the speckled hen and the striped tiger.[5] When a person depicts such a creature, he or she must (it is said) depict it as having a determinate *number* of (visible) speckles or stripes. But when a person imagines such a creature, it may be futile to inquire how many speckles or stripes the imagined creature possessed, because the person imagining it may simply have failed to think about the matter one way or another. On the other hand, it seems that imagining is not as *completely* non-committal about such things as describing is. If I ask you to imagine a striped tiger, I would expect you to be able to say whether you imagined it as lying down or as moving and as facing you or as seen from one side. The bare description of a situation as being one which includes a striped tiger is, by contrast, completely silent about such matters. So perhaps imagining does involve some degree of analogue representation. But maybe

[5] For discussion of the example of the tiger and its stripes and a defence of a descriptional view of imagination, see Daniel C. Dennett, *Content and Consciousness* (London: Routledge and Kegan Paul, 1969), pp. 132–41, reprinted in Block (ed.), *Readings in Philosophy of Psychology, Volume 2* and in Ned Block (ed.), *Imagery* (Cambridge, MA: MIT Press, 1981). Somewhat confusingly, Dennett uses 'depictional' as synonymous with 'descriptional' and contrasts both with 'pictorial'.

it is more like drawing a map or a diagram than painting a picture.

However, the trouble with the foregoing approach to the question just raised is that it still relies on dubious appeal to our powers of introspection. Isn't there a more objective way to settle the matter? Some empirical psychologists certainly think so. They believe that experimental evidence supports the contention that analogue modes of representation are involved in some of our thinking processes. One well-known experimental technique involves showing subjects pictures, projected on to a screen, of pairs of asymmetrically shaped objects, constructed out of uniformly sized cubic blocks. In some cases, both objects in a pair are exactly the same in shape, but one is depicted as having been rotated through a certain angle with respect to the other. In other cases, the two objects in a pair are subtly different in shape as well as in orientation. In each case, after the picture has been removed from the screen, subjects are asked to say whether or not the depicted pair of objects had the same shape. One of the findings is that, when the two objects in a pair have the same shape, the length of time it takes subjects to determine that this is so is roughly proportional to the size of the angle through which one of the objects is depicted as having been rotated with respect to the other. The proffered explanation of this finding – and one which seems to be corroborated by the introspective reports of the subjects concerned – is that subjects solve this problem by 'mentally rotating' a remembered 'image' of one of the objects to determine whether or not it can be made to coincide with their remembered 'image' of the other object. The length of time which it takes them to do this depends, it is suggested, on the size of the angle through which they have to 'rotate' one of the 'images' – on the seemingly reasonable assumption that their 'speed of mental rotation' is fairly constant – thus explaining the experimentally established correlation between the length of time which subjects take to reach their verdict and the size of the angle through which one of the objects was depicted as having been rotated with respect to the other. If subjects had stored the relevant information about the depicted objects in a 'digital' rather than in an 'imagistic' form, it is urged, there would have been no reason to expect such a correlation.[6]

In another series of experiments which has been claimed to support the hypothesis that 'imagistic' modes of representation are involved in human thinking, subjects learn to draw a map of a fictional island containing a number of depicted objects in various locations, such as a hut, a tree, a rock, and so forth. Then they are asked to imagine the map and focus mentally on a given location on it. Finally, a word is presented to them, which may or may not name an object on the map, and they are asked to 'look' for the object and determine whether or not it is on the map. It is found that subjects take more time to reach a verdict about objects which are depicted on the map as being far away from the location initially focused on than they do about objects which are depicted as being closer to it, whence it is hypothesised that they arrive at their answers by 'mentally scanning' a remembered 'image' of the map, taking more time to scan between locations which are far apart than they do between locations which are close together. If subjects stored information about the locations of objects in a 'digital' form, it is once again urged, this sort of correlation would not be expected.[7] However, an objection to such an interpretation both of these experiments and of the previous ones is that, strictly speaking, all that we can safely conclude is that subjects solve these problems by engaging in exercises of the imagination – and that the cognitive processes involved in imagination, whatever they may be, are similar to those involved in perception. Thus, it is plausible to suggest that the cognitive

[6] A fuller account of the 'mental rotation' experiments may be found in R. N. Shepard and J. Metzler, 'Mental Rotation of Three-Dimensional Objects', *Science* 171 (1971), pp. 701–3. See also Roger Brown and Richard J. Herrnstein, 'Icons and Images', in Block (ed.), *Imagery*.

[7] For a fuller description of the 'map-scanning' experiments, see Stephen M. Kosslyn, Steven Pinker, George E. Smith and Steven P. Shwartz, 'On the Demystification of Mental Imagery', *Behavioral and Brain Sciences* 2 (1979), pp. 535–81, partly reprinted in a revised form in Block (ed.), *Imagery*.

processes involved in *imagining* that one is scanning a map are similar to those involved in *actually* scanning a map. But whether those cognitive processes involve 'digital' or 'analogue' modes of representation seems to be a further question which is not settled by the fact that similar processes are involved in both cases. For reasons explained earlier, we must be careful to avoid the fallacy of supposing that *imagining* that one is scanning a map must somehow involve a process of *actually* scanning an 'imaginary' map, or an 'image' of a map. *Maps* undoubtedly involve an analogue mode of representation, but it doesn't follow that our *cognition* of maps involves an analogue mode of representation.[8]

Despite this word of caution, there doesn't seem to be any very compelling reason to *deny* that human thinking could involve elements of analogue representation. Against this, it is sometimes urged that images are unsuited to the role of being vehicles of thought because they are always inherently *ambiguous* – and that such ambiguity can only be removed by processes of interpretation which could not themselves essentially involve imagery, on pain of engendering an infinite regress. Often cited in illustration of this sort of ambiguity is Wittgenstein's example of a picture of a man walking up a hill.[9] It is pointed out that this could equally be a picture of a man sliding down a hill. If one tries to remove the ambiguity by adding an arrow pointing uphill, this will succeed only on the assumption that the arrow signifies the direction in which the man is going rather than the direction from

---

[8] For doubts about the alleged imagistic implications of the map-scanning experiments, see Pylyshyn, *Computation and Cognition*, ch. 8 and 'The Imagery Debate: Analog Media versus Tacit Knowledge', in Block (ed.), *Imagery*. The imagistic view is further defended by Stephen Kosslyn in his 'The Medium and the Message in Mental Imagery: A Theory', in Block (ed.), *Imagery* and, much more comprehensively, in Kosslyn's *Image and Brain: The Resolution of the Imagery Debate* (Cambridge, MA: MIT Press, 1994). A position intermediate between those of Kosslyn and Pylyshyn is defended by Michael Tye in his *The Imagery Debate* (Cambridge, MA: MIT Press, 1991).

[9] Wittgenstein's example of the picture of a man walking up a hill is to be found in his *Philosophical Investigations*, trans G. E. M. Anscombe, 2nd edn (Oxford: Blackwell, 1958), p. 54. This and similar examples are discussed by Fodor in his *The Language of Thought*, pp. 179ff.

which he is coming. Thus, a further act of interpretation is required to remove the ambiguity inherent in the image – and this will always be so, no matter how many more pictorial elements we add to the image. However, it is equally true that *non*-imagistic modes of representation, such as written sentences, are inherently ambiguous, since the same sequence of written words could mean quite different things in different languages. The real point at issue here concerns the distinction between 'original' and 'derived' intentionality, not the distinction between 'digital' and 'analogue' modes of representation. If mental representations – be they digital or analogue – are to have original intentionality, then they must represent whatever they do represent for a reason which does not depend on their being *interpreted* by us in any way. But the fact that humanly constructed analogue representations, such as pictures, do not represent independently of being interpreted by us in certain ways does not by any means imply that elements of analogue representation cannot be involved in human thought processes.

THOUGHT AND COMMUNICATION

So far, we have focused on the question of whether the mode of representation involved in human thought processes is quasi-linguistic in nature or whether, alternatively, it includes elements of analogue representation of an 'imagistic' kind. We have come to no very firm conclusion, but have left open the possibility that quite a wide range of modes of representation are involved. It would not be surprising if that were so. After all, the human brain is not the product of careful planning or design but rather of evolutionary happenstance, so one might expect our cognitive processes to exploit a hotchpotch of different representational strategies rather than a single, uniform one. Moreover, as we have seen, there is no compelling reason to suppose that our powers of introspection provide reliable insight into the modes of mental representation that we (or our brains) deploy. It may be that at least some of our thinking goes on in a 'language of thought', but, if so, conscious reflection on our thoughts certainly does not reveal this to be the case. However, there is another kind of question that we may ask about the relation between thought and language, this time about what connection there is, if any, between our capacity to think and our capacity to express and communicate our thoughts in a *public* language, such as English or French.

Some behaviourists have held the view that thinking just *is*, in effect, suppressed speech.[10] On this view, as children we learn first to speak, by imitating our elders, and then we learn to suppress the sound of our speech and thereby learn to think silently. One of the many difficulties with this implausible doctrine is that learning to speak is not simply a matter of learning to make certain noises – a parrot can easily do that – but rather a matter of learning how to use words to express one's thoughts. And this implies that a speaker must already be a thinker. However, it doesn't imply that any thought that can be expressed in words is a thought that someone could have who had never learned to speak – understanding 'speaking' in a broad sense, to include the use not just of auditory but also of visual language, such as American Sign Language.[11] Indeed, it is hard to see how someone could have, say, the thought that tomorrow is Tuesday, if he or she had never learned a public language. What sorts of thoughts, then, if any, *are* available to a creature incapable of expressing or communicating its thoughts in a public language? Many apparently languageless animals, such as dogs and apes, are clearly capable of intelligent behaviour. But do they really lack language, or any mode of communication relevantly similar to language? And what does the alleged intelligence of their behaviour imply about their capacity for thought?

---

[10] A version of the doctrine that thought is suppressed speech is defended by John B. Watson, the founder of scientific behaviourism, in his *Behaviourism*, 2nd edn (Chicago: University of Chicago Press, 1958), pp. 238ff.

[11] For more about American Sign Language, which is an independent language in its own right, see Oliver Sacks, *Seeing Voices: A Journey into the World of the Deaf* (Berkeley and Los Angeles: University of California Press, 1989).

It is not in dispute that many species of animals utilise signalling codes to communicate with one another. Thus, in chapter 4, we discussed the system of alarm-calls used by vervet monkeys to alert their fellows to the presence of various kinds of predator. But such a system of calls differs fundamentally from human language. A true language has syntactical structure as well as vocabulary, enabling its users to construct novel messages almost without limit. This is the basis of the *productivity* of language mentioned earlier in this chapter. By contrast, animal systems of calls are inflexible and narrow in their range of application. Notoriously, attempts have been made to teach true language – usually some form of sign language – to chimpanzees, but without striking success. Occasionally, it seems, a chimpanzee may, on its own initiative, put together two signs in a novel combination, in a way which seems to be semantically significant. But this is still far removed from a human infant's capacity to construct syntactically complex sentences.[12] Yet chimpanzees are undoubtedly clever animals, often displaying considerable ingenuity in their practical and social activities. So to what extent can we attribute powers of *thought* to them? If their cleverness implies that they have capacities for thought akin to our own, why is it that they seem incapable of learning to express their thoughts in language in anything like the way in which humans can?

One possible answer to this last question is that the human capacity for language is a species-specific trait which has little to do with our intelligence. On this view, humans talk much in the way that birds fly and fishes swim: talking is just a kind of activity that evolution has equipped us to engage in and for which we accordingly have an innate propensity. Chimpanzees and other intelligent animals lack this propensity and hence find it as difficult and unnatural to learn to talk as humans do to learn to fly or swim. I shall discuss this

---

[12] For an overview and discussion of attempts to teach sign language to apes, see Merlin Donald, *Origins of the Modern Mind: Three Stages in the Evolution of Culture and Cognition* (Cambridge, MA: Harvard University Press, 1991), pp. 127–37.

sort of view more fully later in the present chapter. For the time being, I shall only remark that it is hard to suppose that a capacity for language has nothing whatever to do with intelligence. Clever though chimpanzees may be, human beings have intellectual capacities which far outstrip those of other primates, and it seems extremely unlikely that this has nothing to do with our ability to use language. Thus, for example, human beings can solve algebraic equations, design aeroplanes, construct theories about the origins of the universe, and ponder over ethical and legal problems. Chimpanzees, it seems safe to say, can do none of these things. But, equally, it is hard to imagine how human beings could do these things if they did not possess language.

DO ANIMALS THINK?

We are prone to describe and explain animal behaviour in an anthropomorphic way, that is, in a way which unwarrantably likens it to human behaviour. When a dog hears the sound of its owner's feet as he returns home from work, it may snatch up its lead and run to meet him, wagging its tail, as if to express a desire that its owner take it for a walk. But should we literally attribute a *propositional attitude* state to the dog – a desire *that its owner take it for a walk*? We cannot attribute such an attitudinal state to the dog unless we are also prepared to attribute to it the *concepts* which possession of such a state implies: in this case, the concept of an *owner*, the concept of a *walk*, the concept of *itself*, and the concept of *future time*. But it is extremely implausible to suppose that a dog can possess such concepts.[13] To this it might be replied that, while a dog may not possess these *human* concepts, perhaps it can instead possess certain *canine* concepts, which we

---

[13] Scepticism about the possibility of attributing propositional attitude states to languageless animals is expressed by Donald Davidson in his 'Thought and Talk', in Samuel Guttenplan (ed.), *Mind and Language* (Oxford: Clarendon Press, 1975), reprinted in Davidson's *Inquiries into Truth and Interpretation* (Oxford: Clarendon Press, 1984). For discussion of Davidson's view, see John Heil, *The Nature of True Minds* (Cambridge: Cambridge University Press, 1992), ch. 6.

necessarily lack. On this view, the best that we can do by way of describing the content of the dog's desire is to say that it desires 'that its owner take it for a walk', but the inadequacy here is ours rather than the dog's. However, it is difficult to make coherent sense of such a view. What possible reason could we have to attribute to a creature concepts which it is supposedly impossible for us to understand? Precisely to the extent that we cannot understand what a creature is (supposedly) thinking, to that extent we are in no position to attribute any concepts to it whatever. It won't do just to say that the dog *must* be thinking, and therefore deploying concepts of some sort, because its behaviour is so manifestly intelligent. For either one means here, by 'intelligent behaviour', *behaviour which involves thinking* – in which case the claim just made is simply circular – or else one means something like *behaviour which is well-adapted to the animal's needs*, in which case it is an altogether open question whether it involves thinking of any kind. It is very often possible to explain intelligent behaviour in an animal, in this second sense of 'intelligent behaviour', without supposing that the animal engages in thinking of any kind – and where this can be done, it is clearly more economical to do so than to appeal to an explanation involving the attribution of thought. Thus, in the case of the dog just described, one may quite reasonably explain its behaviour in terms of its having learned to associate the sound of its owner's approaching footsteps with the experience of having the lead attached and being taken out for a walk. Having a capacity to make such an association requires the dog to possess acute senses, but does not require it to possess any concepts or to do any thinking.

Sometimes, however, animals appear to engage in *practical reasoning* in order to solve a problem which confronts them – and if that is really what they are doing then, indeed, it seems that we must be prepared to attribute thoughts to them. Examples which are often cited in this context are those of the chimpanzees which, apparently, learnt without prompting to fit two sticks together and rake in some bananas which were lying beyond their reach outside their

cage, or to push a box beneath some bananas hanging over-
head and climb up it to reach them. Yet, even here, it is
questionable whether genuine reasoning and therefore
thought was involved in the tasks. Even the cleverest of these
chimpanzees was defeated, it seems, when the bananas lying
outside the cage were so placed that it was necessary for the
animal to push them *away* from itself before raking them in.[14]
Practical or means-end reasoning often requires an agent to
perform a sequence of tasks which initially seem to take it
further away from its ultimate goal, because that is the only
or the best way to achieve it. Humans are very good at doing
this, but it is debatable whether animals can do it at all.
It requires forward planning and a grasp of the connection
between present action and future satisfaction of desire. An
intriguing series of animal experiments, which seems to illus-
trate this point well, involved rigging up a feeding bowl in
such a fashion that it would recede from an animal if the
animal tried to approach it, but would come within the
animal's reach if the animal tried to back away from it. The
animals concerned failed to master this problem, which
humans can solve with ease.[15] Part of the explanation, perhaps, is that only human beings can dissociate their current
actions from the immediate satisfaction of present desires,
because they are able to represent in thought the future satisfaction of a desire as being a consequence of current action.

Clearly, if an animal is incapable of engaging in conceptual
thinking, then it cannot be a language-user in any serious
sense, because it has no thoughts to communicate by means
of language. But more is required of a language-using creature merely than that it be capable of engaging in conceptual

---

[14] The famous chimpanzee studies by Wolfgang Köhler are described in his book
The Mentality of Apes, 2nd edn (New York: Viking, 1959). See also Dorothy L.
Cheney and Robert M. Seyfarth, *How Monkeys See the World: Inside the Mind of
Another Species* (Chicago: University of Chicago Press, 1990), especially p. 276.

[15] The implications of the feeding bowl experiment and other investigations are
discussed in Cecilia Heyes and Anthony Dickinson, 'The Intentionality of Animal
Action', *Mind and Language* 5 (1990), pp. 87–104. See also their 'Folk Psychology
Won't Go Away: Response to Allen and Beckoff', *Mind and Language* 10 (1995),
pp. 329–32.

thinking. It needs to possess certain quite specific concepts. In particular, it needs to be able to conceive of its fellow creatures, with which it communicates by means of language, as having thoughts to communicate. In short, it needs to have something like a 'theory of mind', and thus the concept of a *thought* or *belief* as a state of mind with a propositional content which can be communicated from one thinker to another. This in turn entails that it must have some grasp of the concepts of *truth* and *falsehood*, since it must be able to conceive of the beliefs of another thinker as being correct or incorrect. It must even have some grasp of the concept of a *concept*, as an ingredient of the propositional content of a thought or belief. But although some non-human primates, such as chimpanzees, enjoy a fairly complex social life, it is very questionable whether they possess a theory of mind in anything like the foregoing sense.[16] This, then, may help to explain why such creatures, despite their undeniable ingenuity, are incapable of learning to use language in the way that humans do.

A further question which arises at this point is whether there is any half-way house between those creatures which are altogether incapable of conceptual thinking and those creatures, like ourselves, which possess a fully fledged theory of mind. Some philosophers, notably Donald Davidson, have argued that a creature cannot *have* beliefs unless it has the *concept* of belief, which would imply that no such half-way house exists and that a capacity for conceptual thinking and a capacity for language go hand in hand.[17] Against this, it might be urged that some non-linguistic animals certainly have *perceptual* states and thus – if perceptual states have conceptual content – that such animals deploy concepts. However, we should again be wary of the dangers of anthropo-

---

[16] On the question of whether chimpanzees have a 'theory of mind', see David Premack, ' "Does the Chimpanzee have a Theory of Mind?" Revisited', in Richard Byrne and Andrew Whiten (eds.), *Machiavellian Intelligence: Social Expertise and the Evolution of Intellect in Monkeys, Apes, and Humans* (Oxford: Clarendon Press, 1988).

[17] See Davidson, 'Thought and Talk', in his *Inquiries into Truth and Interpretation*, p. 170.

morphism. Many animals have highly refined powers of sensory discrimination which should not be conflated with an ability to deploy concepts. Thus, pigeons can be trained to discriminate visually between triangles and squares, but it would be extravagant to suggest that they therefore possess the concepts of triangularity and squareness.[18] To possess a concept, one must possess certain general beliefs involving that concept and relating it to other concepts which one possesses. For example, we should not attribute possession of the concept of a *tree* to someone unless we are prepared to attribute to that person certain general beliefs concerning trees, such as that trees are living things which grow from the ground and have branches, roots and leaves. The mere ability to discriminate visually between trees and other objects, such as rocks, and to engage in distinctive behaviour with respect to them, such as nest-building, is not enough to constitute possession of the concept of a tree.

Indeed, once we recognise that a concept-using creature must possess a whole *system* of concepts, coherently interrelated by a system of general beliefs, we can see why we should be very cautious about attributing concepts to animals which lack the cognitive capacity for language. Such a system of general beliefs will have to involve some highly sophisticated concepts, such as the concepts of *space* and *time*, which are arguably simply not available in the absence of language. A creature which does not merely differentiate sensorily between objects in its environment but perceives them *as objects* and thus as falling under concepts – such as the concept of a *tree*, a *mountain*, a *river*, a *rock*, or a *house* – must also grasp the fact that such objects continue to exist unperceived and can be re-encountered at other times and places. Many animals, such as pigeons and bees, can reliably navigate their way about their natural environment with the aid of such sensory cues as the direction of the sun, but there is no

---

[18] For doubts about whether nonlinguistic animals can be said to possess concepts, see Nick Chater and Cecilia Heyes, 'Animal Concepts: Content and Discontent', *Mind and Language* 9 (1994), pp. 209–46.

reason to suppose that they conceive of that environment in terms of a unified framework of places and times.[19] Lacking the conception of such a framework, animals are tied to the here and now in a way that humans are not. Humans, and language-users generally, are free to roam in thought over all the vast stretches of space and time and thus to reflect on past happenings and contemplate future possibilities. No creature lacking this freedom can have a conception of *itself* as an enduring subject of experience with a personal history and a capacity to choose between alternative courses of action.[20]

NATURAL LANGUAGE AND CONCEPTUAL SCHEMES

We may be inclined to conclude, in the light of the foregoing considerations, that the human capacity for conceptual thinking is something unique to our species and intimately related to our ability to express and communicate thoughts in a public language – though, rather than say that language depends on thought or thought on language, as though these were mutually exclusive alternatives, it may be more plausible to say that language and thought are *inter*dependent. However, if such an interdependency exists, then it raises further important questions, in view of the great diversity of languages spoken by human beings across the world. To what extent, if any, are the concepts which a person is capable of deploying dependent upon the vocabulary and syntax of the natural language which he or she has learnt to speak? Answers to this question have varied widely. Thus, it is often alleged that Eskimos have many more words for different

[19] For discussion of the navigational capacities of animals and their implications for animal spatial cognition, see John Campbell, *Past, Space, and Self* (Cambridge, MA: MIT Press, 1994), ch. 1.
[20] I say more about the gulf between human and animal cognitive capacities in my 'Personal Experience and Belief: The Significance of External Symbolic Storage for the Emergence of Modern Human Cognition', in Chris Scarre and Colin Renfrew (eds.), *Cognition and Culture: The Archaeology of Symbolic Storage* (Cambridge: McDonald Institute for Archaeological Research, 1998). See also John McDowell, *Mind and World* (Cambridge, MA: Harvard University Press, 1994), pp. 114–24.

kinds of snow than do Europeans and consequently a larger repertoire of concepts for thinking about snow. In fact, this claim appears to be completely unfounded, although the myth is very difficult to eradicate.[21] Again, it is often remarked that the colour vocabulary of languages varies widely, from which it is sometimes inferred that speakers of different languages have different colour concepts and even *see* coloured things in quite different ways. However, the range of hues which human beings are able to distinguish is pretty much determined by the physiology of our visual system, quite independently of the colour concepts which we happen to deploy.[22] It would be foolish to conclude, just because speakers of a certain language have no word which translates into English as 'blue' as opposed to 'green', that therefore they cannot visually distinguish blue things from green things. After all, English speakers can distinguish many different hues for which the English language has no name. Moreover, where English fails to supply a name for a certain hue, it still provides us with the resources with which to describe it: for example, one might describe a certain unnamed hue as being 'the colour of kiwi fruit'. This example brings out the difficulty inherent in any claim to the effect that the *vocabulary* of a language restricts the range of concepts expressible in it. For, given the productivity of language which its syntactical structure confers upon it, it is often (perhaps, indeed, always) possible to translate a single word in one language by a complex phrase in another, even if the second language lacks a single word which will do the job on its own.

---

[21] For an amusing debunking of the myth about Eskimo words for snow, see Geoffrey K. Pullum, *The Great Eskimo Vocabulary Hoax and Other Irreverent Essays on the Study of Language* (Chicago: University of Chicago Press, 1991), ch. 19.

[22] For discussion of the relation between colour perception and colour vocabulary, see Paul Kay and Chad K. McDaniel, 'The Linguistic Significance of the Meanings of Basic Color Terms', *Language* 54 (1978), pp. 610–46, reprinted in Alex Byrne and David R. Hilbert (eds.), *Readings on Color, Volume 2: The Science of Color* (Cambridge, MA: MIT Press, 1997). For an opposing view, see B. A. C. Saunders and J. van Brakel, 'Are There Nontrivial Constraints on Color Categorization?', *Behavioral and Brain Sciences* 20 (1997), pp. 167–228.

A rather more interesting suggestion, however, is that the *grammar* or *syntax* of a language imposes constraints upon the 'conceptual scheme' deployed by its speakers. This thesis is generally known as the 'Sapir-Whorf hypothesis', named after two American linguistic anthropologists, Edward Sapir and Benjamin Lee Whorf.[23] By a *conceptual scheme*, here, is meant something like an overall system of categories for classifying items in the world which speakers want to talk about. The grammatical categories of Indo-European languages seem to map onto the ontological categories of Western metaphysics and this, it is suggested, is no accident. Thus substantive nouns, such as 'table' and 'tree', denote *substances*. Adjectives, such as 'red' and 'heavy', denote *properties*. Verbs, such as 'walk' and 'throw', denote *actions*. Prepositions, such as 'under' and 'after', denote *spatial and temporal relations*. And so on. But other families of languages, such as the American Indian languages studied by Sapir and Whorf, allegedly have different grammatical categories, suggesting that speakers of them operate with a conceptual scheme quite different from ours. Thus, Whorf claimed that speakers of Hopi do not operate with an ontology of substances – persisting material things and stuffs – and do not think of space and time separately, as Western Europeans do. Indeed, he implied that their ontology is rather closer to the ontology of modern relativistic physics, which talks in terms of *events* and a unified *spacetime*. At the same time, he suggested that it is not really possible for us to grasp this alien conceptual scheme, so radically different is it from the one embedded in our own language. He even went so far as to suggest that speakers of these alien languages inhabit a different *world* from ours, because categorial distinctions are something which speakers impose or project upon reality

---

[23] For Whorf's views, see *Language, Thought and Reality: Selected Writings of Benjamin Lee Whorf*, ed. John B. Carroll (Cambridge, MA: MIT Press, 1956). For a critical evaluation of them, see Michael Devitt and Kim Sterelny, *Language and Reality: An Introduction to the Philosophy of Language* (Oxford: Blackwell, 1987), ch. 10.

rather than discover within it. Clearly, this is a strongly anti-realist or relativist way to think about the ontological structure of the world that one inhabits.

It should not be surprising that there is some degree of correspondence between grammatical and metaphysical categories, though whether this correpondence indicates a relationship of dependency between syntax and metaphysics – and if so, in which direction – is a further question. What is altogether more contentious, however, is the suggestion that speakers of one language may simply be unable to grasp the conceptual scheme adopted by speakers of another – that, in some cases, there is no real possibility of translating between two languages, because the conceptual schemes associated with them are so radically incommensurable. The problem with this thesis, as with the earlier suggestion that non-human animals operate with concepts which we cannot grasp, is that it appears to undermine itself. For the only evidence we can have that a community of creatures are genuine *language*-users is evidence that enables us to interpret certain of their actions as attempts to communicate specific thoughts by means of language. But if we are, allegedly, unable to grasp the contents of their thoughts, then we are prevented from interpreting their actions in that way. Thus, it seems, we can only have reason to regard other creatures as language-users if we can suppose ourselves able to *translate* much of what they say, which requires them not to operate with a conceptual scheme radically incommensurable with our own. This sort of consideration, as Donald Davidson has emphasised, puts pressure on the very idea of a 'conceptual scheme' and the anti-realist or relativist views which generally accompany it.[24]

The difficulty which we have just exposed is readily illustrated by tensions in Whorf's own claims. Thus, on the one hand he urges that it is not really possible for Western Europeans to grasp the Hopi conceptual scheme, so different is it

[24] See Donald Davidson, 'On the Very Idea of a Conceptual Scheme', in his *Inquiries into Truth and Interpretation*.

from ours. But then, paradoxically, he attempts to back up this claim by describing to us – *in our own language*, of course – some of the ways in which their conceptual scheme allegedly differs from ours, such as in not separating time from space. But evidently we must, after all, be able to grasp something of that scheme, if Whorf is to succeed in this attempt. Indeed, he himself must have been able to grasp something of it, despite having a Western European background. Furthermore, Whorf implicitly concedes that Western European languages, despite their alleged bias towards a substance ontology, have not prevented speakers of them from devising various different ontological frameworks in the course of formulating new scientific theories. Indeed, he even suggests that one of these frameworks – that presupposed by Einstein's General Theory of Relativity – is closer to the conceptual scheme of Hopi speakers than to that of traditional Western metaphysics.

The most, it seems, that we can safely conclude is that there is some connection between the syntax of a natural language and the 'common-sense' or 'intuitive' metaphysics espoused by speakers of that language – but that this does not in any way prevent those speakers from constructing novel and very diverse metaphysical theories nor from understanding the 'intuitive' metaphysics of speakers of other natural languages, no matter how different their syntax may be. Speakers of different languages may conceptualise the world in somewhat different ways, but we all inhabit the *same* world and necessarily have a good many beliefs in common. Beliefs are made true or false by states of affairs in the world, not by us, and a creature most of whose beliefs were false would have poor prospects for survival. But if I and another creature had radically different beliefs, we could not plausibly *both* have beliefs which were mostly true. And I cannot coherently suppose my own beliefs to be mostly false. Hence, it seems, I can only have reason to regard another creature as possessing beliefs to the extent that I can consider it to share many of my own beliefs and many of those beliefs to be true. Radical relativism is a doubtfully coherent doctrine and certainly not one that is supported by anthropological-cum-linguistic evidence of the kind which Whorf advanced.

KNOWLEDGE OF LANGUAGE: INNATE OR ACQUIRED?

Earlier on, I touched on the thesis that the human capacity for language is a species-specific trait. More particularly, it is has been claimed, most famously by the linguist Noam Chomsky, that all humanly learnable languages share certain fundamental syntactical features or 'linguistic universals', knowledge of which is innate in all human beings.[25] This innate knowledge is supposed to explain various otherwise inexplicable facts about human language-learning. First of all there is the fact that all human children (apart from those that are severely mentally handicapped) are able to learn, as their first language, any one of the thousands of human languages spoken on the planet – whereas no creature of another species has ever succeeded in doing so. Moreover, all children learn to speak at pretty much the same rate, developing their ability in very much the same way, quite independently of their level of general intelligence. They do this quite rapidly in their early years and manage it without being explicitly taught by their elders. Somehow, children easily acquire the ability to construct and understand novel sentences, correctly formulated according to the syntactical rules of the language which they are learning, despite the fact that the only empirical data which they have to go on are the highly selective and often unfinished or interrupted utterances of speakers around them.

---

[25] Chomsky's current views are very readably presented in his *Language and Problems of Knowledge* (Cambridge, MA: MIT Press, 1988). See also the entry 'Chomsky, Noam', written by himself, in Samuel Guttenplan (ed.), *A Companion to the Philosophy of Mind* (Oxford: Blackwell, 1994), pp. 153–67. Chomsky now contends that not only the syntax of natural language but also the concepts expressible in it have an innate basis. The latter claim is also advanced by Jerry Fodor in 'The Present Status of the Innateness Hypothesis', in his *Representations: Philosophical Essays on the Foundations of Cognitive Science* (Brighton: Harvester Press, 1981). For criticism of this claim, see Hilary Putnam, *Representation and Reality* (Cambridge, MA: MIT Press, 1988), ch. 1. Fodor has recently changed his mind about the innateness of concepts: see his *Concepts: Where Cognitive Science Went Wrong* (Oxford: Oxford University Press, 1998).

Clearly, children cannot simply be learning by a process of imitation or inductive extrapolation from the linguistic data to which they have been exposed, because those data on their own are generally insufficient to enable them to predict correctly whether a certain sequence of words, which they have not previously heard, is compatible with the syntactical rules of the language which is being spoken by their elders. Unless there is some constraint on the possible form of those rules, which is already implicitly grasped by the children, it seems that it must be impossible for them to achieve what they do. But if they already know, tacitly or implicitly, that the language which they are learning has a syntax which conforms to certain general principles, then they may be in a position to use the linguistic data to which they have been exposed to eliminate all but one possible set of syntactical rules for the language in question. In effect, they can reason like scientists who use empirical data to eliminate all but one of a finite number of mutually exclusive hypotheses concerning some range of natural phenomena.[26]

But how seriously can we take this analogy with scientific reasoning? And how literally can we talk of children having an innate *knowledge* of syntactical principles which linguists themselves have managed to discover only by means of extensive empirical research? Such innate knowledge, if it exists, will have to be *represented* in the mind or brain in some fashion, but how? Of course, if there is an innate 'language of thought' or 'brain code', of the sort discussed earlier in

---

[26] For the analogy between language-learning and scientific reasoning, see Noam Chomsky, *Language and Mind*, 2nd edn (New York: Harcourt Brace Jovanovich, 1972), pp. 88ff. In his more recent work, Chomsky rather distances himself from this analogy. This is partly because he no longer thinks that different languages are, strictly speaking, governed by different sets of syntactical rules, but rather that a single set of very general grammatical principles applies to all human languages, which differ from one another in respect of the different values they take for certain 'parameters'. He now sees language-acquisition as a matter of the mind – or, rather, a dedicated module within it – setting the values of these parameters on the basis of the linguistic data made available by experience. However, it is not clear that these changes can help to alleviate worries of the sort that I am about to raise. For wide-ranging discussion of Chomsky's views, see Alexander George (ed.), *Reflections on Chomsky* (Oxford: Blackwell, 1989).

this chapter, then that could provide the required vehicle of representation. Then, indeed, the task of learning one's 'first' language could be assimilated to that of learning a 'second' language: it could be done by learning to translate it into a language which one already knows, namely Mentalese, with the aid of already known general principles of human grammar. An apparent difficulty with this proposed assimilation is that it seems to conflict with the earlier claim that there is something distinctive and remarkable about the ease with which we learn our 'first' language. Perhaps the two propositions can be reconciled by emphasising that learning to translate into Mentalese is something that is done unconsciously by a module of the brain especially dedicated to that purpose, rather than by exercising our general powers of intelligence. However, many philosophers will feel uncomfortable with the suggestion that a part of our brain does unconsciously something akin to what scientists do when they settle upon the truth of a hypothesis by eliminating various possible alternatives. This looks suspiciously like an example of the 'homuncular fallacy' – the fallacy, that is, of trying to explain how human beings achieve some intellectual task by supposing that they have inside their heads some agency, with some of the intellectual powers of a human being, which does that task for them. (Literally, 'homunculus' means 'little man'.) Such an 'explanation' threatens to be either vacuous, or circular, or else vitiated by an infinite regress. We may agree that children could not possibly learn their 'first' language by mere inductive extrapolation from the linguistic data to which they are exposed. But we should not too readily suppose that the only alternative hypothesis is that they learn by drawing on innately known principles of universal grammar. Perhaps we should just hope that someone will one day devise an explanatorily adequate hypothesis which seems less extravagant. Such a hypothesis may conceivably be made available by the 'connectionist' models of cognition to be explored in the next chapter. For it has been advanced on behalf of such models that they can simulate, with surprising fidelity, salient features of children's acquisition of certain grammatical rules – such as the rules governing the past tense of English verbs – without invoking anything akin to innate knowledge of universal grammar.[27]

CONCLUSIONS

As we have seen in this chapter, questions about the connections between thought and language are many, complex, and highly contentious. But they divide into two main areas of concern: (1) questions to do with whether thought itself involves a linguistic or quasi-linguistic medium or mode of representation, and (2) questions to do with whether a capacity for genuine propositional thinking goes hand-in-hand with a capacity to express and communicate thoughts in a public or natural language. These two areas of concern are in principle distinct. Thus, it would be possible for a philosopher to maintain that animals incapable of communicating thoughts in a public language may none the less *have* thoughts whose vehicle or medium is a quasi-linguistic 'brain code'. On the other hand, those philosophers and psychologists who believe that thinking *just is* either 'suppressed speech' or imagined 'silent soliloquy', and thus has natural language as its medium, will obviously have to deny that languageless animals and pre-linguistic human infants are capable of thought. However, we have concluded, albeit only tentatively, (1) that human thinking quite possibly exploits various modes of mental representation, some of them of an 'analogue' or 'imagistic' character, and yet (2) that there is probably a relationship of mutual dependency between having a capacity for genuine conceptual thinking and having an ability to express and communicate thoughts in a public language. We have seen reason to doubt whether it is

---

[27] See D. E. Rumelhart and J. L. McClelland, 'On Learning the Past Tenses of English Verbs', in David E. Rumelhart and James L. McClelland (eds.), *Parallel Distributed Processing, Volume 2: Psychological and Biological Models* (Cambridge, MA: MIT Press, 1986). For discussion, see William Bechtel and Adele Abrahamsen, *Connectionism and the Mind: An Introduction to Parallel Processing in Networks* (Oxford: Blackwell, 1991), chs. 6 and 7.

legitimate to attribute concepts to animals incapable of true language, even including animals with the advanced practical and social skills of chimpanzees. But it is debatable whether an ability to learn a language is, as some innatists maintain, simply a species-specific trait of human beings which has little to do with our level of general intelligence. Finally, even granting that there is an intimate relation between thought and its public linguistic expression, it does not seem justifiable to maintain, with the linguistic relativists, that a speaker's natural language confines his or her thoughts within the scope of a specific 'conceptual scheme', much less that it imposes a particular ontological structure on the speaker's world.

8

Human rationality and artificial intelligence

Our supposed rationality is one of the most prized possessions of human beings and is often alleged to be what distinguishes us most clearly from the rest of animal creation. In the previous chapter we saw, indeed, that there appear to be close links between having a capacity for conceptual thinking, being able to express one's thoughts in language, and having an ability to engage in processes of reasoning. Even chimpanzees, the cleverest of non-human primates, seem at best to have severely restricted powers of practical reasoning and display no sign at all of engaging in the kind of theoretical reasoning which is the hallmark of human achievement in the sciences. However, the traditional idea that rationality is the exclusive preserve of human beings has recently come under pressure from two quite different quarters, even setting aside claims made on behalf of the reasoning abilities of non-human animals. On the one hand, the information technology revolution has led to ambitious pronouncements by researchers in the field of artificial intelligence, some of whom maintain that suitably programmed computers can literally be said to engage in processes of thought and reasoning. On the other hand, ironically enough, some empirical psychologists have begun to challenge our own human pretensions to be able to think rationally. We are thus left contemplating the strange proposition that machines of our own devising may soon be deemed more rational than their human creators. Whether we can make coherent sense of such a suggestion is one issue that we may hope to resolve in the course of this chapter. But to be in a position to do so, we need to examine more closely the nature and basis of some of the surprising claims being made by investigators in the fields of artificial intelligence and human reasoning research.

Some of the key questions that we should consider are the following. How rational, really, are ordinary human beings? Do we have a natural ability to reason logically and, if so, what are the psychological processes involved in the exercise of that ability? What, in any case, do we – or should we – mean by 'rationality'? Could an electronic machine literally be said to engage in processes of thought and reasoning simply by virtue of executing a suitably formulated computer programme? Or can we at best talk of computers as *simulating* rational thought-processes, rather as they can simulate meteorological processes for the purposes of weather-forecasting? Would a genuinely intelligent machine have to have a 'brain' with a physical configuration somewhat similar to that of a human brain? Would it need to have autonomous goals or purposes and perhaps even emotions? Would it need to be conscious, be able to learn by experience, and be capable of interacting intentionally with its physical and social environment? How far are intelligence and rationality a matter of possessing what might be called 'common sense'? What *is* common sense, and how do we come by it? Could it be captured in a computer programme? Without more ado, let us now start looking at some possible answers to these and related questions.

RATIONALITY AND REASONING

It seems almost tautologous to say that rationality involves reasoning – though we shall see in due course that matters are not quite so straightforward as this. If we start with that assumption, however, the next question which it seems obvious to raise is this: what kinds of reasoning are there? Traditionally, reasoning has been divided into two kinds in two different ways. On the one hand, a distinction has long been drawn between *practical* and *theoretical* reasoning, the former having successful action and the latter knowledge, or at least true belief, as its goal. On the other hand, reasoning or rational argument has also traditionally been divided into *deductive* and *inductive* varieties. In a deductive argument, the premises entail or logically necessitate the conclusion, whereas, in an inductive argument, the premises or 'data' merely confer a degree of probability upon a given hypothesis. These two distinctions are independent of one another, so that both practical and theoretical reasoning can involve either deductive or inductive argument, or indeed a mixture of the two.

Purely deductive argument has fairly limited scope for application, beyond the realm of formal sciences such as mathematics. None the less, it has often been regarded as the most elevated form of reasoning, perhaps out of deference to the intellectual status of mathematics in Western culture since the time of the ancient Greeks. Aristotle was the first person to formulate a rigorous formal theory of deductive reasoning, in the shape of his system of syllogistic logic. A syllogism is a deductive argument with two premises and a single conclusion of certain prescribed forms, such as 'All philosophers are talkative; all talkative people are foolish; therefore, all philosophers are foolish', or 'Some philosophers are foolish; all foolish people are vain; therefore, some philosophers are vain'. As these examples make clear, a deductively valid syllogism – one in which the premises entail the conclusion – need not have true premises or a true conclusion: though if it *does* have true premises, then its conclusion must also be true. In more recent times, the theory of formal deductive reasoning has undergone a revolution in the hands of such logicians as Gottlob Frege and Bertrand Russell, the founders of modern symbolic or mathematical logic. Modern students of philosophy are mostly familiar with these developments, because a training in elementary symbolic logic is now usually included in philosophy degree programmes. But an interesting empirical question is this: how good at deductive reasoning are people who have not received a formal training in the subject? Indeed, how good are people who *have* received such a training – that is, how good are they at apply-ing what they have supposedly learnt, outside the examina-tion hall? We can ask similar questions concerning people's inductive reasoning abilities, but let us focus first of all on the case of deduction.

One might expect the questions that we have just raised to receive the following answers. On the one hand, we might not be surprised to learn that people who are untrained in formal logic frequently commit fallacies of deductive reasoning. On the other hand, we would perhaps hope to confirm that a training in formal logic generally helps people to avoid many such errors. However, since a basic compet-ence in deductive reasoning would seem to be a necessary pre-requisite of one's being able to learn any of the tech-niques of formal logic, and since most people seem capable of learning at least some of those techniques, we would also expect there to be definite limits to how poorly people can perform on deductive reasoning tasks even if they have not had the benefit of a training in logical methods. This, how-ever, is where we should be prepared to be surprised by some of the claims of empirical psychologists engaged in human reasoning research. For some of them claim that people exhibit deep-rooted biases even when faced with the most elementary problems of deductive – and, indeed, inductive – reasoning. These biases, they maintain, are not even eradic-ated by a formal training in logical methods and may well be genetically 'programmed' into the human brain as a result of our evolutionary history.

THE WASON SELECTION TASK

Perhaps the best-known empirical findings offered in sup-port of these pessimistic claims derive from the notorious Wason selection task.[1] The task has many different vari-

---

[1] For further details about the Wason selection task, see Jonathan St. B. T. Evans, *Bias in Human Reasoning: Causes and Consequences* (Hove: Lawrence Erlbaum Associ-ates, 1989), pp. 53ff. See also Jonathan St. B. T. Evans, Stephen E. Newstead and Ruth M. J. Byrne, *Human Reasoning: The Psychology of Deduction* (Hove:

ants, but in one of its earliest forms it may be described as follows. A group of subjects – who must have no prior knowledge, of course, of the kind of task which they are about to be set – are individually presented with the following reasoning problem. The subjects are shown four cards, each with just one side displayed to view, and are told that these cards have been drawn from a deck each of whose members has a letter of the alphabet printed on one side and a numeral between 1 and 9 printed on the other side. Thus, for example, the four cards might display on their visible sides the following four symbols respectively: A, 4, D, and 7. Then the subjects are told that the following hypothesis has been proposed concerning just these four cards: that if a card has a vowel printed on one side, then it has an even number printed on the other side. Finally, the subjects are asked to say which, if any, of the four cards ought to be turned over in order to determine whether the hypothesis in question is true or false. Quite consistently it is found that most subjects say, in a case like this, either that the A-card alone should be turned over or else that only the A-card and the 4-card should be turned over. Significantly, very few subjects say that the 7-card should be turned over. And yet, apparently, this is a serious and surprisingly elementary blunder, because if the 7-card should happen to have a vowel on its hidden side, it would serve to falsify the hypothesis. Why do so many subjects apparently fail to appreciate this? The answer, according to some psychologists, is that they simply fail to apply elementary principles of deductive reasoning in their attempts to solve the problem. Instead, these subjects must arrive at their 'solutions' in some other, quite illogical way – for instance, by selecting those cards which match the descriptions mentioned in the proposed

Lawrence Erlbaum Associates, 1993), ch. 4. For a good general introduction to the psychology of reasoning, with a philosophical slant, see K. I. Manktelow and D. E. Over, *Inference and Understanding: A Philosophical and Psychological Perspective* (London: Routledge, 1990); they discuss the Wason selection task in ch. 6.

hypothesis (the cards displaying a vowel and an even number). Such a method of selection is said to exhibit 'matching bias'.

However, the Wason selection task raises many more questions than it succeeds in answering. First of all, are the psychologists in fact *correct* in maintaining, as they do, that the cards which ought to be turned over are the A-card and the 7-card, in the version of the task described above? Notice that what is at issue here is not an empirical, scientific question but rather a *normative* question – a question of what action *ought* to be performed in certain circumstances, rather than a question of what action *is*, statistically, most likely to be performed. Notice, too, that since we are concerned with right or wrong *action*, it would seem that, properly understood, the Wason selection task is a problem in *practical* rather than *theoretical* reasoning. However, once this is realised, we may come to doubt whether the task can properly be understood to concern purely deductive reasoning. It may be, indeed, that subjects are tackling this task, and quite appropriately so, by applying good principles of *inductive* reasoning. Consider, by way of analogy, how a scientist might attempt to confirm or falsify a general empirical hypothesis, such as the hypothesis that if a bird is a member of the crow family, then it is black. Clearly, he would do well to examine crows to see if they are black, which is analogous to turning over the A-card to see if it has an even number printed on its other side. But it would be foolish of him to examine non-black things, just on the off-chance that he might happen upon one which is a crow and thereby falsify the hypothesis: and this is analogous to turning over the 7-card to see if it has a vowel printed on its other side. Of course, it can't be disputed that if the 7-card *does* have a vowel printed on its other side, then it does serve to falsify the hypothesis in question. However, it is unlikely that many subjects will want to dispute this fact, so to that extent they cannot be accused of being illogical. But what subjects are in fact asked is not whether this is so: rather, they are asked which cards *ought to be turned over* in order to verify or falsify the hypothesis, and this is a question of practical reasoning whose correct answer is not just obviously what the psychologists assume it to be.[2]

The lesson which many psychologists are apt to draw from the Wason selection task is, unsurprisingly, quite different from the one suggested above. Many of them say that what it shows is that people are not good at reasoning deductively with purely abstract materials, such as meaningless letters and numerals. In support of this, they cite evidence that people perform much better (by the psychologists' own standards) on versions of the selection task which involve more realistic materials, based on scenarios drawn from everyday life – especially if those scenarios permit the selection task to be construed as a problem of detecting some form of *cheating*. In these versions, the cards may be replaced by such items as envelopes or invoices, with suitable markings on their fronts and backs – and the 'improved' performance of subjects is sometimes put down to our having inherited from our hominid ancestors an ability to detect cheating which helped them to survive in Palaeolithic times.[3] However, by changing the format of the task and the hypothesis at issue, one may be changing the logical nature of the task so that it ceases to be, in any significant sense, the 'same' reasoning task. Hence it becomes a moot point whether differences in performance on different versions of the task tell us anything at all about people's reasoning abilities, since there may be no single standard of 'correctness' which applies to all versions of the task. It is perfectly conceivable that most subjects give the 'correct' answers in both abstract and realistic versions of the task, even though they give

---

[2] I discuss this and related points more fully in my 'Rationality, Deduction and Mental Models', in K. I. Manktelow and D. E. Over (eds.), *Rationality: Psychological and Philosophical Perspectives* (London: Routledge, 1993), ch. 8.

[3] See L. Cosmides, 'The Logic of Social Exchange: Has Natural Selection Shaped How Humans Reason? Studies with the Wason Selection Task', *Cognition* 31 (1989), pp. 187–276. For discussion, see Evans, Newstead and Byrne, *Human Reasoning*, pp. 130ff. For more on evolutionary psychology in general, see Denise Dellarosa Cummins and Colin Allen (eds.), *The Evolution of Mind* (New York: Oxford University Press, 1998).

different answers in each case, because the different versions may *demand* different answers. The difficulty which we are faced with here, and which makes the Wason selection task such a problematic tool for psychological research, is that in many areas of reasoning it is still very much an open question how people *ought* to reason. The norms of right reasoning have not all been settled once and for all by logicians and mathematicians. Indeed, they are by their very nature *contestable*, very much as the norms of moral behaviour are.[4]

THE BASE RATE FALLACY

A moment ago, I suggested that people might be tackling abstract versions of the selection task by applying good principles of inductive reasoning. But people's natural capacities to reason well inductively have also been called into question by empirical psychologists. Most notorious in this context is the alleged 'base rate fallacy'. The best-known reasoning task said to reveal this fallacy is the cab problem.[5] Subjects are given the following information. They are told that, on a certain day, a pedestrian was knocked down in a hit-and-run accident by a taxicab in a certain city and that an eye-witness reported the colour of the cab to be blue. They are also told that in this city there are two cab companies, the green cab company owning 85 per cent of the cabs and the blue cab company owning the remaining 15 per cent. Finally, they are told that, in a series of tests, the witness proved to be 80 per cent accurate in his ability to identify the colour of cabs, in viewing conditions similar to those of the accident. Then subjects are asked the following question: what, in your estimation, is the probability that the accident-victim was knocked

---

[4] For further reading on the Wason selection task and related matters, see Stephen E. Newstead and Jonathan St. B. T. Evans (eds.), *Perspectives on Thinking and Reasoning: Essays in Honour of Peter Wason* (Hove: Lawrence Erlbaum Associates, 1995).

[5] See A. Tversky and D. Kahneman, 'Causal Schemata in Judgements under Uncertainty', in M. Fishbein (ed.), *Progress in Social Psychology, Volume 1* (Hillsdale, NJ: Lawrence Erlbaum Associates, 1980).

down by a blue cab? Most subjects estimate the probability in question as being in the region of 80 per cent (or 0.80, measured on a scale from 0 to 1). However, a simple calculation, using a principle known to probability theorists as Bayes' theorem, reveals the 'true' probability to be approximately 41 per cent, implying that it is in fact more likely that a *green* cab was involved in the accident. If that is correct, the implications of people's performance on this task are alarming, because it suggests that their confidence in eye-witness testimony can be far higher than is warranted. Psychologists explain the supposed error in terms of what they call *base rate neglect*. They say that subjects who estimate the probability in question as being in the region of 80 per cent are simply ignoring the information that the vast majority of the cabs in the city are green rather than blue, and are depending solely on the information concerning the reliability of the witness. Base rate neglect is similarly held to be responsible for many people – including trained physicians – exaggerating the significance of positive results in diagnostic tests for relatively rare medical conditions.

However, as with the Wason selection task, it is possible to challenge the psychologists' own judgement as to what the 'correct' answer to the cab problem is. It may be urged, for instance, that subjects are *right* to ignore the information concerning the proportions of green and blue cabs in the city, not least because that information fails to disclose *how many* cabs of each colour there are. If the numbers of cabs of either colour are small, nothing very reliable can be inferred about the chances of a pedestrian being knocked down by a green rather than a blue cab. It is interesting that when, in probabilistic reasoning tasks like this, subjects *are* given information in terms of absolute numbers rather than percentages, they tend *not* to ignore it – in part, perhaps, because they find the calculations easier.[6] Suppose one is told, for instance,

[6] See Gerd Gigerenzer, 'Ecological Intelligence: An Adaptation for Frequencies', in Cummins and Allen (eds.), *The Evolution of Mind*, ch. 1. For fuller discussion of the base rate problem, see Gerd Gigerenzer and David J. Murray, *Cognition as*

that there are 850 green cabs in the city and 150 blue cabs, and that out of 50 cabs of both colours on which the witness was tested, he correctly identified the colour of 40 and mistakenly identified the colour of 10. Then it is relatively easy to infer that the witness might be expected *correctly* to report 120 of the *blue* cabs to be blue (40 out of every 50), but *mistakenly* to report 170 of the *green* cabs to be blue (10 out of every 50), making the expected ratio of correct reports of a blue cab to total reports of a blue cab equal to 120/(120 + 170), or approximately 41 per cent. It is debatable whether this implies that the psychologists' answer to the cab problem is, after all, correct. But even if we agree that subjects do sometimes perform poorly on such probabilistic reasoning tasks, we should recognise that we may have to blame this on the *form* in which information is given to them rather than on their powers of reasoning.

There is, in any case, something distinctly paradoxical about the idea that psychologists – who, after all, are human beings themselves – could reveal by empirical means that ordinary human beings are deeply and systematically biased in their deductive and inductive reasonings.[7] For the theories of deductive logic and probability against whose standards the psychologists purport to judge the performance of subjects on reasoning tasks are themselves the product of human thought, having been developed by logicians and mathematicians during the last two thousand years or so. Why should we have any confidence in those theories, then, if human beings are as prone to error in their reasonings as some psychologists suggest? Of course, part of the value of having such theories is that they can help us to avoid errors of reasoning:

Intuitive Statistics (Hillsdale, NJ: Lawrence Erlbaum Associates, 1987), pp. 150–74.

[7] For further doubts on this score, see L. Jonathan Cohen, 'Can Human Irrationality be Experimentally Demonstrated?', *Behavioral and Brain Sciences* 4 (1981), pp. 317–70. For an opposing view, see Stephen Stich, *The Fragmentation of Reason: Preface to a Pragmatic Theory of Cognitive Evaluation* (Cambridge, MA: MIT Press, 1990), ch. 4. Cohen's views are also discussed, and defended by him, in Ellery Eells and Tomasz Maruszewski (eds.), *Probability and Rationality: Studies on L. Jonathan Cohen's Philosophy of Science* (Amsterdam: Rodopi, 1991).

if ordinary people, untrained in logical methods, had been naturally flawless reasoners, the work of Aristotle, Frege and Russell would have had no practical value. But unless we suppose that Aristotle, Frege and Russell, who were just as human as the rest of us, were capable of reasoning correctly a good deal of the time, we can have no reason to suppose that their theories have any value whatever.

MENTAL LOGIC VERSUS MENTAL MODELS

Many psychologists believe that people's performance on reasoning tasks provides evidence not only of biases in their reasoning, but also of *how* people reason, that is, of the psychological processes involved in human reasoning. Concentrating on the case of deductive reasoning, there are two major schools of thought at present which maintain, respectively, that we reason by deploying a system of *mental logic* and that we reason by manipulating *mental models*.[8] This difference of approach corresponds, roughly speaking, to the distinction between *syntactical* and *semantic* methods of proof in logical theory. Syntactical methods have regard only to the formal structure of premises and conclusions, whereas semantic methods have regard to their possible interpretations as expressing true or false propositions. Thus, for example, so-called 'natural deduction' methods are syntactical, whereas truth-table methods are semantic. We need not, here, consider the details of this distinction, important though it is for logical theory. Our concern, rather, is with the corresponding distinction between 'mental logic' and 'mental models' theories of deductive reasoning processes.

The mental logic approach contends that ordinary human beings untrained in formal logical methods naturally deploy certain formal rules of inference in their deductive reasoning

---

[8] A third school of thought, invoking 'pragmatic reasoning schemas', will not be discussed here, though it is favoured by some evolutionary psychologists. For an overview of the three different approaches, see P. N. Johnson-Laird and Ruth M. J. Byrne, *Deduction* (Hove: Lawrence Erlbaum Associates, 1991), ch. 2.

processes.[9] For example, one such rule might be the rule known to logicians as *modus ponens*, which licenses us to infer a conclusion of the form '*Q*' from premises of the forms 'If *P*, then *Q*' and '*P*'. *Which* rules of inference people actually deploy is regarded as an empirical matter, to be settled by appeal to evidence of how people perform on various reasoning tasks. Thus, it might be surmised that, in addition to *modus ponens*, people also deploy the rule known as *modus tollens*, which licenses us to infer a conclusion of the form 'Not *P*' from premises of the form 'If *P*, then *Q*' and 'Not *Q*'. However, an alternative possibility is that people adopt a more roundabout strategy for deriving such a conclusion from such premises. For instance, it might be that, presented with premises of the form 'If *P*, then *Q*' and 'Not *Q*', people first of all adopt a hypothesis of the form '*P*', then apply the rule of *modus ponens* to 'If *P*, then *Q*' and '*P*' to get '*Q*', and finally infer 'Not *P*' from the resulting contradiction between '*Q*' and 'Not *Q*' by applying the rule of inference known to logicians as *reductio ad absurdum*. If this more roundabout method is indeed their strategy in such cases, then we would expect people to be quicker and more reliable in inferring a conclusion of the form '*Q*' from premises of the forms 'If *P*, then *Q*' and '*P*' than they are in inferring a conclusion of the form 'Not *P*' from premises of the forms 'If *P*, then *Q*' and 'Not *Q*'. And experimental findings would appear to bear out this expectation. We see, thus, that it may be possible to amass indirect evidence of what rules of inference people deploy in their reasoning, without having recourse to the dubious testimony of introspection.

However, adherents of the mental models approach contend that the available empirical evidence favours an account of deductive reasoning processes which does not invoke formal rules of inference at all.[10] Consider, thus, an inference

---

[9] For a fuller description and a defence of the mental logic approach, see D. P. O'Brien, 'Mental Logic and Human Irrationality: We Can Put a Man on the Moon, So Why Can't We Solve those Logical-Reasoning Problems?', in Manktelow and Over (eds.), *Rationality*, ch. 5.

[10] For a fuller account and a defence of the mental models approach, see Johnson-Laird and Byrne, *Deduction*.

from the premises 'Either Tom is in London or Tom is in Paris' and 'Tom is not in London' to the conclusion 'Tom is in Paris'. A mental logic theorist might contend that this inference is carried out in the following manner. First one recognises the premises to be of the forms 'Either P or Q' and 'Not P', then one applies the rule known as *disjunctive syllogism* to derive a conclusion of the form 'Q', and finally one recognises that 'Tom is in Paris' qualifies as a conclusion of this form in this context. One objection to this sort of account is that it seems very cumbersome, involving as it does a transition from specific sentences to schematic forms and back again, with inferential procedures being carried out on the schematic forms. Another is that it seems to imply that people should reason just as well with 'abstract' materials as they do with 'realistic' ones, which, as we saw earlier, is thought to conflict with evidence from the Wason selection task. The mental models approach suggests that we conduct the foregoing type of inference in a quite different and more direct way. First of all, it suggests, we envisage in what possible circumstances each of the premises would be true – that is to say, we construct certain 'models' of the premises. Then, when we try to combine these models, we see that some of them must be eliminated as inconsistent, and we discover that in all the remaining models the conclusion is true. Thus, both a situation in which Tom is in London and a situation in which Tom is in Paris provides a model of the premise 'Either Tom is in London or Tom is in Paris', but only one of those situations can consistently be combined with a situation in which Tom is not in London, and it is a situation in which the conclusion, 'Tom is in Paris', is true. Hence we draw this conclusion from the premises.

On the face of it, the mental models approach is not only simpler than the mental logic approach, but more intuitively plausible. And its adherents claim, as I have already remarked, that the empirical evidence favours it. Unsurprisingly, none of these points would be conceded by the advocates of the mental logic approach and the debate between the two schools seems to have reached something of an impasse. It is not clear whether philosophers have much of value to contribute to this debate, beyond voicing a degree of scepticism concerning the whole business. It is certainly an odd idea, bordering on the paradoxical, to suppose that ordinary people, quite untutored in formal logical methods, effortlessly deploy in their reasoning formal logical rules which logicians themselves have only discovered and codified during many centuries of painstaking work. The fact that ordinary people's alleged knowledge of these rules is supposed to be 'tacit' rather than 'explicit' does not help much to alleviate the air of paradox. On the other hand, it is not entirely clear what real substance there is to the rival approach of the mental models theorists.[11] For the very process of constructing 'models' of certain premises, attempting to combine them, eliminating some of these combinations as inconsistent, and discovering the remainder to be ones in which a certain conclusion is true, *itself* appears to demand reasoning quite as complex as the sorts of inference which it is supposed to explain. In fact, what it seems to demand is nothing less than a degree of *logical insight* – that is, an ability to grasp that certain propositions entail certain other propositions. Insight of this sort is arguably integral to our very ability to engage in propositional thought of any kind at all.

Suppose, for example, that we discovered someone who grasped the proposition that Tom is in London and grasped the proposition that Tom is in Paris (as well as the negations of those propositions), but simply failed to grasp the following: that if the proposition that *either* Tom is in London *or* Tom is in Paris and the proposition that Tom is not in London are both true, then the proposition that Tom is in Paris must also be true. What could we plausibly say of such a person, but that he must fail to grasp the concept of *disjunction*, that is, the meaning of the words 'either . . . or'? How-

---

[11] For trenchant criticism of the mental models approach by an adherent of the mental logic approach, see Lance J. Rips, 'Mental Muddles', in Myles Brand and Robert M. Harnish (eds.), *The Representation of Knowledge and Belief* (Tucson: University of Arizona Press, 1986). See also my 'Rationality, Deduction and Mental Models'.

ever, someone who failed to grasp this concept would scarcely be able to engage in propositional thought at all. We cannot, it seems, coherently separate *some* ability to engage in correct logical reasoning from even a minimal ability to have thoughts with propositional content – though this is not, of course, to belittle the problem of explaining the latter ability.

But why, then, do we bother to construct and learn systems of logic and why are we prone to commit logical fallacies in our reasoning? The answer, plausibly, is that logical insight, indispensable though it is, has a very limited scope of application. In the simplest inferences, we can just 'see' that the premises entail the conclusion: failure to see this would constitute a failure to understand the propositions in question. But in more complicated cases, involving highly complex propositions or lengthy chains of reasoning, we need to supplement logical insight with formal methods – just as we use formal techniques of arithmetic to supplement our elementary grasp of number relations. The formal methods are no substitute for logical or arithmetical insight, nor can the latter be explained by appeal to the former (as the mental logic approach would have us suppose), since insight is needed in order to apply the formal methods. But this is not to deny the utility of those methods as a means to extend our logical or computational capacities beyond their natural range.

So, one possible answer to the question 'How do we reason?' could be this. We conduct elementary deductive inferences simply by deploying the logical insight which is inseparable from propositional thinking. Beyond that severely restricted range of inferences, however, our ability to reason effectively is largely determined by what technical methods we have managed to learn and how well we have learnt to apply them. People untutored in such methods have nothing but their native wit to rely upon and it should be unsurprising that they fail to solve reasoning problems which really demand the application of formal methods. For this reason, it seems singularly pointless to subject such people, as psychologists sometimes do, to complex reasoning tasks involving Aristotelian syllogisms, for syllogistic reasoning is quite as formal and artificial as anything to be found in modern textbooks of symbolic logic. Moreover, we should recognise that formal methods of deductive and probabilistic reasoning are really designed to be carried out *on paper*, not *in our heads* – so that when we engage in acts of reasoning using them, parts of our physical environment literally become adjuncts of our reasoning processes. Empirical psychologists who overlook this fact are misconceiving human reasoning to be a wholly internal operation of the mind.

TWO KINDS OF RATIONALITY

Earlier on, I remarked that it seems almost tautologous to say that rationality involves reasoning. But further reflection may lead us to qualify that judgement. When we describe a person as being 'rational' or 'reasonable', we need not be ascribing to him or her especially good powers of reasoning, that is, an especially well-developed capacity to engage in inductive and deductive argument. Indeed, it has often been remarked that the madman may reason quite as well as a sane person does, but is distinguished by the extravagance of the premises which he assumes to be true. Someone who believes himself to be made of glass may reason impeccably that he will shatter if struck, and take the appropriate avoiding action: his error lies in his beliefs, not in what he infers from them. Nor will it do to blame his error on his having acquired those beliefs by faulty processes of reasoning, for even the sanest and most reasonable person acquires relatively few of his or her beliefs by processes of reasoning.

It seems, then, that there are two distinct notions of rationality.[12] Rationality in the first sense, which we have been concerned with so far in this chapter, is an ability to reason well,

---

[12] The view that there are two kinds of rationality is a pervasive theme in Jonathan St. B. T. Evans and David E. Over, *Rationality and Reasoning* (Hove: Psychology Press, 1996): see especially pp. 7ff.

whether deductively or inductively. It is this kind of rationality which psychologists presumably think they are investigating when they study people's performance on reasoning tasks. Rationality in the second sense is a more diffuse notion: roughly speaking, a rational (or 'reasonable') person in this sense is one who is well-adjusted to his or her social and physical environment, who acts appropriately in the light of his or her goals, and whose goals are sensible and attainable given the available resources. Possessing this second kind of rationality may well involve possessing the first kind of rationality in some degree, but clearly involves much more besides. Not least, it involves possessing a good measure of 'common sense'. Characterising this latter quality is no easy matter, though I shall have more to say about it later in this chapter.

In this context, it is worth remarking that, even if we accept the pessimistic judgement of some psychologists regarding the reasoning abilities of ordinary people, as supposedly revealed by their performance on reasoning tasks, these experimental findings have no very clear bearing on the question of how rational people are in our *second* sense of 'rationality'. How rational people are in this sense is primarily revealed by how they behave in the circumstances of everyday life, not by how they perform on artificial tasks in laboratory conditions. Indeed, one might question the sanity – the rationality – of anyone who took such tasks too seriously, given that the associated costs and benefits to the subjects concerned are relatively trivial in comparison with those regularly encountered in everyday life. Perhaps, then, ironically enough, the allegedly mediocre performance of ordinary people on the reasoning tasks which psychologists set them is testimony to their rationality in the broader sense.

ARTIFICIAL INTELLIGENCE AND THE TURING TEST

I remarked at the beginning of this chapter that human claims to be uniquely rational have come under pressure from investigators in the rapidly expanding field of artificial intelligence, or AI. It is customary, in this context, to distinguish between 'strong' and 'weak' AI, proponents of the latter maintaining merely that aspects of intelligent human behaviour can be usefully simulated or modelled by appropriately programmed computers, whereas advocates of the former hold that in virtue of executing a suitably written programme a machine could literally be said to think and reason.[13] Clearly, it is strong AI whose claims are philosophically controversial and whose credentials we must therefore investigate.

It is indisputable that suitably programmed computers can perform tasks which human beings can only carry out by exercising their powers of understanding and reason. Thus, for example, playing chess is an intellectually demanding task for human beings and we regard people who can play chess well as being highly intelligent. Notoriously, however, there now exist chess programmes which enable computers to match the performance of world-class human chess-players. Does this imply that those computers are exercising powers of understanding and reason when they execute these programmes? One may be inclined to answer 'No', on the grounds that such programmes do not, it seems, replicate the kind of thinking processes which human players engage in when they play chess. For one thing, these programmes exploit the immense information storage capacity of modern computers and their extremely rapid calculating ability, enabling a machine to evaluate many thousands of possible sequences of chess moves in a very short period of time. Human beings, by contrast, have a short-term memory of very limited capacity and carry out calculations much more slowly and much more erratically than computers do. A human being, then, could never hope to play chess by following the sorts of procedures which a chess-playing computer

[13] John Searle makes the distinction between 'strong' and 'weak' AI in his influential but controversial paper, 'Minds, Brains, and Programs', *Behavioral and Brain Sciences* 3 (1980), pp. 417–24, reprinted in Margaret A. Boden (ed.), *The Philosophy of Artificial Intelligence* (Oxford: Oxford University Press, 1990). I discuss some of Searle's views more fully later.

executes. It may be said that this, indeed, makes it all the more remarkable that a human being can, nonetheless, match the performance of a computer at chess. And it may be suggested that the lesson is that true intelligence involves intuition or insight rather than mere calculating power, on however massive a scale. Thus, the experienced human chess-player, despite being unable to compute and evaluate the thousands of possible sequences of moves open to him at a given stage of the game, may simply 'see' that a certain line of attack or defence is strategically promising, even if he has never encountered precisely such a situation before.

Here, however, it may be objected that the notion of 'intuition' or 'insight' is altogether too vague to be of any use in the present context. How can we *tell* whether a creature – be it living or a machine – is carrying out a task by employing intuition or insight rather than by means of 'mere' calculation? Perhaps, for all we know, what we fondly call the employment of intuition or insight just *is* a matter of complex computation, albeit at a sub-personal level which is inaccessible to introspective awareness. More-over, even when I judge another human being to be intelli-gent, I surely do so on the evidence of his or her observable behaviour, verbal and non-verbal, not on the basis of specu-lations concerning his or her supposed capacity for intuition or insight. By this standard, it seems, the significant differ-ence between a chess-playing computer and a human being has nothing to do with *how* they play chess – something which they may do equally well, even if they deploy differ-ent strategies – but consists, rather, in the fact that a chess-programme only enables a computer to accomplish *one* of the indefinitely large number of intelligent things that an ordinary human being can do. On this view, if we were to encounter a computer whose programme enabled it not only to play chess, but also to converse about the weather, write poetry, place bets on horse races, advise people concerning their medical problems, and so on – switching appropriately between one such activity and another according to circumstances and performing each of them at least as well as an average human being – then to deny it intelligence would be quite unreasonable.

It is a view like this which informs the well-known *Turing test* of artificial intelligence, named after its progenitor, the computer pioneer Alan Turing.[14] Simplifying somewhat, the test may be described in essence as follows. Suppose that you are confined to a room equipped with a typewriter keyboard and printer on one side and another keyboard and printer on the other side. By means of these devices you can send and receive typewritten messages to and from the occupants of the two adjoining rooms. One of the occupants is another ordinary human being who speaks your language, while the other occupant is a computer executing a programme designed to provide responses to questions expressed in that language. You are allotted a limited period of time, say ten minutes or so, during which you are at liberty to send whatever questions you like to the two occupants and to scrutinise their answers. Your task is to try to determine, on the basis of those answers, which room contains the human being and which the computer. The computer is said to pass the test if you cannot tell except by chance which of the two occupants is human.

Turing himself, who first proposed this test in 1950, somewhat ambitiously predicted that a computer would succeed in passing it by the year 2000. (At the time I write this, no computer has incontrovertibly passed the test.) According to Turing and his followers, we should equate the intelligence of a computer which passes the Turing test with that of an ordinary human being. And, on the face of it, that seems entirely reasonable. For suppose that, instead of a computer, another human being occupied the second room. Shouldn't the fact that this occupant's answers to your questions were indistinguishable to you from those of another ordinary human being suffice to convince you of his or her intelligence? We demand no better evidence of intelligence than

[14] See Alan M. Turing, 'Computing Machinery and Intelligence', *Mind* 59 (1950), pp. 433–60, reprinted in Boden (ed.), *The Philosophy of Artificial Intelligence*.

this, it seems, when we engage in a telephone conversation with a human stranger, so why should we harbour any doubts when our communicant happens to be a computer? To demand further evidence in the latter case smacks of anthropocentric prejudice, for what further evidence could we reasonably demand? It is surely irrelevant that a computer may not look at all like a human being and has a different internal constitution. After all, would it be rational to harbour doubts about the intelligence of one of your friends if you were suddenly to discover that, instead of being made of flesh and bones, he or she was composed internally of metal rods, wires and silicon chips?

Perhaps, however, one cannot justly be accused of anthropocentric prejudice for insisting that evidence of intelligence should consist of more than just an appropriate range of verbal responses, for this is to ignore *non-verbal* behaviour as a proper source of such evidence. The Turing test represents a curiously 'disembodied' conception of intelligence. It is true that evidence of intelligent non-verbal behaviour is not immediately available to us when we converse with a human stranger over the telephone, but the circumstances of everyday life suffice to make us justifiably confident that we *could* obtain such evidence, at least in principle. We could have the call traced, track down the caller, and confront him or her in person. Then we would discover him or her to be a creature capable of all sorts of intelligent non-verbal behaviour. By contrast, when we enter the room containing the computer which has passed the Turing test, all we may find is an inert metal box sitting on a table, quite incapable of engaging in any physical activity at all apart from the electronic activity going on inside it. Our doubts about the intelligence of the room's occupant need have nothing to do, then, with the fact that it is composed of metal and silicon, and to that extent need not be an expression of prejudice in favour of biological organisms of any kind. If this line of objection is correct, it is not enough for a computer to be deemed intelligent that it can pass the Turing test: it must also be able to interact intelligently with its physical environment, which will require it to have the equivalent of animal sensory and motor systems. In short, the computer will have to be a sophisticated kind of robot.

Against this, it may be objected that, by these standards, a human being who has been completely paralysed by a stroke but nonetheless retains all of his or her intellectual faculties – that is, a victim of so-called 'locked in' syndrome – should not be deemed intelligent. But there is a crucial difference between such a human being and a physically inert computer which has passed the Turing test, namely, that the human being has *lost* a capacity for physical interaction with its environment, whereas the computer has never had one. It is questionable whether we can make sense of the idea of there being an intelligent creature which has never acquired a capacity to interact physically with its environment, because so much of the knowledge which intelligence demands apparently has to be acquired through active exploration of one's environment, both physical and social. The idea that such knowledge can simply be 'programmed' into a computer directly is highly dubious, as we shall see more fully in due course.

SEARLE'S 'CHINESE ROOM' THOUGHT-EXPERIMENT

There are other doubts that can be raised about the Turing test. Amongst the best known of these are some that John Searle has raised in the context of his much-debated 'Chinese room' thought-experiment.[15] Imagine the following scenario. A monoglot English-speaking person is confined to a room containing a typewriter keyboard, a printer, and an operation manual written in English. The keyboard is designed to produce Chinese characters rather than letters of the Roman alphabet. Outside the room, a monoglot Chinese-speaking

---

[15] See Searle, 'Minds, Brains, and Programs'. For comments and criticism, see the peer review commentary in the same issue of *Behavioral and Brain Sciences*. See also Margaret A. Boden, 'Escaping the Chinese Room', in Boden (ed.), *The Philosophy of Artificial Intelligence*.

person has another such keyboard and printer, allowing him to send messages written in Chinese into the room. The Chinese speaker is permitted ask whatever questions he likes in these messages. On receiving a message, the English speaker inside the room has to consult the operation manual, which tells him what string of Chinese characters to type out in response. Let us suppose that the manual has been so written that, when the Chinese speaker receives the responses to his questions, he is unable to distinguish them from those of a native Chinese speaker. In that case, it seems, the Turing test has been passed. By the standards of that test, the Chinese speaker outside the room ought to conclude that he is communicating with an intelligent being inside the room. And, of course, in a sense that is precisely what he is doing, since the English speaker *is* an intelligent being. However, the English speaker inside the room has no understanding of Chinese whatever. The implication, it seems, is that passing the Turing test demands no understanding of the questions posed in the course of that test and consequently that the test is no test of genuine intelligence, since genuine intelligence does demand understanding.

The direct relevance of this thought-experiment to the problem of artificial intelligence can be seen if we suppose that, instead of the room containing a human being, it contains a computer programmed to obey the instructions embodied in the operation manual. (Of course, it is an open question whether such an operation manual could really be written, but let us assume for the sake of argument that it can; if it can't, then it would appear that the hopes of strong AI supporters must be dashed in any case.) If a human being can follow these instructions, then so too, surely, can a computer, since they are simply rules specifying what string of Chinese characters should be sent out in response to a given incoming string. The rules are purely formal or syntactical, having regard merely to the shape and order of Chinese characters in a string. But then, since a computer executing this programme will pass the Turing test, as judged by the Chinese speaker outside, Turing and his followers must hold that the Chinese speaker would be justified in attributing intelligence to such a computer. And yet, it seems, the computer no more understands Chinese than did the English-speaking person. Moreover, unlike the English-speaking person, there is surely nothing else that the computer understands, so our conclusion should apparently be that the computer understands *nothing whatever*. But how can something which understands nothing whatever justifiably be deemed intelligent? The lesson seems to be that intelligence cannot consist in the mere execution of a computer programme, which is a set of purely formal rules for transforming certain strings of symbols into others. Rather, to the extent that intelligence involves the deployment of symbols at all, it must include an understanding of what those symbols *mean*: it must involve not just *syntax*, but also *semantics*.

However, the foregoing argument may be accused of begging the question against advocates of the Turing test, on the grounds that we have simply assumed that the computer does *not* understand Chinese. It is true enough that the English-speaking person in the original version of the thought-experiment does not understand Chinese. But the computer executing its programme is not equivalent to the English-speaking person alone: rather, it is equivalent to the combination of the English-speaking person *and the operation manual*, for the latter is what corresponds to the computer's programme. What corresponds to the English-speaking person is the computer's central processor, which executes the programme. The advocate of the Turing test can happily concede that the central processor by itself does not understand Chinese, any more than the English-speaking person does: rather, he will say, what understands Chinese is the whole *system* consisting of the computer's central processor, its data storage banks, and the programme which it is running. In like manner, then, he may urge that the system consisting of the English-speaking person and the operation manual *does* understand Chinese, even though the person alone does not.

Searle has responded to this objection (the so-called 'systems reply') by urging that, even if the English-speaking person were to memorise the operation manual by heart, he would still not understand Chinese – and yet now he would constitute the whole system inside the room. The problem at this point is that we are entering deep into counterfactual territory. An operation manual that would suffice for the purposes of the Turing test would be immense and consequently impossible for an ordinary human being to memorise by heart. But if, *per impossibile*, a human being *were* to be able to memorise such a manual, who is to say whether or not he would as a consequence be able to understand Chinese? Rather than pursue pointless speculation about such matters, it is more helpful to emphasise what Searle takes to be the crucial lesson of the Chinese room thought-experiment. This is that intelligent thought and understanding cannot consist merely in the making of transitions between strings of symbols in accordance with formal rules – and yet the latter, seemingly, is all that a computer is doing when it is executing a programme. Hence, a computer cannot be said to be intelligent purely in virtue of executing a programme. To the extent that the Turing test implies otherwise, it must surely be mistaken.

But perhaps the Turing test doesn't imply otherwise. It only provides a criterion for the ascription of intelligence and has nothing to say about what intelligence consists in. Moreover, it would seem false to say that all that a computer which passes the test is doing is to execute a programme, for this is to ignore the verbal exchange that is going on between the computer and the person who is putting questions to it. The computer's part in that exchange is determined by its programme, no doubt, but it amounts to more than just the making of transitions between strings of symbols in accordance with formal rules – it also involves the sending out of appropriate verbal messages in response to incoming ones. In view of these and other complications, it simply isn't clear what lesson, if any, can be drawn from the Chinese room thought-experiment concerning the prospects for strong AI. Even so, it should be recognised that Searle has raised some deep and important issues which the advocates of strong AI cannot afford simply to ignore.

THE FRAME PROBLEM

I suggested earlier that one reason for denying that a chess-playing computer is intelligent might be that it is incapable of doing *anything but* play chess – anything, that is, which would be deemed an intelligent activity if performed by a human being. The idea that a creature or machine could be intelligent in virtue of performing *just one* kind of activity in an intelligent manner seems highly questionable. It is true that a few human beings are so-called *idiots savants*. These are individuals who, despite having a fairly low level of general intelligence by human standards, are outstandingly talented in one area of intellectual endeavour, be it musical, mathematical, or linguistic.[16] However, even these people are not totally devoid of intellectual ability in a wide range of other areas. Part of what it is to be an intelligent being, it seems, is to be versatile and flexible in one's range of responses, especially to novel or unexpected circumstances. That is why the so-called *tropistic* behaviour of many lower forms of animal life, superficially intelligent though it may appear to be, does not reveal them to be genuinely intelligent creatures but quite the reverse. Such a creature will repeatedly carry out some complex scheme of behaviour in response to a predetermined stimulus, never learning to adapt it to new circumstances or to abandon it when it becomes unproductive.

Intelligence requires knowledge, but it also requires an ability to extend one's knowledge in the light of new experience and an ability to apply one's knowledge appropriately in relevant circumstances. Is it possible to confer these abilities upon a computer simply by endowing it with the right sort of

---

[16] See Michael J. A. Howe, *Fragments of Genius: The Strange Feats of Idiots Savants* (London: Routledge, 1989). For a more detailed case study, see Neil Smith and Ianthi-Maria Tsimpli, *The Mind of a Savant: Language Learning and Modularity* (Oxford: Blackwell, 1995).

programme? That seems unlikely. While it is often possible to capture, in a computer programme, a body of expert knowledge within a restricted domain – for example, some of the diagnostic knowledge of a skilled medical practitioner – it is not at all clear how one could embody *relevantly applicable general knowledge* in a computer programme. Perhaps one might hope to do so simply by combining a host of different specialised programmes, each designed to capture some specific aspect of human knowledge, either practical or theoretical. For instance, one such programme might try to capture the knowledge required to order a meal in a restaurant, while another might try to capture the knowledge required to render assistance in the event of a fire. The problem, however, is that in the circumstances of everyday life we constantly have to shift from engaging in one intelligent activity to engaging in another, in the light of new information and our own priorities – and our ability to do this effectively is itself a mark of our intelligence.

Imagine that one is busily ordering a meal in a restaurant, when suddenly a fire-alarm rings and one sees smoke billowing from windows across the street. Then one has to decide whether to carry on ordering the meal or to do something about the fire. Neither the meal-ordering programme nor the fire-assistance programme by itself will specify what to do in these circumstances, since each is dedicated exclusively to its own domain. And yet if a programmer tried to build in cross-connections between all of his specialised programmes in order to overcome this sort of limitation, he would rapidly discover that that this would do no good – for there is no end to the number of different ways in which one intelligent activity may need to give way to another in the course of an intelligent creature's everyday life. Suppose, for instance, that the programmer were to include in his meal-ordering programme the following provision for action in the event of a fire: in this event, the programme specifies that the meal should be abandoned and the fire-assistance programme be followed instead. But *would* an intelligent and responsible person necessarily try to assist with the fire in these circumstances? Not necessarily, because, once more, unexpected contingencies may demand some other course of action. For instance, just as one is thinking of calling the fire brigade, one might notice a small child outside the restaurant about to run in front of a car: in that case one may very reasonably decide to rush out and try to save the child instead of assisting with the fire – unless, of course, some further complication arises which causes one to change one's mind yet again. And this is just a single example of countless kinds of contingency which *could* arise, most of which no one will ever encounter or even envisage. That being so, it appears to be impossible in principle for the computer programmer to take all such contingencies into account in advance, even in the case of so mundane an activity as that of ordering a meal in a restaurant.

The problem confronting the advocates of strong AI here is sometimes known as the *Frame Problem*.[17] It consists in the apparent impossibility of writing a programme which not only embodies the general knowledge available to an average human being but which also specifies how that knowledge is to be applied appropriately in relevant circumstances. For it seems to be impossible to specify in advance what all the 'relevant' circumstances and 'appropriate' applications might be. Another way of describing the difficulty is to say that there is plausibly no set of algorithms, or computational rules, which can embody the qualities of common sense and sound judgement which characterise a rational human being of average intelligence. Whether the challenge posed by this problem can be met by the advocates of strong AI remains to be seen. It would be foolhardy, however, to proclaim too firmly that the challenge *cannot* be met. We should recognise that human ingenuity has often managed to overcome the restrictions which some human beings have tried to impose

---

[17] See the articles in Zenon W. Pylyshyn (ed.), *The Robot's Dilemma: The Frame Problem of Artificial Intelligence* (Norwood, NJ: Ablex, 1987). See also Daniel C. Dennett, 'Cognitive Wheels: The Frame Problem of AI', in C. Hookway (ed.), *Minds, Machines and Evolution* (Cambridge: Cambridge University Press, 1984), reprinted in Boden (ed.), *The Philosophy of Artificial Intelligence*.

upon it. Ironically, if we were to succeed in developing artificial intelligence, that might provide the strongest possible testimony to the superiority of our own intelligence.

CONNECTIONISM AND THE MIND

We are perhaps unduly impressed by computers which effortlessly and rapidly perform tasks which we find intellectually daunting, such as playing chess to grandmaster level or carrying out complex mathematical calculations. It is noteworthy that these activities are rule-governed and self-contained and thus well-suited to implementation by means of a computer programme. Carrying out the steps of a programme, however, is a purely mechanical procedure and to that extent, some would say, the very antithesis of genuinely intelligent behaviour. We would not, I think, have a high regard for the intelligence of someone who played a game of skill by laboriously following the steps laid down in a computer programme – though we might have a high regard for the intelligence of the person who wrote the programme.

On the other hand, we are perhaps not sufficiently impressed by the intelligence of some of the things that human beings do effortlessly but which it is very difficult to make computers do. I have in mind here such humble and mundane activities as walking across a room without bumping into anything, packing a suitcase, and making a sandwich from ingredients located in the typical kitchen. One reason why these things are difficult for computers to do is that they are *not* self-contained and straightforwardly rule-governed activities. As such, they all come up against the Frame Problem. Another reason is that these tasks require the agents performing them to have sophisticated perceptual and motor capacities: they must be able to recognise a great variety of objects perceptually and to move their limbs in ways which take into account the physical properties and spatial relations of those objects. These capacities do not seem to be readily amenable to programming. Human beings have to acquire them by learning from experience and it seems likely that machines, too, could only ever acquire them in that way. But it seems unlikely that an ability to learn from experience is something that could be conferred upon a machine simply by endowing it with the right sort of programme, along with sensors and movable limbs.

If one wanted to create an intelligent machine, would it not be sensible to try to model it on creatures which we already know to be intelligent – ourselves? This is to invert the approach of traditional AI, which attempts to throw light upon the nature of human intelligence by comparing human thought to the execution of a computer programme. The human brain, however, is constructed very differently from an electronic computer of traditional design. It consists of billions of nerve cells or neurones, each connected to many others in a complicated and tangled network. Electrical activity in certain neurones may stimulate or depress such activity in other neurones, depending on how the neurones in question are connected. The whole network is constantly undergoing changing patterns of activation as nerve cells in sensory organs are stimulated by events in the environment and interact with neurones in the brain. Thus, there is no 'central processor' in the brain comparable to that found in a computer of traditional design. To the extent that we can describe the brain as an 'information processor' at all, it is one which utilises *parallel* rather than *serial* processing on a massive scale.[18]

The distinction between serial and parallel processing may be crudely illustrated by the following simple example. Suppose that we have the task of counting the books in a library. One way of accomplishing the task would be to get one person to do the whole job by counting every book on every shelf. Another way would be to allot each shelf to a different person, whose task it would be to count the books on that

---

[18] For a general introduction to parallel processing, see J. L. McClelland, D. E. Rumelhart and G. E. Hinton, 'The Appeal of Parallel Distributed Processing', in David E. Rumelhart and James L. McClelland (eds.), *Parallel Distributed Processing: Explorations in the Microstructure of Cognition, Volume 1: Foundations* (Cambridge, MA: MIT Press, 1986).

shelf, and then to add together the totals reported by each person to get the final sum. Both methods should deliver the same answer, but the second method may well be quicker because many people are working on different parts of the task simultaneously, or 'in parallel'. It may also be more reliable, because if one of the people counting makes a mistake or abandons the job, the overall count may still be approximately correct – whereas if the same happens to the single person using the first method, a serious error or no answer at all may result. Another difference between the two methods is that the single person using the first method must have more advanced numerical abilities than the many people using the second method, since he must be capable of counting up to a much higher number. Electronic computers of traditional design work in a way comparable to our first method: a single, high-powered central processor carries out all of the steps of a programme in a sequential fashion in order to solve an information-processing problem. But, more recently, so-called *connectionist* machines have been designed, whose architecture is more comparable to that of an animal brain or nervous system. In these, an information-processing task is not only shared, as in our illustrative example, but also there is continual interaction between different parts of the system.

Connectionist machines consist of many simple processing units arranged in layers and connected to one another in multiple ways.[19] Typically, such a machine has three layers of units: a layer of input units, a layer of intermediate or 'hidden' units, and a layer of output units. Each unit in a layer is connected to some or all of the units in the next layer. In the simplest case, units might have only two possible

---

[19] For a simple and clear example of a working connectionist system, see Paul M. Churchland, *Matter and Consciousness*, revised edn (Cambridge, MA: MIT Press, 1988), pp. 156–65. Churchland is an enthusiastic supporter of the connectionist approach to the mind: see his *The Engine of Reason, the Seat of the Soul: A Philosophical Journey into the Brain* (Cambridge, MA: MIT Press, 1995). See also William Bechtel and Adele Abrahamsen, *Connectionism and the Mind: An Introduction to Parallel Processing in Networks* (Oxford: Blackwell, 1991).

states of activation: on and off. The state of activation of an intermediate unit or an output unit will depend upon the activation states of the units in previous layers which are connected to it and upon the 'strengths' or 'weights' of those connections. These connection-strengths can be modified, so as to alter the ways in which patterns of activation flow through the system of units. The activation state of an input unit will depend on the data being fed into the machine, which might derive, for example, from a sensor device. The activation state of the machine's output units constitute its response to the data being fed into it. Even from this simplified description, one can see how such a machine resembles an animal brain or nervous system and why, consequently, it is often described as an artificial neural net.

Simple though neural nets seem to be, they can be made to perform remarkable tasks which are difficult to accomplish using traditional AI methods. For example, they are good at pattern-recognition tasks, such as the task of 'recognising' letters of the alphabet printed in different fonts or in partially degraded forms. Moreover, they can continue to perform reasonably well even when some of their units are malfunctioning, so they are robust and reliable. Like an organic nervous system, however, they need to undergo a 'training' regime in order to be able to perform such tasks: this involves making adjustments to the connection-strengths between units so as to attune a machine's responses to the data which are fed into it. There are algorithms, or computational rules, which dictate how these adjustments should be made in the 'training' period, during which the machine is exposed to samples of the kind of data involved in its allotted task. It is not altogether fanciful, then, to think of such a machine as acquiring its abilities by a process of trial and error, and even as 'learning from experience'.

Interesting though these matters may be from a technical point of view, we need to ask how significant they are for the philosophy of mind. Some philosophers think that they are immensely significant. They hold that if artificial neural nets provide a good model of how the human mind works, then many of our cherished ideas about human cognition will have to be abandoned – for example, our 'folk-psychological' assumption that cognition involves propositional attitude states, such as beliefs.[20] The problem is that whereas a computer of traditional design stores and processes discrete representations of information, in the form of strings of machine code, connectionist machines, to the extent that they may be said to 'represent' information at all, do so in a 'widely distributed' fashion. That is to say, no one piece of information is locatable in any particular set of units, but rather all of the information which such a machine is handling is embodied in its overall pattern of activation and connection-strengths. Thus, any attempt to identify distinct beliefs with distinct representational states of a person's brain will, it seems, be undercut by connectionist models of human cognition. If so, such models present a serious challenge not only to folk psychology but also to functionalism in the philosophy of mind – indeed, they seem to give succour to the advocates of eliminative materialism (see chapter 3). Against such models, however, their detractors maintain that they are incapable of dealing with the higher reaches of human cognition, such as linguistic comprehension and reasoning, where traditional AI models appear to be more promising.[21]

In fact, though, we are not forced to choose between two stark alternatives, traditional AI and connectionism, when it comes to deciding how best to model aspects of human

---

[20] See, especially, William Ramsey, Stephen P. Stich and Joseph Garon, 'Connectionism, Eliminativism, and the Future of Folk Psychology', in J. E. Tomberlin (ed.), *Philosophical Perspectives, 4* (Atascadero, CA: Ridgeview Press, 1990), reprinted in William Ramsey, Stephen P. Stich and David E. Rumelhart (eds.), *Philosophy and Connectionist Theory* (Hillsdale, NJ: Lawrence Erlbaum Associates, 1991) and in Cynthia Macdonald and Graham Macdonald (eds.), *Connectionism: Debates in Psychological Explanation, Volume 2* (Oxford: Blackwell, 1995).

[21] See Jerry A. Fodor and Zenon W. Pylyshyn, 'Connectionism and Cognitive Architecture: A Critical Analysis', *Cognition* 28 (1988), pp. 3–78, reprinted in Macdonald and Macdonald (eds.), *Connectionism*. For an opposing view, see Paul Smolensky, 'On the Proper Treatment of Connectionism', *Behavioral and Brain Sciences* 11, (1988), pp. 1–74, reprinted in Macdonald and Macdonald (eds.), *Connectionism*. See also, in the same volume, the subsequent exchanges between Smolensky and Fodor *et al.*

cognition. Hybrid approaches are possible.[22] Thus, connectionist models, with their ability to handle pattern-recognition tasks, might be drawn on to account for some of our sensory and perceptual capacities, while traditional models could be drawn on to account for our powers of logical inference. The fact that the human brain has a physical organisation somewhat akin to that of a connectionist machine should not lead us to assume that its *functional* organisation is best described by purely connectionist models. It is worth remarking that most experimentation with connectionist models is actually carried out using computers of traditional design rather than connectionist machines. But, just as a serial processing machine can be used to model the workings of a connectionist one, so, in principle, could a connectionist machine be used to model the workings of a serial one. Thus, even if the human brain is a 'connectionist machine' at the level of its physical organisation, this does not preclude it from supporting computational activities which are best described by traditional AI models.

In fact, there is a sense in which any machine whatever that can be called a 'computer', whatever its particular design or architecture, is equivalent to any other, because each is equivalent in its computational capacities to what is now known as a 'universal Turing machine'.[23] (A Turing machine is a very simple device consisting of an indefinitely long tape, recording information in symbolic code, and a reading head which prints or erases symbols and moves the tape to the left or right in accordance with a pre-set programme or 'machine table'.) Of course, the design of a machine can make a big difference to how efficiently and quickly it processes information but, in principle, any func-

---

[22] See further Andy Clark, *Microcognition: Philosophy, Cognitive Science, and Parallel Distributed Processing* (Cambridge, MA: MIT Press, 1989), ch. 7.

[23] This point is explained by Turing himself, without going into too many technicalities, in his 'Computing Machinery and Intelligence'. For a more technical account, see Richard C. Jeffrey, *Formal Logic: Its Scope and Limits*, 2nd edn (New York: McGraw-Hill, 1981), ch. 6, or George S. Boolos and Richard C. Jeffrey, *Computability and Logic*, 3rd edn (Cambridge: Cambridge University Press, 1989), ch. 3 and ch. 6.

tion that can be computed by a computer of one design can be computed by one of any other design. Because of this equivalence, it may even be urged that connectionist models provide no answer to the challenge raised by Searle's Chinese room thought-experiment, if indeed that challenge is thought to be a serious one. If Searle is right in urging that computation as such has nothing to tell us about cognition because it involves only 'syntax' and not 'semantics', then his point would seem to apply as well to connectionist as to traditional AI models.

It seems, then, that the advent of connectionism does nothing to divert or resolve the long-standing philosophical questions concerning the possibility of artificial intelligence. Perhaps we shall, in time, be able to build robotic machines of connectionist design which appear to learn through processes of education and socialisation akin to those undergone by human children in their formative years and which appear to act as autonomous agents, motivated by their own goals. Such machines would surely deserve to be called 'intelligent', and they would certainly be 'artificial'. To that extent, the dream of artificial intelligence would have been realised. However, it is quite conceivable that the makers of these machines would no more understand the basis of their cognitive capacities than current neuroscientists understand the cognitive capacities of the human brain. In particular, there is no guarantee that *computation* provides the key to cognition.

CONCLUSIONS

In this chapter, we have seen that it is not as easy as some scientists would have us believe to demonstrate empirically that human beings are irrational or that machines can think. Neither possibility should be dogmatically ruled out, but the empirical and theoretical claims advanced in favour of them are open to many doubts. On the one hand, the way people perform on reasoning problems is open to many different interpretations and often there is no settled answer to the question of what a 'correct' solution to such a problem is. Normative questions of how to reason correctly are not, in any case, the business of empirical scientists but rather of logicians, mathematicians, decision theorists and philosophers – and all of the latter are frequently in dispute with each other over precisely such questions. The very notion of 'rationality' – which we have seen to be deeply ambiguous – is normative in character and hence not one whose application can be determined on purely empirical grounds.

On the other hand, the prospects for artificial intelligence are not as favourable as some of its devotees would have us suppose. The notion of 'intelligence', like that of 'rationality', is a contentious one and there is no indisputably correct criterion for its application. The Turing test is open to the objection that it is inspired by behaviourist assumptions and focuses too narrowly on verbal evidence of intelligence. It may also be vulnerable to attack by appeal to Searle's Chinese room thought-experiment. The Frame Problem seems to present a formidable challenge to traditional, programmed-based AI models, while connectionist models appear to be limited in their potential range of application to fairly low-level cognitive activities. More fundamentally, it is not even clear yet that computation of *any* kind, whether involving serial or parallel processing, provides the key to human cognitive capacity. Computation clearly is *one* of our cognitive capacities – one that we have found so useful that we have developed machines to do it for us. But to regard the operations of those machines as providing a model for *all* of our cognitive activities looks suspiciously like the overworking of a metaphor. It appears to ignore too many facets of our mental life which are inseparable from human cognition, such as sensation and emotion, and to disregard the biological aspects of our nature which make us purposive, goal-seeking creatures. A creature without goals could not really be said to reason, since reason aims at truth or successful action. That being so, machines of our making cannot really be said to reason, because they surely have no goals of their own to pursue.

How, then, can they provide us with adequate models of our own reasoning and thinking capacities? We would do well, for the time being, to maintain a healthy scepticism concerning the prospects for artificial intelligence.

9

Action, intention and will

An important point which emerged from the last chapter is that even so 'intellectual' an aspect of the human mind as our ability to reason cannot be divorced from our nature as autonomous goal-seeking creatures endowed with complex motivational states, involving intentions, sensations and emotions. Even purely theoretical reasoning, which aims at truth, is a goal-directed activity which requires motivation. Nor can we simply aim at truth in the abstract. Advance in the sciences is made by focusing on particular problems, which have to be perceived as problems if investigators are to be motivated to attempt to solve them. Human beings, like other primates, are creatures naturally endowed with a high degree of curiosity. A being devoid of all curiosity could never engage in processes of reasoning, for it would have no motive to form hypotheses, to seek empirical data in confirmation or refutation of them, or to select certain propositions as the premises of an argument. Human curiosity is a trait which, in all probability, our evolutionary history has conferred upon us as a consequence of natural selection. Curiosity may have killed the cat, as the saying goes, but if, as seems plausible, a moderately high degree of curiosity tends to increase a creature's chances of survival, we modern humans may well have it at least partly because our ancestors' less curious rivals did not survive to pass on their genes. However, if a universal human trait such as curiosity is to be explained in such an evolutionary way, it must be questionable whether it is one which could simply be manufactured artificially and 'installed' in a computer. Its biological roots are surely too deep for that to make sense. And this, perhaps, is the most fundamental reason for denying that computers could be, in any literal sense, rational beings.

If this conclusion is supported by reflection on the nature of theoretical reasoning, all the more so must it be supported by considerations to do with the nature of practical reasoning, whose quite explicit goal is action satisfying the reasoner's desires. It is to the character of intentional action and its motivation that we shall turn our attention in this chapter. Amongst the questions that we should explore are the following. First of all, what do we, or should we, mean by an 'action'? In particular, how should we distinguish between a person's actions and things which merely 'happen to' that person? Next, is it correct to describe some actions as 'intentional' and others as 'unintentional' – and if so, what does this difference consist in? Or should we say, rather, that one and the same action may be intentional under one description of that action but unintentional under another description? More generally, how should actions be *individuated* – what counts as 'one and the same action', as opposed to two distinct actions? Is it a distinctive feature of all actions that they involve *trying* – and is trying just a matter of what some philosophers have called 'willing'? What, if anything, should we mean by 'freedom of will', and do we have it? What is it that motivates us to act? What roles do such mental states as beliefs, desires, intentions, and emotions have in the motivational structure of human agency? And how are our reasons for action related to the causes of our actions?

AGENTS, ACTIONS AND EVENTS

In everyday language, we commonly draw a distinction between things that a person *does* – his or her *actions* – and things that merely 'happen to' a person. For example, if a person trips and falls, we say that his falling is just an event which happens to him, whereas if a person jumps down from a step we say that his jumping is an action that he is performing. What is the difference that we are alluding to here?

To a casual observer, someone's falling could look exactly like his jumping. Indeed, if we just focus on the way in which the person's body moves, we may not be able to discern any difference at all between the two cases. Because of this, we may be tempted to say that the difference must be purely mental, to do with the psychological states of the person in question and their causal relation to his bodily movement. According to such an approach, an action of jumping just *is* a certain bodily movement, but one that is caused by a certain kind of mental state, or combination of mental states – such as, perhaps, an appropriate combination of belief and desire. On this view, that very bodily movement, or one exactly similar to it, could have occurred without being an action at all, if it had had different causes – for instance, if it had been caused by circumstances entirely external to the person concerned, such as a sudden gust of wind. To take this view is to deny, implicitly, that actions constitute a distinct ontological category of their own: it is to hold that they are simply events which happen to have mental causes of certain appropriate kinds.

But there is a problem with this view. It appears to trade on an ambiguity in the expression 'bodily movement'. In one sense of this expression, a bodily movement is a certain kind of motion in a person's body: so let us call a bodily movement in this sense a *bodily motion*. In another sense, however, a bodily movement is a person's *moving* of his or her body in a certain kind of way – and from now on let us reserve the expression 'bodily movement' exclusively for this use. The underlying point here is that the verb 'to move' has both an intransitive and a transitive sense.[1] We employ the former when, for example, we say that the earth *moves* around the sun. We employ the latter, however, when we say that a person *moves* his limbs in order to walk. Now, it seems clear, when a person trips and falls, his falling is merely a *bodily motion*, but when a person jumps down from a step he is enga-

---

[1] On the distinction between the transitive and intransitive senses of 'move', see Jennifer Hornsby, *Actions* (London: Routledge and Kegan Paul, 1980), ch. 1.

ging in a form of *bodily movement*. For a person to engage in a form of bodily movement is for that person to *make his body move* in a certain way – that is, it is for that person to cause or bring about a certain kind of motion in his body. But if a person's action of jumping is his *causing* a certain bodily motion, it surely cannot simply be *identical* with that bodily motion. Indeed, it now begins to look doubtful whether we can properly describe an action such as this as being an *event* at all, since it appears to be, rather, a person's *causing* of an event. And this suggests that actions do, after all, constitute a distinct ontological category of their own.

An important point to note about the foregoing characterisation of action is that it employs what appears to be a distinctive concept of causation – what is sometimes called 'agent causation'.[2] This is standardly contrasted with so-called 'event causation'. A typical statement of event causation would be this: 'The explosion caused the collapse of the building'. Here one event is said to be the cause of another event. But in a statement of agent causation, a person – an *agent* – is said to cause, or to be the cause of, an event, as in 'John caused the collapse of the building'. Very often, when we make a statement of agent causation like this, we can expand the statement by saying *how* the agent caused the event in question. Thus, we might say that John caused the collapse of the building *by detonating some dynamite*. But notice that to detonate some dynamite is itself to perform a certain kind of action, involving agent causation: for to detonate some dynamite is to cause the dynamite to explode, that is, it is to cause a certain event, the explosion of the dynamite. And, once again, we may be able to say *how* that event was caused: for instance, we might say that John caused the

---

[2] On the notion of agent causation, see, especially: Richard Taylor, *Action and Purpose* (Englewood Cliffs, NJ: Prentice-Hall, 1966), ch. 8 and ch. 9; Arthur C. Danto, *Analytical Philosophy of Action* (Cambridge: Cambridge University Press, 1973), ch. 3; and Roderick M. Chisholm, 'The Agent as Cause', in Myles Brand and Douglas Walton (eds.), *Action Theory* (Dordrecht: D. Reidel, 1976). But see also Chisholm, *Person and Object: A Metaphysical Study* (London: George Allen and Unwin, 1976), pp. 69–7, and, for discussion, Hornsby, *Actions*, pp. 96ff.

explosion of the dynamite *by pushing the plunger of the detonator.*

Now, it is easy to see that we have started here on a regress, which had better not be an infinite one. John caused the collapse of the building by denotating the dynamite; he caused the explosion of the dynamite by pushing the plunger; he caused the depression of the plunger by moving his arm ... But what about the motion of his arm – how did John cause *that* event? Here we are talking about John engaging in a kind of bodily movement, that is, about him *moving his arm* in a certain way and thus causing a certain kind of motion in it. But – except in unusual circumstances – it doesn't seem that one causes motion in one's arm *by doing something else*, in the way that one causes the collapse of a building by detonating some dynamite. One could, of course, cause motion in one's arm by pulling on a rope attached to it, using one's other arm – but that certainly would be unusual. Normally, it seems, one causes motion in one's arm *just by moving it.* For that reason, actions like this are often called *basic* actions and it is widely assumed that these are restricted to certain kinds of bodily movement.[3]

Not many philosophers, it should be said, are happy to regard the notions of agent causation and basic action as primitive or irreducible. Most would urge that agent causation must, ultimately, be reducible to event causation. Consider, thus, John's action of moving his arm, in the 'normal' way – that is, as a case of 'basic' action. Suppose, for instance, that John simply raises his arm, as a child in school might do in order to attract the teacher's attention. Here John causes the rising of his arm, a certain bodily motion and thus a certain event. If we ask John *how* he caused this event, he is likely to say that he did so simply by raising his arm – not by doing anything *else*. But that doesn't imply that nothing else caused the event in question. Indeed, it is plausible to suppose that the rising of John's arm was caused by a whole

---

[3] For the notion of a 'basic action', see Arthur C. Danto, 'Basic Actions', *American Philosophical Quarterly* 2 (1965), pp. 141–8, and also Danto, *Analytical Philosophy of Action*, ch. 2. For further discussion, see my *Subjects of Experience* (Cambridge: Cambridge University Press, 1996), pp. 144–5 and 150–2.

chain of preceding *events*, occurring in John's muscles and central nervous system. Now, were these events that *John* caused? It is unlikely that John himself will say so, since he will very probably profess himself quite ignorant of the events in question. Moreover, to suppose that John did cause these events seems to conflict with the claim that John's raising his arm was a 'basic' action. But an alternative proposal would be to say that John's causing the rising of his arm – his 'basic' action – *consisted in* these other events causing the rising of his arm. This would be to reduce an instance of agent causation to one of event causation. On this view, to say that agent *A* caused event *e* is to say that certain other events involving *A* caused *e* – in particular, certain events in *A*'s central nervous system.

An objection to this view, however, is that we then seem to lose sight of the distinction between the agent's *actions* and those events that merely 'happen to' the agent – for events going on in an agent's central nervous system seem to belong to the latter category. Even if we try to temper the proposal by urging that some of these events in the agent's central nervous system will in fact be (identical with) certain *mental* events, such as the onset of the agent's desire to raise his arm, it may still seem that the proposal really *eliminates* agency rather merely 'reducing' it. For a picture then emerges of the person as being a mere vehicle for a stream of causally interrelated events of which he is in no serious sense the author or originator. On the other hand, it may seem difficult to resist this picture, given that causal determinism reigns in the physical world. For there seems to be no scope to allow *John* to be the cause of the rising of his arm in any sense which makes his causation of this event supplementary to or distinct from its causation by prior physical events. I shall not attempt to resolve this issue here, but we shall return to it later in the chapter.

INTENTIONALITY

In the previous section, I mentioned one popular view according to which actions, rather than constituting a distinct ontological category of their own, are simply events which happen to have mental causes of certain appropriate kinds. The events in question are taken to be bodily movements – in the sense, now, of *bodily motions* – and the mental causes are propositional attitude states, such as beliefs and desires, or, more accurately, events which are the 'onsets' of such states. This sort of view is typically advanced in association with an account of the important notion of *intentionality*. However, the term 'intentionality' is ambiguous, as well as being open to confusion with the quite distinct term 'intensionality' (spelt with an 's' rather than with a 't'), so some preliminary verbal clarification is necessary at this point.

'Intensionality' with an 's' is a term used in philosophical semantics to characterise linguistic contexts which are 'non-extensional'. Thus, '*S* believes that . . .' is a non-extensional, or *intensional*, context because, when it is completed by a sentence containing a referring expression, the truth-value of the whole sentence thus formed can be altered by exchanging that referring expression for another with the same reference. For example: 'John believes that George Eliot was a great novelist' may be true while 'John believes that Mary Ann Evans was a great novelist' is false, even though 'George Eliot' and 'Mary Ann Evans' refer to one and the same person. Now, as I have indicated, 'intentionality' with a 't', as well as being distinct from 'intensionality' with an 's', is itself ambiguous. It has a technical, philosophical sense, in which it is used to describe the property which certain entities – notably, contentful mental states – have of being 'about' things beyond themselves (see chapter 4 and chapter 7). Thus, John's belief that George Eliot was a great novelist is an *intentional state* inasmuch as it is 'about' a certain person and, indeed, 'about' novelists. Clearly, there are certain close connections between intentionality with a 't' in this sense and intensionality with an 's', which I shall return to shortly. Finally, however, there is also the more familiar, everyday sense of 'intentionality' with a 't', in which it is used to characterise *actions*. Thus, in this sense we may speak of John *intentionally* raising his arm and in doing so *unintentionally* poking his neighbour in the eye. And, of course, in this sense we also speak of people having *intentions* to perform certain actions, usually at some time in the future. Talk of such intentions is especially liable to give rise to confusion, because an *intention to act* is clearly an *intentional mental state*, in that it is 'about' a future action, but, furthermore, '*S* has the intention that . . .' is an *intensional context*. So all three notions are in play in this case.[4]

Now, what exactly do we mean when we say, for instance, that John reached towards the salt-cellar *intentionally* and contrast this with the fact that in doing so he knocked over his glass *unintentionally*? Our first thought might be that we are talking here of two different kinds of action, intentional and unintentional ones. But, on second thoughts, we might wonder whether John's reaching towards the salt-cellar and his knocking over the glass should really be regarded as two distinct actions. Perhaps, after all, they are one and the same action, described in two different ways. That, certainly, would be the opinion of those philosophers who hold that actions just *are* bodily motions with mental causes of certain appropriate kinds – the view mentioned at the beginning of this section. For, according to this view, both John's reaching towards the salt-cellar and his knocking over the glass – assuming, as we are, that he does the latter 'in' doing the former – are one and the same bodily motion, with the same mental causes. Insofar as this bodily motion brings John's hand closer to the salt-cellar, it may be described as an action of reaching towards the salt-cellar, and insofar as it has as one of its effects the event of the glass's falling over, it may be described as an action of knocking over the glass. But how can one and the same action be at once intentional and

---

[4] It is in fact a debated issue whether intentions constitute a genuine species of mental state or whether talk of 'intentions' is reducible to talk of beliefs, desires and the actions they cause: see Bruce Aune, *Reason and Action* (Dordrecht: D. Reidel, 1977), pp. 53ff, and Donald Davidson, 'Intending', in his *Essays on Actions and Events* (Oxford: Clarendon Press, 1980). In view of their controversial status, I shall say little explicitly about intentions in this chapter, focusing instead on what it is for an action to be 'intentional'.

unintentional? Very easily, if '*S* intentionally did ...' is an *intensional context* ('intensional' with an 's', of course). For if that is so, it is possible to complete this phrase by two different descriptions of one and the same action to produce two sentences which differ in their truth-values. Let the descriptions in question be, as in our example, 'the reaching towards the salt-cellar' and 'the knocking over of the glass': then '*S* intentionally did the reaching for the salt-cellar' may be true even though '*S* intentionally did the knocking over of the glass' is false. (Of course, '*S* intentionally did the knocking over of the glass' is an extremely stilted way of saying '*S* intentionally knocked over the glass', but is a useful reconstruction for present purposes because it explicitly exploits a singular term referring to an action.)

Philosophers who adopt the foregoing approach to intentional action typically say that an action is only intentional or unintentional *under a description* and that one and the same action may be intentional under one description but unintentional under another. This enables them, moreover, to offer a simple and superficially appealing account of the distinction between actions and those events which merely 'happen to' people. They can say that an action is simply an event – more precisely, a bodily motion – which is intentional under *some* description.[5] Thus, John's knocking over of his glass, although unintentional (under that description), is still an *action* of John's, because it *is* intentional under the description 'reaching towards the salt-cellar'. But, for example, John's blinking involuntarily as someone waves a hand in his face is *not* an action of his, because it is not intentional under *any* description.

This, of course, still leaves the philosophers who hold this view with the task of saying what it is for an action to be intentional under a certain description. And here they tend

---

[5] For the idea that an action is an event that is intentional under some description, see Donald Davidson, 'Agency', in Robert Binkley, Richard Bronaugh and Ausonio Marras (eds.), *Agent, Action, and Reason* (Toronto: University of Toronto Press, 1971), reprinted in Davidson, *Essays on Actions and Events.*

to adopt the following sort of account.[6] Let S be a person and e be an event which is a motion of S's body. Then, it is suggested:

(I) Event e is intentional of S under the description of doing D if and only if e was caused by (the onsets of) certain propositional attitude states of S which constituted S's reasons for doing D in the circumstances.

For example: the motion of John's hand was intentional of John under the description of *reaching towards the salt-cellar* because it was caused by beliefs and desires of John's which constituted, for John, his reasons for *reaching towards the salt-cellar*. But, although this motion of John's hand may also be described as the action of knocking over his glass, the beliefs and desires which caused it did *not* constitute, for John, reasons *for knocking over the glass*, and consequently the action was not intentional of John under this description. The beliefs and desires in question might include, for example, John's belief that the salt-cellar was full and his desire to have more salt on his food. (In more sophisticated accounts of this kind, the more general notion of a 'pro-attitude' may be invoked, rather than the specific notion of 'desire'; but, certainly, it is generally held that purely cognitive states, such as beliefs are commonly taken to be, cannot by themselves provide motivating reasons for action.[7] We shall deal

---

[6] The account of intentionality which follows is loosely modelled on one that appears to be implicit in the work of Donald Davidson: see, especially, his 'Actions, Reasons, and Causes', *Journal of Philosophy* 60 (1963), pp. 685–700, reprinted in his *Essays on Actions and Events*. But Davidson's subtle views have evolved considerably over the years, as he explains in the introduction to the latter book, and so I avoid direct attribution to him of any doctrine that I describe in the text. For critical discussion of Davidson's views, see Ernest LePore and Brian McLaughlin (eds.), *Actions and Events: Perspectives on the Philosophy of Donald Davidson* (Oxford: Blackwell, 1985), part I, and Bruce Vermazen and Merrill B. Hintikka (eds.), *Essays on Davidson: Actions and Events* (Oxford: Clarendon Press, 1985).

[7] The term 'pro-attitude' is Davidson's: see his 'Actions, Reasons, and Causes'. The doctrine that cognitive states by themselves can never motivate action is traceable to David Hume: see his *Treatise of Human Nature*, ed. L. A. Selby-Bigge and P. H. Nidditch (Oxford: Clarendon Press, 1978), bk. II, part III, sect. III, 'Of the influencing motives of the will' (pp. 413–18).

with the topic of reasons for action in more detail later. At the same time, we shall look at a problem of 'deviant causal chains' besetting (I), similar to one which besets the causal theory of perception discussed in chapter 6.)

The foregoing account of action and intentionality is an attractive package, but is open to doubt on a number of grounds. Some philosophers may feel that, because the account abandons any distinctive notion of agent causation, it cannot really capture the difference between genuine actions and those events which merely 'happen to' people. Other philosophers may disagree with the account's view of the causal antecedents of action, perhaps on the grounds that it acknowledges no role for the concept of *volition*. This is an issue to which we shall return shortly. Yet other philosophers may dispute the account's assumptions concerning the *individuation* of actions – and it is to these doubts that we shall turn next.

THE INDIVIDUATION OF ACTIONS

In a famous example due to Elizabeth Anscombe, a man is described as poisoning the inhabitants of a house by pumping contaminated water into its supply from a well, which the inhabitants drink with fatal consequences.[8] There are various ways of describing what this man is doing: he is moving his arm, he is depressing the handle of the pump, he is pumping water from the well, he is contaminating the water-supply to the house, he is poisoning the inhabitants of the house, and he is killing the inhabitants of the house. But are these six *different* things that he is doing, or just six different ways of describing one and the same thing? Normally, when we say that a person is doing two or more different things at once, we have in mind something like the performance of a juggler, who is juggling with several clubs while simultaneously balancing a ball on a stick which he holds in his mouth. But this

---

[8] Elizabeth Anscombe's example may be found in her *Intention*, 2nd edn (Oxford: Blackwell, 1963), pp. 37ff.

is not how we think of the man in Anscombe's example. The theory of action which we looked at in the previous section may appear to explain this, for it implies that there is just *one* thing that the man is doing – moving his arm – which can be variously described in terms of its many different effects. For example, one of the effects of what the man is doing is the death of the inhabitants of the house, which is why, according to this theory, we can describe what he is doing as 'killing the inhabitants of the house'.

However, there is a difficulty with this view of the matter. For suppose we ask *where* and *when* the man is killing the inhabitants of the house. Presumably, if his killing the inhabitants just *is* (identical with) his moving his arm, the killing takes place where and when the arm-moving does. But the arm-moving takes place outside the house and quite some time before the death of the inhabitants. So, it seems, we have to say that the man kills the inhabitants outside the house and quite some time before they die. But that is surely absurd. No doubt defenders of the view in question can suggest ways of deflecting this kind of objection.[9] There is, however, an alternative approach to the individuation of actions which clearly does not have these counterintuitive consequences but which will still allow us to distinguish between the case of the man in Anscombe's example and that of the juggler.

This alternative approach invokes once more the notion of *agent causation*. In Anscombe's example, there are various different events which happen as a result of the motion of the man's arm – events such as the motion of the pump-handle, the motion of the contaminated water and, ultimately, the death of the inhabitants of the house. Each of these events, including the motion of the man's arm, is caused or brought about by the man, who can be described as the agent of all of them. If we think of an action as *an agent's causing or bringing about of an event*, then it seems that

[9] For discussion, see Judith Jarvis Thomson, 'The Time of a Killing', *Journal of Philosophy* 68 (1971), pp. 115–32.

we should indeed say that there are several different actions being performed by the man, since several different events are brought about by him. But these actions, although different, are not *wholly distinct*, because the events in question are linked to one another in a single causal sequence: motion in the man's arm causes motion in the pump-handle, which causes motion in the water, which ultimately causes – via various other events – the death of the inhabitants of the house. On this view, indeed, it seems reasonable to say that some of these actions are related to others as *parts to a whole*. Thus, we might say, *part* of the man's action of pumping the water is his action of moving his arm, since it is *by* moving his arm that he pumps the water. But, we might add, there is *more* to his action of pumping the water than just his moving his arm, since the former additionally involves the motion of his arm causing, via the motion of the pump-handle, the motion of the water. Matters are quite different in the case of the juggler, since the different actions which the juggler is performing do not bear causal and therefore part-whole relations to one another – rather, they are wholly distinct. So, on this view, the way to distinguish between the case of Anscombe's man and the case of the juggler is *not* to say that the man is doing *just one thing* whereas the juggler is doing many different things, but rather to say that the man is not doing many *wholly distinct* things whereas the juggler is.[10]

This still leaves us with the question of where and when the man in Anscombe's example kills the inhabitants of the house. But now we see that this question may not be altogether well-conceived. For if an action is an agent's causing or bringing about of an event, to ask where and when an action took place is to ask where and when the causing of an event took place. Even in the case of event causation, how-

---

[10] The approach to the individuation of actions proposed here is similar to one advocated by Irving Thalberg in his *Perception, Emotion and Action* (Oxford: Blackwell, 1977), ch. 5. See also Judith Jarvis Thomson, *Acts and Other Events* (Ithaca, NY: Cornell University Press, 1977), ch. 4.

ever, such a question is problematic. Suppose that an earthquake (one event) causes the collapse of a bridge (another event). We can ask where and when the earthquake took place and where and when the collapse of the bridge took place. But can we sensibly ask where and when the earthquake's *causing* of the collapse took place? I am not sure that we can. One event's causing of another is not *itself* an event and so should not be assumed to have a time and a location in the way that events clearly do. By the same token, however, an *agent's* causing of an event is not itself an event, so that if this is what an action is, we should not assume that actions have, in any straightforward sense, times and locations. Of course, the events which an action involves have times and locations and, as we have seen, an action may involve a long causal sequence of such events. So perhaps we can say that, in a derivative sense, an action occupies all the times and locations that are occupied by the events which it involves. This would imply that, in Anscombe's example, the man's action of killing the inhabitants of the house begins beside the well when his arm begins to move and ends inside the house when the inhabitants die. I think that this would be the verdict of common sense, too, so to that extent it may be said that common sense supports the present view of action rather than the view discussed earlier.

INTENTIONALITY AGAIN

Of course, if we do adopt this alternative view of actions and their individuation, we shall have to think again about what it means to describe an action as being 'intentional'. If we can no longer say that John's reaching towards the salt just *is* (identical with) his knocking over his glass, we cannot say that we have here one and the same action which is intentional under one description and unintentional under another. And if we abandon the idea that actions are intentional or unintentional only 'under a description', we shall have to abandon, or at least modify, the account of intentionality sketched earlier in this chapter. What could we say instead, adopting the agent causation approach to action? Here is one possibility. Suppose we take our task to be that of analysing what it means to say that an agent A causes or brings about an event e *intentionally*. For present purposes, we are assuming the notion of agent-causation to be primitive and hence in need of no further analysis, so that our task consists in finding a plausible analysis of the adverb 'intentionally' as it is used in the foregoing construction. The proposal I have in mind is simply as follows:[11]

(II)   Agent A brings about event e *intentionally* if and only if A brings about e, knowing that he is bringing about e and desiring e.

For example, in the case described by Anscombe, (II) allows us to say that the man brought about the death of the inhabitants of the house *intentionally* if he brought about the death of the inhabitants, knowing that he was bringing about their death and desiring their death. To this it might be objected that the man cannot have brought about the death of the inhabitants intentionally unless he also brought about the motion of the water intentionally, which (II) fails to require. But the objection is mistaken, since an agent who intentionally brings about a remote event need not have a complete knowledge of the causal chain through which he brings about that event. For instance, the man in Anscombe's example may not understand the workings of the pump or even that the handle that he is moving operates a pump: but if he knows that he is bringing about the motion of the handle and that this will somehow result in the death of the inhabitants of the house, whose death he desires, then I think he can properly be said to be bringing about their death intentionally, as (II) implies.

It may be wondered whether (II) harbours a problem inas-

---

[11] A fuller account and defence of this approach to intentionality may be found in my 'An Analysis of Intentionality', *Philosophical Quarterly* 30 (1980), pp. 294–304. I have simplified the analysis somewhat for the purposes of this book. For a similar approach, see Anthony Kenny, *Will, Freedom and Power* (Oxford: Blackwell, 1975), ch. 4.

much as the context '*A* brings about . . .' is an *extensional* (non-intensional) one whereas the context '*A* knows that he is bringing about . . .' is an *intensional* one. On the contrary, it is the fact that the latter is an intensional context which explains, according to (II), why the context '*A* brings about . . . *intentionally*' is itself an intensional one. Let us see how this works. Suppose it is true that *A* brings about *e* and that $e = e^*$. Then it follows that *A* brings about e^*. This is because '*A* brings about . . .' is an extensional context. Now suppose, however, that it is true that *A* brings about *e* *intentionally* and that $e = e^*$. In that case, it does *not* follow that *A* brings about e^* intentionally. For example, suppose that *A* brings about the death of Napoleon intentionally. Now, since Napoleon is (identical with) Bonaparte, the death of Napoleon is (identical with) the death of Bonaparte. However, we cannot conclude that *A* brings about the death of Bonaparte intentionally. Why not? According to (II), the reason is that *A* may know that he is bringing about the death of Napoleon and yet not know that he is bringing about the death of Bonaparte, even though these events are one and the same, because '*A* knows that he is bringing about . . .' is not an extensional context.

Notice that, according to (II), an action may be *non-intentional* for either or both of two different reasons. If *A* brings about *e* *non*-intentionally, this may either be because *A* does not know that he is bringing about *e* or because *A* does not desire *e*. Suppose, for instance, that a bomber-pilot drops bombs on a munitions factory, knowing that he is bringing about the death of civilian workers but not desiring their death – he only desires the destruction of the factory. Then it seems correct to say, as (II) implies, that the pilot is *not* bringing about the death of the workers *intentionally*. At the same time, however, it seems wrong to say that the pilot is bringing about the death of the workers *un*intentionally, given that he knows that he is bringing about their death. This suggests that 'unintentional' does not simply mean 'not intentional' but, rather, that *A* brings about *e* *unintentionally* if and only if *A* brings about *e* *not* knowing that he is bringing about *e*. Hence, some actions, like the bomber-pilot's, can be neither intentional nor unintentional.

TRYING AND WILLING

On the view of actions which regards them as bodily motions whose causes are the onsets of certain complexes of belief and desire, there seems to be no clear place for the notion of *trying*, nor for the traditional notion of an *act or exercise of the will*. But, equally, the agent-causation approach may seem to leave little scope for these notions either. According to the latter approach, an action is an agent's bringing about of an event. But when we try to do something and fail, it seems that there may be no event that we bring about – and yet we still seem to be 'active' rather than merely 'passive'. Traditionally, such a situation would have been described as one in which an agent performs an 'act of will', or 'wills' to do something, but, for some reason, his will is ineffective – for example, he may suddenly have become paralysed, or his limbs may have been prevented from moving by an irresistible external force. According to this *volitionist* theory, an act of will is conceived as a special 'executive' operation of the mind which occurs *after* the onset of relevant beliefs and desires and which – if it is effective – sets in train a causal sequence of events leading to a desired motion of the body.[12] Here it is worth recalling Wittgenstein's famous question: 'What is left over if I subtract the fact that my arm goes up from the fact that I raise my arm?'.[13] The volitionist would answer that what is left over is the fact that I *willed* to raise my arm.

But acts of will, or 'volitions', have in recent times been

---

[12] Volitionism was widely accepted by philosophers of the early modern period, notably John Locke: see my *Locke on Human Understanding* (London: Routledge, 1995), ch. 6. In recent times it has enjoyed a modest revival: see, for example, Lawrence E. Davis, *Theory of Action* (Englewood Cliffs, NJ: Prentice-Hall, 1979), ch. 1, and Carl Ginet, *On Action* (Cambridge: Cambridge University Press, 1990), ch. 2. I myself defend a version of volitionism in my *Subjects of Experience*, ch. 5.

[13] Ludwig Wittgenstein poses his famous question in his *Philosophical Investigations*, trans. G. E. M. Anscombe, 2nd edn (Oxford: Blackwell, 1958), p. 621.

looked upon unfavourably by many philosophers, including Wittgenstein himself.[14] Why is this? One reason, it seems, is that it is suspected that volitionism is committed to the view that all we ever *do*, really, is to 'will' certain events to happen – and the rest is up to nature rather than to us. This view is frowned upon because it seems to depict us as disembodied 'egos' mysteriously attached to our physical bodies, which move (or fail to move) in various ways at the command of our will. But, although some volitionists may be committed to this picture of human agency, it is far from clear that it is their volitionism which commits them to it. A careful volitionist would not, in any case, say that to exercise the will is to will *some event to happen*: rather, he would say that it is to will *to do something*, that is, to perform some action.[15] And then it is perfectly clear that such a volitionist is not committed to the view that all we ever do, really, is to will: for if we will to do something *and are not obstructed*, then we succeed in *doing* that thing, which is more than just willing to do it.

Another reason why volitionism is sometimes rejected is that it is doubted whether there is any 'common element', such as a volition is thought to be, between a successful action and a failed attempt. The doubt raised here is similar to that raised in the philosophy of perception by advocates of the 'disjunctive' theory, who reject the idea that there is a common element, in the form of a perceptual 'experience', between veridical perception and hallucination (see chapter 6). The philosophers who raise this sort of doubt tend to adopt the view that, in a case of successful action, the agent's *trying* to perform that action is just identical with the action performed – so that, for example, when I try to raise my arm

---

[14] Perhaps the severest critic of volitionism in modern times was Gilbert Ryle: see his *The Concept of Mind* (London: Hutchinson, 1949), ch. 3. I respond to Ryle's criticisms in my *Locke on Human Understanding*, pp. 126ff, and in my *Subjects of Experience*, pp. 152ff.

[15] Here I disagree with H. A. Prichard: see his 'Acting, Willing, Desiring', in his *Moral Obligation: Essays and Lectures* (Oxford: Clarendon Press, 1949). I explain why in my *Subjects of Experience*, pp. 146ff.

and succeed in doing so, my trying to raise it just *is* (identical with) my raising it.[16] They acknowledge, of course, that I can also try to raise my arm and fail to do so, whether because I am paralysed or because an external force is restraining my arm. And in this case, obviously, my trying to raise my arm cannot be identified with my action of raising it nor, it seems, with any other physical action of mine. Yet my trying to raise my arm in this case is not *nothing*: at least some sort of mental event seems to have occurred which constitutes my trying, unsuccessfully, to raise my arm. The philosophers in question may concede this, however: their point is just that it takes further argument to show that a mental event of this sort *also* constitutes my trying to raise my arm when I *succeed* in raising it, which they want to deny. And if no sound argument for this conclusion can be constructed, volitionism may appear to be undermined, for it does assume that willing to raise my arm is the common element between a successful and a failed attempt to raise my arm.

However, although the volitionist does indeed believe in the existence of a common element between a successful action and a failed attempt, in the form of an act of will, he need not identify *trying* with *willing*. That being so, he can acknowledge that *trying* to perform an action is differently constituted in successful and unsuccessful cases. That trying should not be identified with willing, even by the volitionist, is apparent from the fact that sometimes a failed attempt to perform one physical action seems to be constituted not merely by some mental event, but by *another physical action*. For sometimes we try and fail to do something, not because we are paralysed or rendered helpless by an external force, but simply because the objects upon which we act fail to behave in the ways we want and expect them to. For example, an expert darts-player who tries but fails, unexpectedly, to

---

[16] For the view that a successful action is (identical with) a trying, see Hornsby, *Actions*, ch. 3. Hornsby argues plausibly against the commonly held view that trying implies failure or its possibility. See also Brian O'Shaughnessy, *The Will: A Dual Aspect Theory* (Cambridge: Cambridge University Press, 1980), ch. 9.

hit the bull's eye still performs a physical action: he throws the dart. In this case, it seems correct to say that his attempt to hit the bull's eye consists in his wayward throw of the dart. Now, the volitionist may indeed say that, in a case of complete paralysis, trying can only consist in willing. But he need not – and, if I am right, should not – say that trying *always* consists merely in willing. He may say that sometimes – indeed, very often – it consists in much more than that. But that being so, the volitionist cannot be accused of introducing volitions on the unwarranted assumption that a distinctive sort of mental event must constitute trying both in the case of successful actions and in the case of failed attempts.[17]

Yet another objection to volitionism is that, according to some of its critics, volitions cannot be individuated independently of the actions which are supposed to issue from them, which is inconsistent with the general principle that a cause should be identifiable independently of its effects. Thus, it is suggested, we have no way of identifying my supposed volition to raise my arm on a given occasion, other than as something like 'the volition which caused my arm to rise on this occasion'.[18] To see the point of the objection, consider, by way of analogy, the following example. Suppose that a certain explosion occurred and someone decided to let the term 'X' mean 'the cause of this explosion'. Then, clearly, this person would be conveying no information in asserting 'X caused this explosion', other than that the explosion did have a cause. For, provided that the explosion did have a cause, 'The cause of this explosion caused this explosion', though true, is only trivially true. In order to convey substantive information about what caused the explosion, one must be able to identify its cause other than simply as 'the cause of this explosion'. By the same token, then, unless my volition to raise my arm can be identified other than simply as 'the volition which

---

[17] For more on the relation between trying and willing, see my *Subjects of Experience*, pp. 157–61.

[18] For this objection to volitionism, see Richard Taylor, *Action and Purpose*, pp. 68–9. See also A. I. Melden, *Free Action* (London: Routledge and Kegan Paul, 1961), ch. 5. I discuss the objection in my *Locke on Human Understanding*, pp. 124–6.

caused my arm to rise on this occasion', it is vacuous to offer a volitionist account of my action of raising my arm in terms of my volition to raise my arm causing my arm to rise.

However, although we may accept the validity of the foregoing argument, we may question whether one of its premises is true, namely, the premise that volitions cannot be individuated independently of the actions which are supposed to issue from them. Since it is one of the volitionist's central claims that volitions, or acts of will, can sometimes occur in the *absence* of the bodily effects to which they normally give rise – for example, in a case of complete paralysis – it is already implicit in volitionism that volitions are, in principle, identifiable independently of any such effects, in accordance with the general principle mentioned earlier. So it certainly cannot be said that the very *concept* of a 'volition' offends against that general principle. Certainly, the volitionist owes us an account of the individuation of volitions, but there is no obvious reason why it should be inherently more difficult to provide one than it is to provide an account of the identity-conditions of any other kind of mental process or event.

VOLITIONISM VERSUS ITS RIVALS

So far, I have been defending volitionism against various objections, but have said nothing positive in its favour. In order to see what might be said on this score, we need to compare volitionism with its rivals. The two alternative approaches to action which we have looked at are, first, the view that actions are bodily motions whose causes are the onsets of certain complexes of belief and desire and, secondly, the agent-causation theory, which holds that an action is an agent's bringing about of an event. I am assuming that the agent-causation theorist holds that whenever an agent performs an action, there is some *basic* action which he performs, which consists in his bringing about a certain bodily motion. On this view, a *non*-basic action consists, thus, in the agent's bringing about some *further* event *by* bringing about a bodily motion which causes that further event. And the agent-causation theorist takes it as true by definition that a basic action is one which is not done *by* doing anything else whatever.

Against the agent-causation theorist, the volitionist may urge that there *is* in fact something by doing which any agent brings about any event whatever, including his own bodily motions: namely, *willing*. According to volitionism, it is by *willing* to raise my arm that I bring about the rise of my arm. And the volitionist may say that the agent-causation theorist's refusal to acknowledge this renders his own account of action fundamentally mysterious, for it treats certain cases of an agent's bringing about of an event as simply being primitive – that is, as not being amenable to any further analysis or explanation. Moreover, the agent-causation theorist has nothing very obvious to say about cases in which an agent *tries but fails* to perform what the agent-causation theorist would describe as a basic action, such as raising his arm. For in these cases it does not seem correct to say that the agent simply does *nothing*. The volitionist, however, can say that the agent *does* still do something, namely, *will* to perform the action in question.

From this it should be clear that the volitionist regards willing itself as being a kind of action, though not, of course, one which consists in the agent's bringing about of any event. Does this implication of volitionism harbour any difficulties of its own? I do not think so. For willing is conceived to be a kind of *mental* act and many mental acts cannot readily be thought of as involving the bringing about of events of any sort. The act of *thinking* provides a good illustration of this point: when I engage in silent thinking, I *do* something, but what I do does not appear to consist in my causing anything to happen. It may well be the case that in the course of thinking, I experience various forms of auditory or visual imagery, but it would be quite wrong and indeed absurd to regard my thinking as *consisting in* my causing myself to have such experiences.

Let us turn now to volitionism's other rival, the view that actions are bodily motions whose causes are the onsets of certain complexes of belief and desire. The main advantage which volitionism has over this other view is one which it shares with the agent-causation theory, namely, that it does not give the appearance of *eliminating* rather than illuminating the concept of agency. Inasmuch as volitionism regards willing as a primitive and irreducible form of mental *act* – what I described earlier as a special 'executive' operation of the mind, quite distinct from such propositional attitude states as belief and desire – it does not attempt to 'reduce' every case of agency to a special case of event-causation. (At the same time, it does not treat the notion of *agent causation* as primitive, because it analyses an agent's bringing about of an event in terms of that event's being caused by an act of the agent's will. There is no threat of circularity here because, as I remarked a moment ago, willing itself is *not* conceived of as a kind of action which consists in the agent's bringing about of some event.) The objection, then, that the volitionist may have against the second rival theory is that in restricting the mental antecedents of action to beliefs and desires (or the 'onsets' of these), it misses out a crucial element – the element of *choice*. For willing may be thought of as *choosing* to act in one way rather than another – for instance, to buy a lottery ticket or not to, when the opportunity to do so arises. If we are rational, we make our choices *in the light of* our beliefs and desires: but to suppose that our beliefs and desires *causally determine* our actions, as the second rival theory does, seems to eliminate this element of choice and with it any genuine notion of rationality. Here, however, we arrive at the difficult problem of freedom of the will, which we must now look at in more detail.

FREEDOM OF THE WILL

Whether or not we have 'free will' is as much a question for metaphysics as it is for the philosophy of mind and we do not have space here to go into all of its ramifications. Indeed, it may be suspected that the question is somewhat out of place in a book on the philosophy of mind, because it may be doubted whether empirical considerations concerning the nature of the human mind have much bearing upon it. How, it may be wondered, could empirical evidence ever be taken to show that we do or do not have 'freedom of will'? But in fact there are recent empirical findings which do seem to have a bearing on this question, generated by some ingenious experiments of the eminent neurophysiologist Benjamin Libet.[19]

In Libet's experiments, subjects were asked to perform some simple bodily movement, such as flexing a finger, on repeated occasions, each time choosing for themselves when to initiate the action. Subjects were asked to estimate the time at which they chose to initiate a movement by simultaneously noting the clock-position of a revolving spot of light. (Such an estimate is, of course, liable to error, but Libet devised a way of measuring the likely error by another experimental procedure.) Throughout an experiment, a device attached to the subject's scalp was used to record electrical activity in the part of the brain known as the motor cortex, which is concerned with voluntary bodily movement. It was already known that, prior to a voluntary bodily movement, a slow negative shift in electrical potential takes place in the motor cortex, beginning just over half a second before the movement itself. What Libet discovered, however, is that the subject's conscious choice to make the movement occurs only about one *fifth* of a second before the movement begins, and thus significantly *later* than the onset of the brain's so-called 'readiness potential'. The implication seems to be that voluntary movements are not *initiated* by the conscious 'choices' of subjects, but rather by unconscious brain-processes which precede those 'choices'.

What can we conclude from these findings, assuming that they are reliable?[20] One's first thought might be that the

---

[19] See Benjamin Libet, 'Unconscious Cerebral Initiative and the Role of Conscious Will in Voluntary Action', *Behavioral and Brain Sciences* 8 (1985), pp. 529–66, reprinted in his *Neurophysiology of Consciousness* (Boston, MA: Birkhaüser, 1993).

[20] To be fair, some doubts have been raised about Libet's experiments by, for example, Daniel C. Dennett: see his *Consciousness Explained* (Harmondsworth: Penguin Books, 1991), pp. 162ff.

findings show that 'choice' is just an illusion – that when one imagines onself to be moving one's finger of one's own conscious volition, the movement is in fact being caused by prior unconscious processes which also cause one's conscious state of seeming to 'choose' to make the movement. This would mean that conscious 'choices' or 'volitions' are *epiphen-omenal* rather than genuinely efficacious. What clearer empir-ical demonstration of our *lack* of free will could there be? However, matters are not so simple, as Libet himself points out. For one thing, Libet discovered that subjects appear to have a 'veto' power over their voluntary movements, that is, that even *after* the moment of conscious choice, it is still pos-sible for a subject to refrain from making the movement. He suggests, therefore, that even though our conscious choices do not *initiate* our actions, we still exercise control over our actions through our choices to act or not to act. Equally inter-esting, in view of our discussion of volitionism earlier in this chapter, is the fact that Libet's experiments seem to provide empirical support for the very concept of a 'volition', con-ceived as a special kind of 'executive' mental operation. Indeed, it is known from other experimental work that when movements of a subject's limbs are brought about by direct electrical stimulation of the motor cortex, the subject declares emphatically that he is *not* moving his limbs himself, of his own volition.[21]

However, interesting though these findings may be, it may be felt that they do not go to the heart of the problem of free will. Even if it is conceded that Libet's experiments are consistent with the verdict of 'folk psychology' that conscious acts of will or choice have a genuine causal role to play in the genesis of our voluntary bodily movements, the freedom of our will still seems to be under threat when we reflect on the question of whether or not our conscious choices are *themselves* causally determined by prior events and processes.

---

[21] Some of these classic studies of stimulation of the cortex are due to Wilder Pen-field: see his *The Excitable Cortex in Conscious Man* (Liverpool: Liverpool University Press, 1958).

For however we answer this question, the freedom of our will may appear to be compromised. On the one hand, if our conscious choices are simply the causal consequences of long sequences of cause and effect stretching back to times before our birth, it is hard to see in what sense *we* can be responsible for those choices.[22] But, on the other hand, if our conscious choices are *un*caused, or not fully causally determined, it may seem hard to see how they can be anything but random occurrences happening merely by chance – which again seems incompatible with the idea that *we* are responsible for them.

Perhaps, though, there is a way through the horns of this apparent dilemma. As I mentioned earlier, we take it to be a hallmark of the rational person that he makes his choices in the light of his beliefs and desires: but this is not necessarily the same as saying that a rational person is one whose choices are *caused* by his beliefs and desires. Indeed, one's instinct is to say that it is a contradiction in terms to speak of a *choice* being *causally determined* in this way. When we choose how to act in the light of our beliefs and desires, we do not feel ourselves to be *caused* by those beliefs and desires to choose in the way we do. Rather, we conceive of our beliefs and desires as giving us *reasons* to choose. Choosing to act in a certain way *for a reason* can hardly be described as a mere chance occurrence, but neither does it seem proper to conceive of it as being causally determined. Whether this way through the dilemma is really available to us is a question that we shall have to return to, when we discuss in more detail the relationship between reasons for and causes of action.

But even if we find that we can distinguish, in an appropriate way, between reasons and causes, problems still remain.

---

[22] In defence of this claim that free will is incompatible with causal determinism, see Peter van Inwagen, *An Essay on Free Will* (Oxford: Clarendon Press, 1983), ch. 3. I am persuaded by van Inwagen's arguments and consequently reject the rival doctrine that free will is compatible with determinism. But many contemporary philosophers, it has to be said, accept the latter doctrine: see, for example, Daniel C. Dennett, *Elbow Room: The Varieties of Free Will Worth Wanting* (Oxford: Clarendon Press, 1984).

Surely, it may be said, our conscious choices, if they exist, are either parts of the universal network of cause and effect, or they are not: but if they are, then they are causally determined and our will is consequently not 'free', while if they are not, then they are causally inefficacious and 'choice' is an illusion. The problem becomes especially pressing if one presupposes the truth of the (strong) principle of the causal closure of the physical, discussed in chapter 2. As I stated it there, this is the principle that at every time at which a physical state has a cause, it has a fully sufficient physical cause. The principle implies that any bodily motion supposedly caused by an agent's choice has a fully sufficient physical cause at the time of the choice – and that that physical cause likewise has a fully sufficient physical cause at every time prior to the time of the choice. We seem forced to conclude that either (1) the agent's act of 'choosing' is in fact identical with some physical state – presumably, a state of the agent's brain – which is fully causally determined at all previous times by prior physical states, or else (2) the agent's act of 'choosing' is causally inefficacious. Neither alternative seems compatible with the notion that we have 'free will'.

But, again, we should not rush to such a conclusion. As we saw in chapter 2, the strong principle of the causal closure of the physical is contestable. Moreover, we should bear in mind Libet's findings concerning the 'veto' power of the will. Even though unconscious processes in an agent's brain may initiate a certain bodily movement prior to the agent's act of consciously choosing to make that movement, it seems that the movement is not rendered *inevitable* by those brain-processes at the time at which they occur: the agent, it seems, retains the power to permit the movement to go ahead or else to countermand it, for some fractions of a second before the movement takes place. This picture of the role of conscious choice in human action does, I think, make sense and appears to be compatible with the available empirical evidence. But I think it will only make sense to philosophers who do not attempt to reduce the notion of an act of choosing to that of an event that merely 'happens to' a person. To adopt this picture, I think we have to accept the concept of agency – the concept of being 'active' as opposed to 'passive' – as primitive and irreducible. Very arguably, however, we must do this in any case if we are to retain our familiar self-conception as autonomous and rational subjects of experience. And without that self-conception, it seems, rational inquiry itself becomes impossible for us and with it all philosophical argument.

MOTIVES, REASONS AND CAUSES

Why do people act in the ways that they do? Sometimes, in asking such a question, we are inquiring into people's *motives* for acting in certain ways. At other times we are seeking to uncover their *reasons* for acting. And at yet others we want to know the *causes* of their actions. Not all philosophers of action would agree that the notions of motive, reason and cause are perfectly distinct, but some of our ordinary ways of talking suggest that they are. Suppose, for instance, that a youth has been brought before a juvenile court accused of some act of vandalism, such as breaking all the windows in his school. Asked for his *reasons* for behaving in this way, the youth might reply that he had *no* reason – that he did it just because he felt like doing it when the opportunity arose. In particular, he may deny that he did it with premeditation. And, indeed, we might agree that the action was a thoroughly irrational and senseless one. On the other hand, a psychologist might consider that the youth had strong *motives* for acting in this way – for instance, that he did it out of feelings of frustration, bitterness or jealousy. Yet again, a social worker might try to explain the youth's behaviour as being *caused* by his poor home background and ill-treatment in infancy.

One questionable implication of such ways of talking is that actions which proceed from emotional states, such as fear or jealousy, are for that very reason 'irrational' and to be contrasted with actions which proceed from a cool calculation of likely costs and benefits. But the model of the perfectly rational agent as an emotionless calculator is a distorted and shallow one.[23] Sometimes, an 'emotional' response to a situation is not only understandable but *right*, in the sense that we should regard it as a moral defect in a person not to react in that way. And there is, surely, no incompatibility between being rational and being moral. In any case, no sharp distinction can be drawn between acting 'emotionally' and acting 'rationally', given that no sharp distinction can be drawn between emotion and desire. For, as I remarked earlier, it is generally accepted that purely cognitive states, such as beliefs are commonly taken to be, cannot by themselves provide motivating reasons for action – desire (or at least some sort of 'pro-attitude') is additionally required. Indeed, the very mention here of 'motivating reasons' demonstrates that talk of 'motives' and talk of 'reasons' for action cannot be held entirely apart.

In support of the contention that no sharp distinction can be drawn between emotion and desire, I must emphasise that emotions should not be thought of as mere 'feelings' – even if, as in the case of fear, they sometimes involve bodily sensations of certain distinctive kinds – since they are *intentional* states, in the sense of being 'about' things beyond themselves. For example, one may be angry *about* another person's rudeness or anxious *about* an impending job interview. And traditionally, indeed, desire was itself accounted an emotion or 'affect', by philosophers such as Descartes and Spinoza.

A more contestable issue is whether we can hold apart talk of reasons for action and talk of the causes of action. In the previous section, I suggested that to describe a rational person as someone who makes his choices in the light of his beliefs and desires is not necessarily the same as saying that a rational person is one whose choices are *caused* by his beliefs and desires. But this suggestion may be challenged, on the following grounds. Suppose we are seeking a person's reasons

---

[23] For more on the relations between reason and emotion, see Ronald de Sousa, *The Rationality of Emotion* (Cambridge, MA: MIT Press, 1987). See also Thalberg, *Perception, Emotion and Action*, ch. 2, and Anthony Kenny, *Action, Emotion and Will* (London: Routledge and Kegan Paul, 1963), ch. 4.

for performing a certain action. For instance, to use an earlier example, suppose we want to know what John's reasons were for reaching for the salt-cellar. Perhaps, if we ask him, he will tell us himself that he did this because he desired more salt on his food and believed that the salt-cellar was full. But, it may be urged, John's having this desire and this belief, although it *gave him* a reason for acting as he did, did not actually *constitute* his reason for so acting unless it was at least partly causally responsible for his action of reaching for the salt-cellar. On this view, the only way in which we can explain the difference between merely having a reason to act in a certain way and actually acting *for* that reason, is to suppose that in the latter case one acts *because* one has the reason, in a *causal* sense of 'because'. This implies that, far from it being the case that reasons for and causes of action are quite distinct, reasons must *be* causes when agents act 'for' reasons.[24]

However, although it is true that there is a difference between merely having a reason to act in a certain way and actually acting *for* that reason, which calls for some explanation, it is not incontestable that the only way to explain this difference is the one just proposed. Indeed, against this explanation we may lay the fact, mentioned earlier, that when we choose how to act in the light of our beliefs and desires, we do not feel ourselves to be *caused* by those beliefs and desires to choose in the way we do. Moreover, the theory of action which maintains that reasons are causes is beset with a problem of 'deviant causal chains' similar to the one affecting the causal theory of perception which we discussed in chapter 6. Indeed, the problem is arguably more intractable in the case of this theory of action.

To see how the problem arises here, consider another example of John's behaviour at the dining table. Suppose, this time, that John actually desires to knock over his glass,

---

[24] For this line of argument that reasons must be causes, see Davidson, 'Actions, Reasons, and Causes'. Many philosophers, however, have denied that reasons can be causes: see, for example, Taylor, *Action and Purpose*, ch. 10.

perhaps in order to create a diversion while he steals a dia-
mond necklace from the woman seated next to him. He
therefore reaches towards the salt-cellar, as if to pick it up,
with the intention of knocking over his glass in a show of
clumsiness. However, so excited is he with the prospect of
securing the necklace, that his very desire to knock over the
glass causes his hand to tremble as it approaches the glass
and he really *does* knock it over accidentally rather than intentionally. At this point, let us recall the causal analysis of
intentionality examined earlier, where S is a person and e is
an event which is a motion of S's body:

(I)   Event e is intentional of S under the description of doing
      D if and only if e was caused by (the onsets of) certain
      propositional attitude states of S which constituted S's
      reasons for doing D in the circumstances.

It appears that (I) implies, mistakenly, that John in our latest
example knocked over his glass *intentionally*: for, according to
the theory of action now under consideration, the motion of
John's hand was indeed caused by beliefs and desires of his
which constituted his reasons for *knocking over his glass* on this
occasion. That is to say, John had at this time certain beliefs
and desires, which gave him a reason for knocking over the
glass, *and his having those beliefs and desires was causally responsible
for his knocking over the glass*, whence it follows from (I) that
John knocked over the glass intentionally. And yet, plainly,
he did not.[25]

   What emerges from this example, I think, is that the difference between merely having a reason to act in a certain
way and actually acting *for* that reason, *cannot* be explained
simply by saying that in the latter case one acts *because* one

---

[25] Discussing a similar example, Donald Davidson says that he 'despair[s] of spelling
out . . . the way in which attitudes must cause actions if they are to rationalize
them': see his 'Freedom to Act', in Ted Honderich (ed.), *Essays on Freedom of Action*
(London: Routledge and Kegan Paul, 1973), reprinted in Davidson, *Essays on
Actions and Events* (see p. 79). For one interesting attempt to solve the problem of
deviant causal chains, see Christopher Peacocke, *Holistic Explanation: Action, Space,
Interpretation* (Oxford: Clarendon Press, 1979), ch. 2.

has the reason, in a *causal* sense of 'because'. Indeed, being *caused* to act in a certain way by the beliefs and desires which give one a reason to act in that way actually seems to be incompatible with acting in that way *for* that reason. If that is so, then the problem is not simply one of finding an 'appropriate' causal relation between reasons and actions which excludes 'deviant' examples like the one which we have just examined: rather, the theory of action which maintains that reasons are causes must be rejected altogether. (Note, incidentally, that the alternative analysis of intentionality mooted earlier – (II) above – is not defeated by this example, since we can plausibly say that John did *not* know that he was bringing about the event of the glass's falling over. He did believe, and believe truly, that he was bringing about an event of that *type*, but did not know that he was bringing about the *particular* event of that type which occurred.)

There is one other issue that I should mention which bears upon the question of how reasons for action are related to causes of action: this is the problem of so-called *weakness of will*, or (to use the Greek word for it) *akrasia*. Sometimes people fail to take what they apparently believe, all things considered, to be the best (most desirable) course of action available to them in certain circumstances. One interpretation of such a situation is that the person involved cannot *really* have a stronger desire to take the course of action in question rather than any other, despite what he might say to the contrary. And, indeed, if reasons *are* causes, it is hard to see how any alternative interpretation is possible. For, on this view, the reasons *for* which an agent acts are the beliefs and desires which actually cause him to act in the way he does, from which it appears to follow that if an agent does not act in accordance with a professed desire, it must be because it was overridden by another, stronger desire, which was his real reason for action. However, on the alternative view that choices to act made in the light of one's beliefs and desires are not *caused* by those beliefs and desires, it seems to be at least possible, albeit irrational, to fail to choose a course of action which one desires above all others. In other words, it seems that, on this view, the phenomenon of weakness of will really is possible and, indeed, that its name is entirely apt. However, the complexity of the issue is too great for it to be examined any further here, so I shall leave it now, with the warning that it would be rash to try to adjudicate between the two rival views on the basis of so contentious a matter.[26]

CONCLUSIONS

In this chapter, we have looked at three different theories of action: (1) the theory which takes actions to be bodily motions whose causes are the onsets of certain complexes of belief and desire, (2) the agent-causation theory, which holds that an action is an agent's bringing about of an event and takes the latter notion as primitive and irreducible, and (3) the volitional theory, which contends that all action involves a special 'executive' operation of the mind, variously called a 'volition', 'act of will', or 'choice'. As may be suspected, my own sympathies lie with the volitional theory because, like the agent-causation theory, it does not seek to eliminate the notion of agency or reduce it to something else, and yet it is not committed to a distinctive and seemingly mysterious species of causation. I believe that volitionism is implicit in our common-sense or 'folk-psychological' ways of thinking and talking about action, that it can be defended against the standard philosophical objections to it, and that it is consistent with or even confirmed by empirical investigations into the neurophysiology of action. But I should emphasise that volitionism is, none the less, still a minority opinion amongst contemporary philosophers of mind.

We have also explored questions to do with intentionality, freedom of the will, and the motivational basis of human agency. On the matter of intentionality and the related ques-

---

[26] For Donald Davidson's characteristically subtle treatment of the problem of weakness of will, see his 'How is Weakness of the Will Possible?', in Joel Feinberg (ed.) *Moral Concepts* (Oxford: Oxford University Press, 1970), reprinted in Davidson, *Essays on Actions and Events*.

tion of how actions are to be individuated, we examined two rival approaches, tentatively favouring one which is congenial to the agent-causation theory and volitionism. Unsurprisingly, we arrived at no firm solution to the problem of free will, but it seems that it does at least make sense to suppose that our conscious choices to act could be both causally efficacious and rational without being fully causally determined by prior physical events. There is no clear-cut case for saying that the reasons for which an agent acts must be causes of his actions. Indeed, there is a case for saying, to the contrary, that our familiar self-conception as autonomous and rational subjects of experience requires us *not* to think of ourselves as being caused to act by the beliefs and desires which constitute our reasons for action. Perhaps that self-conception may be challenged as being ultimately incoherent, given a fully naturalistic view of human beings and the world which they inhabit. I am not at all sure that such a challenge would be warranted, but I am fairly confident that our current self-conception is not one that we could easily abandon. Moreover, I strongly suspect that philosophy itself could not survive its abandonment.

10

Personal identity and self-knowledge

In chapter 1, I described the philosophy of mind as being the philosophical study of minded things just insofar as they are minded. And the general term which I introduced to refer to something with a mind was *subject of experience* – interpreting 'experience' here in a broad sense, to include any kind of sensation, perception or thought. I take it that the term 'subject of experience' is more extensive than the term 'person' – that is, that although all persons are (at least potentially) subjects of experience, not all subjects of experience are persons. This is because I think that at least some non-human creatures, such as chimpanzees, are certainly subjects of experience and yet that they may not be persons. It is perfectly conceivable that there should be non-human persons, but it is open to question whether any actually exist. What, then, is distinctive of persons as opposed to other subjects of experience? Just this, I suggest: persons are *selves* – that is to say, they are subjects of experience which have the capacity to recognise themselves as being individual subjects of experience. Selves possess reflexive self-knowledge. By 'reflexive self-knowledge' I mean, roughly speaking, knowledge of one's own identity and conscious mental states – knowledge of who one is and of what one is thinking and feeling. As we shall see, there are some complexities involved in spelling out this notion in a completely satisfactory way, if indeed that can ultimately be achieved. But – again, roughly speaking – having the kind of reflexive self-knowledge which makes one a person goes hand-in-hand with possessing a 'first-person' concept of oneself, the linguistic reflection of which resides in an ability to use the word 'I' comprehendingly to refer to oneself.

But what sort of thing does the word 'I' refer to, assuming that it does indeed refer to something? What sort of thing am I? In raising this question, of course, we return to some of the issues discussed in chapter 2. There we saw that different philosophers have offered very different answers to this question, some holding that 'I' refers to a certain body – 'my' body – some that it refers to something altogether non-physical, such as an immaterial soul or spirit, and some that it refers to something which is a combination of body and soul. Yet another possible answer is that 'I' refers to a collection of thoughts and feelings – 'my' thoughts and feelings. But it may surprise us that philosophers can disagree so radically about what sort of thing 'I' refers to and yet be so certain that it does refer to *something*. Perhaps we should question that assumption. And even if we accept it, perhaps we should question the assumption that 'I' refers to a thing of the *same* sort or kind whenever it is used to refer to something. Perhaps persons or selves do not constitute a *kind* of things, all instances of which share the same identity-conditions. Perhaps to be a person or self is to occupy some role or perform some function – a role or function which could be occupied or performed by things of many different kinds. For example, it might be held that being a person is a role which my body occupies now and has occupied for most of my existence, but that for the first few weeks or months of my existence it did not occupy that role. This would imply that, in my case at least, 'I' refers to my body, but that there was a time when I (that is, my body) existed but was not (yet) a person. We shall look more closely at this and other possibilities in the course of this chapter.

Another set of issues which we should explore concerns our knowledge of our own mental states and their content. How is it that one can seem to have incontestable knowledge of what one is thinking and feeling? Or is our belief that we have such knowledge in fact unfounded? If so, we must still explain the prevalence and tenacity of that belief. However, let us make a start with the phenomenon of self-reference, that is, with the comprehending use of the word 'I'.

THE FIRST PERSON

Although children pick up the use of the first-person pronoun, 'I', quite early in the course of their linguistic development, understanding the semantics of first-person discourse is a surprisingly difficult matter. It is easy enough to say what the linguistic function of the word 'I' is, in a way which will satisfy most people: 'I' is the word (in English) which everyone uses to refer to him or herself. Every human language appears to have a word or expression equivalent to this. But the difficulty which philosophers have in understanding the meaning of the word 'I' arises from the difficulty of spelling out, in a non-circular and illuminating way, what it is to 'refer to oneself' in the special way that is associated with the comprehending use of the word 'I'. I deliberately speak here of the *comprehending* use of the word 'I', because, for instance, even a mindless computer might be said to be 'referring to itself' when it displays some such message on its screen as 'I am ready'. Equally, a parrot could conceivably be taught to utter the words 'I feel hungry' whenever it felt hungry, in which case it might be said to be using the word 'I' to refer to itself – but this wouldn't imply that it had a first-person concept of itself, as appears to be required for the comprehending use of the word 'I'.

The difficulty that I am alluding to can perhaps best be brought out by comparing the comprehending use of the word 'I' to refer to oneself with the comprehending use of various other singular terms to refer to oneself. I can, for instance, use my personal name, 'Jonathan Lowe', to refer to myself. Equally, I can use certain definite descriptions to refer to myself, such as 'the author of this book' or 'the person seated in this chair'. However, it is a curious feature of the word 'I' that it seems to be *guaranteed* to refer to a quite specific person on any occasion of its use, in such a way that the person using it cannot mistake which person it refers to – namely, him or herself. No such feature attaches to other ways of referring to ourselves. I might forget that I am Jonathan Lowe or come to doubt whether I am the author of this book, but I cannot doubt that I am *I*. This might be dismissed as a trivial matter, like the fact that I cannot doubt that Jonathan Lowe is Jonathan Lowe. But that would be too quick and superficial a response. That this is no trivial matter can be brought out by considering the following kind of example. Suppose that, upon entering a strange house and walking along a corridor, I see a human figure approaching me and form the following judgement: 'That person looks suspicious'. Then I suddenly realise that the person in question is *myself*, seen reflected in a mirror at the end of the corridor. Although, in one sense, I knew to whom I was referring in using the demonstrative phrase 'that person' – namely, the person who appeared to be approaching me – there is clearly another sense in which I did *not* know to whom I was referring, since I was unwittingly referring to myself. Clearly, then, when I 'refer to myself' in the way involved in this example, I do not refer to myself in the way I do when I use the word 'I' – for in the latter case there is no similar possibility of my failing to know to whom I am referring.

This feature of the use of the word 'I' is closely linked with the fact that certain first-person judgements exhibit what is sometimes called 'immunity to error through misidentification'.[1] It is perfectly possible to make a mistaken first-person judgement, of the form 'I am *F*', just as it is possible to make a mistaken third-person judgement, of the form '*S* is *F*'. However, whereas '*S* is *F*' can be mistaken in either of two different ways, certain judgements of the form 'I am *F*' can apparently be mistaken in only one way. Compare, for example,

---

[1] The expression 'immunity to error through misidentification' is due to Sydney Shoemaker: see his 'Self-Reference and Self- Awareness', *Journal of Philosophy* 65 (1968), pp. 555–67, reprinted in his *Identity, Cause, and Mind: Philosophical Essays* (Cambridge: Cambridge University Press, 1984) and in Quassim Cassam (ed.), *Self-Knowledge* (Oxford: Oxford University Press, 1994). The inspiration for this notion comes from Ludwig Wittgenstein: see *The Blue and Brown Books*, 2nd edn (Oxford: Blackwell, 1969), pp. 66ff. See also Gareth Evans, *The Varieties of Reference* (Oxford: Clarendon Press, 1982), pp. 179–91.

the two judgements 'John feels angry' and 'I feel angry'. In making the first judgement, I might be mistaken either about *what* John feels or about *who* feels angry. On the one hand, perhaps John really feels jealous rather than angry. On the other hand, perhaps it is not John who feels angry, but another person whom I have mistaken for John. But now consider the second judgement, 'I feel angry'. Here, too, it is possible for me to be mistaken about *what* I feel – maybe I think I feel angry when really what I feel is jealousy. However, what doesn't seem to make sense, in this case, is that I should be mistaken not about *what* is felt but about *who* feels it. It doesn't seem to make sense that I should mistake another person's anger for my own. But not all first-person judgements have this property of immunity to error through misidentification: the only ones that do, it seems, involve the attribution to oneself of some conscious psychological state. Consider, for instance, the judgement 'I am touching the table with my hand', made on the basis of what I can see and feel. It is conceivable, if unlikely, that it is not in fact my hand that is touching the table, but the very similar hand of the person sitting next to me – and that what I can really feel is my hand touching another nearby object. In that case, I am mistaken about *who* is touching the table, in a way in which I could not be mistaken about *who* is feeling angry when I make the judgement 'I feel angry'.

Some philosophers seem to think that, when the word 'I' is used as it is in making the judgement 'I feel angry', it cannot really be functioning as a referring-expression at all, *precisely because* mistaken reference is apparently ruled out in such cases.[2] They take the view that a genuine act of reference to something can occur only if the possibility of mistake or failure exists: as they might put it, where there is no possibility of failure, there is no possibility of success either.

---

[2] For doubts about whether 'I' is a referring expression, see G. E. M. Anscombe, 'The First Person', in Samuel Guttenplan (ed.), *Mind and Language* (Oxford: Clarendon Press, 1975), reprinted in G. E. M. Anscombe, *Metaphysics and the Philosophy of Mind* (Oxford: Blackwell, 1981). For discussion, see Andy Hamilton, 'Anscombian and Cartesian Scepticism', *Philosophical Quarterly* 41 (1991), pp. 39–54.

Hence, they regard the word 'I' in such contexts as no more having a referential function than the word 'it' has such a function in a statement such as 'It is raining'. So what, then, *is* the function of the word 'I' in such contexts, according to these philosophers? Here they are less clear, but they tend to say that sentences like 'I feel angry' are used, in reality, not so much to express *judgements*, which could be true or false, as to make *avowals*. On this view, to say 'I feel angry' is to express *one's feelings*, rather than to express a judgement about what one is feeling. Such an 'avowal' is regarded as a verbal expression of emotion, comparable with such non-verbal 'expressions' of emotion as angry looks and gestures.[3]

However, most philosophers would, I think, be unpersuaded by this doctrine, not least because they would not subscribe to the principle that any genuine act of reference must leave room for the possibility of error. Furthermore, they would regard it as being inherently implausible to suppose that the same word, 'I', could have two radically different functions. For that the word 'I' has a referential function in many contexts of its use seems hardly disputable. How, then, would these philosophers explain why the word 'I' seems incapable of reference-failure? Some of them may attribute this quite simply to its being a so-called *token-reflexive* expression, akin to such expressions as 'here' and 'now'. Just as any utterance of the word 'here' standardly refers to the place at which the word is uttered and any utterance of the word 'now' standardly refers to the time at which the word is uttered, so, on this account, any utterance of the word 'I' standardly refers to the person who is uttering it. Thus, the semantic rule governing the use of the word 'I' precludes the possibility of someone mistakenly using the word 'I' to refer to anyone other than him or herself.[4] How-

---

[3] In the *Philosophical Investigations*, Wittgenstein says at one point: 'When I say "I am in pain", I do not point to a person who is in pain . . . I don't name any person. Just as I don't name anyone when I groan with pain. Though someone else sees who is in pain from the groaning.' See Ludwig Wittgenstein, *Philosophical Investigations*, trans. G. E. M. Anscombe, 2nd edn (Oxford: Blackwell, 1958), p. 404.

[4] For more on token-reflexivity and the comparison between 'I' and 'now', see D. H. Mellor, 'I and Now', *Proceedings of the Aristotelian Society* 89 (1989), pp. 79–94,

ever, although it is important to recognise the token-reflexive character of the word 'I', it does not appear that appeal to this alone can explain all the distinctive features of first-person reference which we have been examining. This is because one cannot capture what is special about the comprehending use of the word 'I' to refer to oneself merely by citing the semantic rule that any utterance of the word 'I' standardly refers to the person uttering it. For that rule imposes no requirement that the person – or, indeed, thing – uttering the word 'I' should have a first-person conception of itself as a self-aware subject of experience: and yet the comprehending use of the word 'I' to refer to oneself does require this.

I have to confess that I know of no wholly satisfactory way of providing a non-circular analysis of the concept of self-reference which is peculiar to the comprehending use of the word 'I'. An ability to think *of oneself as oneself* and to attribute to oneself, thought of in this way, various conscious thoughts and feelings seems to be one which is primitive and irreducible, in the sense that one cannot model this ability on any other more general ability to think of particular objects and attribute properties to them. At some stage in a normal child's intellectual development, it acquires this special ability, but how it achieves this must remain something of a mystery so long as we have no way of characterising the ability in question save in its own terms.[5]

PERSONS AND CRITERIA OF IDENTITY

Given that the word 'I' is guaranteed a reference, on every occasion of its comprehending use, to what sort of thing does

reprinted in his *Matters of Metaphysics* (Cambridge: Cambridge University Press, 1991). See also the papers in part I of Palle Yourgrau (ed.), *Demonstratives* (Oxford: Oxford University Press, 1990) and John Campbell, *Past, Space, and Self* (Cambridge, MA: MIT Press, 1994), ch. 3 and ch. 4.

[5] For wide-ranging further discussion of the concept and development of self-consciousness, from both philosophical and psychological perspectives, see José Luis Bermúdez, Anthony Marcel and Naomi Eilan (eds.), *The Body and the Self*

it refer when it is so used? The quick answer would be that it refers to a particular *person* or *self*. But, as I have been using the terms 'person' and 'self', this is effectively just true by definition and so not especially revealing – for I have characterised a person as being a subject of experience which has a first-person concept of itself. We have not yet established that either persons, or subjects of experience more generally, constitute a distinct *sort* or *kind* of things in the way, say, that stars, oak trees and chairs all constitute distinct kinds of things. The instances of a genuine sort or kind must at least share the same identity-conditions, enabling us to count such instances and trace their careers over time. If someone asks me how many oak trees there are in a certain wood at a certain time, I know, at least in principle, how to discover the answer to that question, because I know what makes one oak tree numerically distinct from another at a given moment of time – namely, the fact that it occupies a distinct and separate region of space of a shape apt to accommodate just one oak tree. Likewise, if someone asks me whether the oak tree now growing in a certain part of the wood is the *same* oak tree as the one which was growing there forty years ago, I know, at least in principle, how to discover the answer to this question, because I understand the *persistence-conditions* of oak trees – that is, I understand what sorts of changes an oak tree can and cannot undergo if it is to survive over time. For instance, I know that oak trees can survive transplantation and hence that it would be rash to assume that this oak tree is identical with a previously encountered one merely because it has the right sort of age and is growing in the same place.

The question that we must ask now is whether subjects of experience, and more specifically *persons*, do indeed constitute a genuine *kind* of things, all instances of which share the same identity-conditions, enabling us to count persons and trace their careers over time. On the face of it, the answer

(Cambridge, MA: MIT Press, 1995). See also José Luis Bermúdez, *The Paradox of Self-Consciousness* (Cambridge, MA: MIT Press, 1998).

to this question is clearly 'Yes'. We seem to assume that we can count persons at least as easily as we can count oak trees and that persons have persistence-conditions determining what sorts of changes they can and cannot undergo if they are to survive over time. It may be that we are a little unclear about what to say in certain borderline cases, but the same is true as regards oak trees, which we none the less consider to constitute a genuine and indeed natural kind of things.

So what *are* the principles which govern how we count persons and trace their careers over time? What we are looking for, here, is what many philosophers would call a *criterion of personal identity*.[6] The general form which a criterion of identity for things of a kind K takes is this:

(C_k) If x and y are things of kind K, then x is identical with y if and only if x and y stand in the relation R_k to one another.

So the question that we must try to answer is this: how do a person P_1 and a person P_2 have to be related to one another if P_1 is to be *identical* with P_2? The problem has two aspects – one concerning the identity of persons *at* a time ('synchronic' identity) and the other concerning the identity of persons *over* time ('diachronic' identity) – the second of which is usually regarded as the more difficult. Clearly, there are many trivial and uninformative answers to the question that has just been raised. It would be true, but only trivially so, to say that P_1 and P_2 must be related by *identity* if they are to be identical with one another. What is sought is a non-trivial and informative answer to the question in hand. More generally, the relation R_k mentioned in a criterion of identity of the form of (C_k) must not be the relation of identity itself, nor any relation which can only be stated in terms which involve or presuppose the identity of things of kind K.

---

[6] For more on the general notion of a criterion of identity, see my 'What Is a Criterion of Identity?', *Philosophical Quarterly* 39 (1989), pp. 1–21, reprinted in Harold W. Noonan (ed.), *Identity* (Aldershot: Dartmouth, 1993) and my 'Objects and Criteria of Identity', in Bob Hale and Crispin Wright (eds.), *A Companion to the Philosophy of Language* (Oxford: Blackwell, 1997).

Some philosophers have maintained that persons have a *bodily* criterion of identity. For instance, some have maintained that a person P_1 and a person P_2 are identical, either at a time or over time, if and only if P_1 and P_2 have the same body. Against this, it may be pointed out that persons can survive the loss of many parts of their bodies. However, this is not a decisive consideration, since it is equally plausible to say that a person's *body* can survive the loss of many of its parts. A more compelling objection, if it can be sustained, would be that different persons can share the same body – as is sometimes alleged to happen in cases of so-called multiple personality syndrome – or that one person can swap bodies with another.[7] The latter possibility is suggested by the seemingly feasible but as yet unattempted procedure of whole-brain transplantation, whereby the brain of one person is transplanted into the skull of another and vice versa. In the light of this apparent possibility, some philosophers are inclined to judge that it is sameness of *brain*, rather than sameness of *body*, which makes for personal identity. However, such a position would appear to be unstable, for the following reason (even setting aside any problem raised by cases of multiple personality syndrome, in which the same brain appears to be shared by two different people). Clearly, the reason why we are inclined to judge that a double brain-transplant operation would constitute a swapping of *bodies* between two people rather than a swapping of their *brains* is that we suppose all the vitally important aspects of human personality to be grounded in features of the brain – in particular, we suppose a person's memories and temperament to be grounded in features of his or her brain. But this suggests that what we *really* take to determine a person's identity are these aspects of human personality and, consequently, that we should deem it possible, at least in principle, for a person to acquire a new brain, provided that the new brain

[7] For a discussion of the implications of multiple personality syndrome, see Kathleen V. Wilkes, *Real People: Personal Identity Without Thought Experiments* (Oxford: Clarendon Press, 1988), ch. 4.

serves to ground all the vital aspects of human personality which were grounded by the old one.[8]

We have been led, by a couple of plausible steps, from a bodily criterion of personal identity, via a brain criterion, to a *psychological* criterion of personal identity. According to simple versions of the latter type of criterion, a person P_1 and a person P_2 are identical, either at a time or over time, if and only if P_1 and P_2 share certain allegedly vital aspects of human personality. But what are these allegedly vital aspects of human personality? Are there, in fact, any aspects of one's personality which cannot change over time? It seems hard to suppose so. People can undergo radical changes of temperament following brain injury and they can suffer extreme forms of amnesia or memory-loss. However, while we may agree that someone's personality may, over an extended period of time, become completely altered, it is less obvious that someone could survive a sudden and radical change of personality, involving both a complete change of temperament and a wholesale exchange of 'old' memories for 'new' ones. This would seem to be more a case of one person *replacing* another than a case of one and the same person surviving a change. So perhaps an acceptable psychological criterion of personal identity should allow a person to undergo major changes of personality over time, but only if these changes take place in a piecemeal and gradual fashion. For example, according to such an approach, a person existing at one time might retain *none* of the memories possessed by that same person at a much earlier time, provided that at the later of any two intervening times separated by only a short interval, he retained many of the memories which he possessed at the earlier of those two times.[9]

---

[8] For further discussion of the implications for personal identity of brain-transplantation and related procedures, see Sydney Shoemaker, *Self-Knowledge and Self-Identity* (Ithaca, NY: Cornell University Press, 1963), pp. 22ff and Bernard Williams, 'The Self and the Future', *Philosophical Review* 79 (1970), pp. 161–80, reprinted in his *Problems of the Self* (Cambridge: Cambridge University Press, 1973).

[9] For more on this idea of *continuity* of memory, see Derek Parfit, *Reasons and Persons* (Oxford: Clarendon Press, 1984), pp. 204ff.

However, even this more plausible version of a psychological criterion of personal identity is subject to an apparently devastating objection. For if we suppose that the aspects of human personality which are relevant to personal identity, such as temperament and memory, are grounded in features of the brain, what is to rule out the possibility of two different brains simultaneously grounding the *same* aspects of human personality? Suppose, for example, that the two hemispheres of a single brain both grounded the same aspects of human personality – the same temperament and memories – but were then separated and transplanted into the skulls of two different human bodies, each of which had previously had its own brain removed.[10] Then, it seems, we would be confronted with two different human persons, each with only half a brain, sharing the same temperament and memories. But this seems to be incompatible with the suggested psychological criterion of personal identity, which implies that persons who share the same temperament and memories are identical. What we seem to be faced with here is a case of *personal fission* – the splitting of one person, P_1, into two distinct persons, P_2 and P_3. The logical laws of identity preclude us from saying that P_2 and P_3 are *both* identical with P_1, since they are not identical with each other. And yet both P_2 and P_3 are related psychologically to P_1 in a way which the proposed psychological criterion of personal identity deems to be sufficient for identity. Accordingly, it seems, that criterion must be mistaken.

One possible response to this objection is to revise the proposed psychological criterion of personal identity in such a way that a person existing at a later time qualifies as ident-

---

[10] The more general implications for the concept of personal identity of the possibility of brain-bisection are discussed by Thomas Nagel in his 'Brain Bisection and the Unity of Consciousness', *Synthese* 22 (1971), pp. 396–413, reprinted in his *Mortal Questions* (Cambridge: Cambridge University Press, 1979). The hypothetical case of brain-bisection followed by separate transplantation of the two hemispheres is discussed by Derek Parfit in his 'Personal Identity', *Philosophical Review* 80 (1971), pp. 3–27, reprinted in Jonathan Glover (ed.), *The Philosophy of Mind* (Oxford: Oxford University Press, 1976). See also Parfit, *Reasons and Persons*, ch. 12.

ical with a person existing at an earlier time only if no process of fission has occurred, that is, only if the person existing at the later time is the *only* person existing at that time who is related in the relevant psychological way to the person existing at the earlier time. However, if this line of response is adopted, it seems to have the implication that questions of personal identity are far less important, morally and emotionally, than we intuitively take them to be.[11] For, according to this view, whether or not I shall still exist tomorrow may depend on the answer to the seemingly unimportant question of whether or not *someone else* very similar to me will exist tomorrow. If I am destined to undergo fission, I shall cease to exist: and yet someone else will exist tomorrow who is related to me psychologically in just the same way in which I am related to my self of yesterday. Indeed, *two* such people will exist tomorrow. However, if what matters to me when I consider my own prospects for survival is simply that someone should exist tomorrow who is related to me psychologically in the same way in which I am related to my self of yesterday, why should I worry if *more than one* such person exists tomorrow? But if I shouldn't worry about this, then it follows, according to the view of personal identity now being proposed, that I shouldn't necessarily worry about there not existing anyone tomorrow who is *identical* with me. Indeed, perhaps I shouldn't think of my 'survival' in terms of *identity* – that is, in terms of there existing in the future someone who will be identical with me – but rather in terms of there being *at least one* (but possibly more than one) person existing in the future who will be related to me psychologically in the way in which I am related to my past self. On this understanding of 'survival', if I undergo fission I shall 'survive' twice over, even though no one existing after the fission will be identical with me.

The upshot of our discussion so far is that we have not found a criterion of personal identity, either bodily or psycho-

---

[11] This is Derek Parfit's view, who also suggests the notion of 'survival' shortly to be discussed: see again his *Reasons and Persons*, ch. 12 and ch. 13.

logical, which is wholly satisfactory, in the sense that its verdicts involve no clash with our intuitive beliefs concerning the nature of personal identity and its moral and emotional significance. Some philosophers may be inclined to draw the conclusion that our intuitive beliefs concerning personal identity are confused or inconsistent, even suggesting that the very concept of a 'person' is in some way confused. An alternative suggestion is that some of the imaginary cases which seem to create difficulties for certain proposed criteria of personal identity are themselves ill-conceived and fail to represent genuine possibilities.[12] But a third possible line of response, which we should not dismiss too lightly, is to raise the suspicion – without in any way intending to impugn the concept of a person – that there is in fact *no* non-trivial and informative criterion of personal identity. Perhaps personal identity is something so basic that it cannot be accounted for in any more fundamental terms. I shall not attempt to adjudicate between these responses here, though my own sympathies lie with the third.[13]

PERSONAL MEMORY

The concept of *memory* has figured quite importantly in our discussion of personal identity so far, but we have not yet scrutinised that concept with the care which it deserves. There is in fact no *single* concept of memory, but many different concepts. Memory of facts is quite different from memory of practical skills and both are quite distinct from what is sometimes called *personal* or *autobiographical* memory. It is the latter kind of memory which is most obviously relevant to questions of personal identity. A personal memory is the

---

[12] For criticism of the appeal to thought experiments in philosophical discussions of personal identity, see Wilkes, *Real People*, ch. 1.

[13] I develop my own views about personal identity more fully in my *Kinds of Being: A Study of Individuation, Identity and the Logic of Sortal Terms* (Oxford: Blackwell, 1989), ch. 7 and in my *Subjects of Experience* (Cambridge: Cambridge University Press, 1996), ch. 2. For more on personal identity quite generally, see Harold W. Noonan, *Personal Identity* (London: Routledge, 1989) and Brian Garrett, *Personal Identity and Self-Consciousness* (London: Routledge, 1998).

remembrance of some past experience or action as one's own:
it is a memory *of experiencing or doing something* – not merely
a memory *that* one experienced or did something. I might
remember *that* I did a certain thing as a child because someone who witnessed me doing it has told me that I did it and
I remember this fact about myself. This is obviously quite
different, however, from my simply remembering *doing* that
thing. As I have just indicated, memories of facts and personal memories are typically reported in different ways, that
is, by sentences which have different grammatical structures.
Thus, on the one hand I might say 'I remember that I went
to the seaside last summer', while on the other I might say
'I remember going to the seaside last summer': the first sentence is most naturally interpreted as reporting a memory of
a fact, whereas the second is most naturally interpreted as
reporting a personal memory.[14]

Another distinction which we should make is between *dispositional* and *occurrent* memory, that is, between having a
capacity to remember something and actually recalling it.
Right now, there are many things which I *can* remember
doing in the past, even though I am not presently recalling
them because I am thinking about other things. The mental
act of recalling some past experience or action involves, it
seems, elements of *present* experience. That is why people
sometimes describe such an act as a 'reliving' of a past
experience, although it is rarely the case that the experience
of 'reliving' a past experience is as 'vivid' as the original
experience. In some ways, then, personal memory experiences are like the experiences involved in acts of *imagination*
(see chapter 7). In both cases, we describe the experiences
involved as exhibiting sensory characteristics, or as falling
within the province of different sense modalities: thus we
discriminate between *visual* and *auditory* memories and ima-
ginings. In an act of visual recall, one remembers how some-

[14] For more on personal or (as it is sometimes called) *experiential* memory, see Richard Wollheim, *The Thread of Life* (Cambridge: Cambridge University Press, 1984),
ch. 4.

thing *looked*, whereas in an act of auditory recall, one remembers how something *sounded*.

A question which may arise here is this: given the resemblance between personal memory experiences and the experiences involved in acts of imagination, how do we distinguish between the two, when we ourselves are undergoing the experiences? How do we tell whether we are remembering something or merely imagining it? This question would be a sensible one if we supposed that there was nothing more to remembering or imagining than simply undergoing some sort of experience but, of course, there is a great deal more. Remembering and imagining are mental *acts* – things we *do*, very often quite intentionally. Thus, if you ask me to try to remember going to the seaside last summer, this is something that I may find that I can readily do, of my own volition. Similarly, I find myself able to *imagine* going to the seaside. But if you then ask me how I know that what I am doing in the first case is *remembering*, rather than *imagining*, going to the seaside last summer, I am not sure what sense I can make of your question. The fact that the attendant experiences may be quite similar is seemingly irrelevant, since I do not judge whether I am remembering or imagining on the basis of what kind of experiences I am undergoing. Rather, I know whether I am remembering or imagining because these are things that I can do intentionally, and one cannot do something intentionally unless one knows that one is doing it. The question that we should really ask, perhaps, is not how I know whether I am remembering or merely imagining going to the seaside last summer, but how I know that I really *did* go to the seaside last summer, given that I 'remember' going.

One may be tempted to answer this question by saying that if I *remember* going to the seaside last summer, I must indeed have gone, because one cannot 'remember' doing something that one has not done – just as one cannot 'know' something that is not the case or 'see' something which does not exist. As we might put it, 'know', 'see' and 'remember' are all verbs of *success* or *achievement*. However, this answer seems to rely on a purely verbal point concerning the conventional meaning of the word 'remember' and so doesn't appear to go to the heart of the matter. Given that one can at least *seem* to remember doing something that one did not do, how does one know, on the basis of seeming to remember, that one really did do it? Perhaps the answer to this question is that one *cannot* know, for sure, that one did something merely on the basis of seeming to remember doing it, but that it is none the less reasonable to believe, on that basis, that one did it, unless one possesses evidence to the contrary. It is doubtful whether we can coherently call into question the veridicality of *everything* that we seem to remember, but we should certainly acknowledge the fallibility of any particular attempt to recall what happened in the past.

Given that one may mistakenly seem to remember doing something that one did not in fact do, the further question arises as to whether one can seem to remember doing something that *someone else* in fact did. Surely, one can. But could it be the case that one seemed to remember doing something and, but for the fact that it was someone else who did it, one *would* be remembering doing it? If personal fission is possible, of the kind envisaged earlier, the answer to this question seems to be 'Yes'. For in such a case, *both* of the persons, P_2 and P_3, into which the original person, P_1, divides seem to remember doing what P_1 did and all that prevents us from saying that P_2 and P_3 both *remember* doing what P_1 did is that neither of them in fact did it, because P_1 did it and neither of them is identical with P_1. Some philosophers introduce the term 'quasi-memory' to describe what is going on in such a case.[15] The concept of quasi-memory is supposed to be more extensive than that of personal memory as ordinarily understood. One can only have a veridical personal memory of doing something that was in fact done by oneself, but one can have a veridical *quasi*-memory of doing something that

---

[15] The notion of 'quasi-memory' is due to Sydney Shoemaker: see his 'Persons and their Pasts', *American Philosophical Quarterly* 7 (1970), pp. 269–85, reprinted in his *Identity, Cause, and Mind*. The notion is adopted by Derek Parfit: see his 'Personal Identity' and his *Reasons and Persons*, pp. 220ff.

was in fact done by someone else, provided that one is related psychologically to that person in the same sort of way in which one is typically related to one's earlier self, as supposedly happens in a case of personal fission. However, not all philosophers are happy with the notion of quasi-memory, some of them suspecting it to be incoherent. If personal fission is possible, it is theoretically possible that – unbeknownst to me – I myself am a product of such fission, in which case many of my personal 'memories' are really only quasi-memories. But it is tempting to urge that personal memory exhibits a form of 'immunity to error through misidentification', in the sense that if I seem to remember doing something, it cannot be the case that I am mistaken only inasmuch as it was not *I* who did the thing in question.[16] If that is so, then it would seem to follow that personal fission is, after all, an impossibility. However, I shall not attempt to resolve this difficult issue here.

One reason why some philosophers defend the notion of quasi-memory is in order to avoid the charge of circularity which is sometimes raised against any psychological criterion of personal identity which appeals to personal memory. Any criterion of personal identity which contends that a person, P_2, existing at one time, is identical with a person, P_1, existing at an earlier time, only if P_2 remembers doing some of the things done by P_1 appears to involve a circularity, because a necessary condition of P_2's *remembering* doing something is that P_2 should actually have done that thing. One cannot establish, then, that P_2 does indeed *remember* doing something done by P_1 until one has established that P_2 is indeed *identical* with P_1, which is what the criterion was supposed to enable us to determine. (Recall my earlier remark that the relation R_k mentioned in a criterion of identity of the form of (C_k) must not be the relation of identity itself, nor any relation

---

[16] For doubts about the coherence of the notion of quasi-memory, see Evans, *The Varieties of Reference*, pp. 242–8, Wollheim, *The Thread of Life*, pp. 111–17 and Andy Hamilton, 'A New Look at Personal Identity', *Philosophical Quarterly* 45 (1995), pp. 332–49.

which can only be stated in terms which involve or presuppose the identity of things of kind K: it is the second constraint which appears to be violated in the case under discussion.) By replacing reference to memory by reference to *quasi*-memory in such a criterion, the charge of circularity can be avoided. But if it should turn out that the concept of quasi-memory is incoherent, the implication would seem to be that no non-circular psychological criterion of personal identity is available, given that the concept of personal memory would have to figure centrally in any such criterion.

MEMORY AND CAUSATION

A question which we have not really addressed so far is this: in virtue of what is a current mental act or state of mine a personal *memory* of some earlier experience or action of mine? Plausibly, some sort of *causal* connection is required between the earlier experience or action and the current mental act or state.[17] But what sort of connection? Not just any causal connection will do. For suppose that someone else witnessed an earlier action of mine and later told me that I had done it, even though I myself had since forgotten doing it. It is conceivable that, after a while, I might forget that I was only told that I did this thing and I might begin to *seem* to remember doing it, even though I really do not. In such a case, my current mental state of seeming to remember doing the thing is causally connected to my original act of doing it, but evidently not in the right kind of way for that mental state to qualify as a genuine personal *memory* of doing that thing. So what *is* the 'right' kind of causal connection?

Here we meet again the problem of 'deviant causal chains', which we met earlier when discussing causal theories of perception (in chapter 6) and causal theories of action (in chapter 9). We know that that problem is in general a difficult one, so we should expect it to prove difficult in the particular

---

[17] A causal account of memory is defended by C. B. Martin and Max Deutscher in their important paper 'Remembering', *Philosophical Review* 75 (1966), pp. 161–96.

case of memory. I shall not attempt to resolve it here. But one obvious thought is that the kind of causal connection that is involved in memory is one that is 'internal' to the person whose memory is in question. It is this thought that sustains various theories of memory which invoke the notion of a memory *trace*, conceived as a physical state of the brain laid down by an original episode of sensory experience and capable of inducing a subsequent memory experience of that original episode. But it has to be said that some philosophers are hostile to this notion and to causal theories of memory in general, for reasons similar to those which motivate their hostility to causal theories of perception.[18] In particular, they consider that such theories foster scepticism about memory and hence about our knowledge of the past. Just as such philosophers may advance a 'disjunctive' theory of perception (see chapter 6) which represents veridical perception as being 'direct', so they may advance the view that veridical memory is 'direct' knowledge of the past. Their opponents, however, are apt to regard such a view as being both obscure and difficult to square with a naturalistic conception of human beings and their psychological capacities. Again, this is not a dispute which I shall try to resolve here.

ANIMALISM

We saw earlier that it is not easy to find any criterion of personal identity which is free from problems. Some philosophers may be inclined to draw the conclusion that the term 'person' does not really denote a distinct *kind* of things, all instances of which share the same identity-conditions. Here we may recall the view, mentioned at the beginning of this chapter, that to be a person or self is to occupy some role or perform some function – a role or function which could be

---

[18] For a survey of attacks on the notion of a memory trace, see John Sutton, *Philosophy and Memory Traces: Descartes to Connectionism* (Cambridge: Cambridge University Press, 1998), ch. 16. See also Norman Malcolm, 'A Definition of Factual Memory', in his *Knowledge and Certainty: Essays and Lectures* (Ithaca, NY: Cornell University Press, 1963).

occupied or performed by things of many different kinds. One version of this view is espoused by the increasingly popular doctrine known as *animalism*.[19] According to animalism, I just *am* my body, that is, I am just a living human organism, which began to exist as a single cell (a zygote) and which will go on existing until its biological death occurs. During some of this time, various kinds of activity in my brain and nervous system sustain the kind of consciousness, including conscious self-awareness, which entitles me to be described as being a 'person'. But I existed before I was a person and I may well go on existing for some time after I cease to be a person. Hence, I am not *essentially* a person, since an essential property is one without which its bearer could not exist. My identity-conditions, therefore, are simply those of a human organism. But if things of another kind – suitably programmed robots, perhaps – could be persons, then they could have identity-conditions quite different from mine. On this view, then, it is simply an error to seek some criterion of identity which applies to all and only those things which could be persons. And it is tempting to blame the problems we met earlier in seeking such a criterion upon this supposed error.

One apparent advantage of animalism is this. If we suppose that I am *not* identical with my body, nor with any part of it such as my brain, and yet that I am still a physical thing extended in space and having physical properties such as weight and solidity, then it seems that I must *coincide* with something distinct from myself. For instance, if my weight and shape are the same as my body's, then I must coincide with my body, which is supposedly distinct from myself. But how can two distinct things exactly coincide – that is, occupy exactly the same region of space at one and the same time? Moreover, if both I and my body have a certain weight and yet are two distinct things, how is it that our combined weight is not twice that of my body? Neither of these apparent diffi-

<hr>

[19] Perhaps the most fully developed defence of animalism to date is by Eric T. Olson: see his *The Human Animal: Personal Identity Without Psychology* (New York: Oxford University Press, 1997).

culties arise for animalism, since it maintains that I am indeed identical with my body.

In fact, however, these supposed difficulties may not be as severe as the animalist suggests for, as I indicated in chapter 2, it may be possible for the opponent of animalism to draw on an analogy with the relation between a statue and the lump of bronze of which it is composed. The statue and the lump of bronze similarly appear to be two distinct things which exactly coincide, their distinctness being implied by the difference between their respective persistence-conditions. There are changes which the statue can survive but which the lump of bronze cannot, and vice versa. And the reason why the 'combined' weight of the statue and the lump of bronze is just that of the lump of bronze alone is that the statue entirely owes what weight it has to the matter of which it is composed. Although the statue and the lump of bronze are *distinct* objects – that is, are not identical with one another – it is not as though they are *separate* objects, as would be two different lumps of bronze. Hence, one possible view of the relationship between me and my body which rivals that of animalism is the view that I am *composed*, or *constituted*, by my body. As I made clear in chapter 2, this is not my own view, but all that I want to urge here is that animalism deserves less credit than some of its supporters imagine merely on account of its avoidance of the supposed difficulties that we have been discussing. For those supposed difficulties have, I think, been exaggerated by the supporters of animalism.

Another alleged difficulty which animalism seems to avoid is this. Clearly, I am the subject of certain mental states – I have certain thoughts and feelings. But, the animalist urges, surely it is equally true that the human organism which is my body has certain thoughts and feelings, in virtue of the activity of its brain and nervous system. However, if I am not identical with my body, then it appears that there are two distinct things having the same or exactly similar thoughts and feelings at one and the same time – I and my body. And this seems absurd. But the absurdity is apparently avoided by maintaining, as the animalist does, that I just *am* (identical with) my body.

However, an opponent of animalism may question the animalist's contention that the human organism which is my body has thoughts and feelings. It is far from being an obvious truth that either my body as a whole or any part of it, such as my brain, literally has thoughts and feelings. It certainly appears to be true that I could not have thoughts and feelings if I did not have a brain which functions in certain ways. But it is equally true that I could not run if I did not have legs which function in certain ways. However, the latter fact does not imply that *my legs* run, so why should the former fact be taken to imply that *my brain* has thoughts and feelings? We have to distinguish between a *subject* of thought and feelings – something that thinks and feels – and something, such as the brain, whose activity renders possible and sustains a subject's thoughts and feelings.

Now, the animalist may readily concede that it is not *my brain* that has thoughts and feelings, because he wants to say that it is *I* who have thoughts and feelings and that I am identical with my body as a whole – a living organism – rather than with one organ within that body, my brain. However, once it is maintained that a *whole body* may literally have thoughts and feelings, it seems difficult to deny that *a brain* may literally have thoughts and feelings, because it appears to be perfectly possible, in principle, for a detached brain to be kept alive and functioning in the ways which enable it to sustain thoughts and feelings. In such a case, the animalist cannot say that it is the person whose brain it is rather than the brain itself which has the thoughts and feelings, because that would commit him to a claim which he rejects – namely, that a person can coincide with something distinct from itself (in this case, a brain). So he must say that it is the brain that has the thoughts and feelings in such a case. However, if a detached but functioning brain has thoughts and feelings, it surely follows that an embodied and functioning brain also has thoughts and feelings. But this means that we can turn the animalist's own objection against himself. For now he appears to be committed to the view that *both* my whole body *and* my brain have thoughts and feelings, that is, once again, that there are two distinct things having the same or exactly similar thoughts and feelings at one and the same time.

In view of this consequence, there is considerable pressure on the animalist to revise his position and maintain, after all, that it is my brain and *not* my whole body that has thoughts and feelings. But then he is committed to the unattractive doctrine that I am identical with my brain, since it would be absurd to deny that *I* have thoughts and feelings. What emerges from these considerations, I think, is that animalism is an unstable theory. It is under threat of collapse into the theory that I am identical with my brain. We can avoid this identity claim by distinguishing between myself, a subject of thoughts and feelings, and my brain, the bodily organ whose activity renders possible and sustains my thoughts and feelings. But once that distinction is in place, there is nothing really to motivate the animalist's original claim that I am identical with my whole body, a living organism. Indeed, if, as seems intuitively plausible, I could survive with my brain detached from the rest of my body, I most certainly cannot be identical with my whole body. Animalism simply runs counter to our deepest intuitions concerning our own persistence-conditions: we believe that we could survive changes which our bodies could not survive. Difficult though it may be to spell out those persistence-conditions in a precise and uncontentious way, it seems clear enough that they differ from the persistence-conditions of living organisms. We can even conceive of surviving a process of change in which our organic bodies and brains are gradually replaced by inorganic bodies and brains, composed of metal and silicon. And, upon reflection, animalism just seems plain wrong in its contention that I could go on existing as an unconscious body after my brain had ceased to be capable of sustaining any conscious thought or feeling. Our considered view, I think, is that a body in this condition is nothing but a living corpse and that the person whose body it was has ceased to exist.

KNOWING ONE'S OWN MIND

I suggested earlier that persons or selves are distinctive amongst subjects of experience in that they not only have thoughts and feelings, but also have knowledge of at least some of their own thoughts and feelings – in particular, their *conscious* thoughts and feelings. Persons can identify their conscious thoughts and feelings as being their own and they often have, or seem to have, reliable and authoritative knowledge of *what* they are consciously thinking and feeling.[20] Assuming that such knowledge really does exist, how is it possible? It is very tempting to offer an *observational* model of our acquisition of such knowledge, that is, to suppose that we discover facts about our own conscious thoughts and feelings by a process of 'introspection' which is analogous to the perceptual processes through which we discover facts about events and states of affairs in the world at large. But there are difficulties with such a model of the sources of self-knowledge. For one thing, it is far from obvious that we do in fact have any sort of 'inner sense' which is analogous to the 'outer senses' of vision, hearing, olfaction and so forth. Furthermore, an observational model of the sources of self-knowledge seems ill-fitted to explaining the special reliability and authority which are assumed to characterise one's knowledge about one's own conscious mental states. We tend to assume that each person is, in general, a better judge of what he himself is consciously thinking or feeling than anyone else can be, even if we concede that no one is completely infallible in such matters. But it is not clear how the observational model can explain this fact, if indeed it is a fact, because observation is, as a rule, a far from reliable source of information, subject as it is to many varieties of bias and illusion.

It may be suggested, on behalf of the observational model, that each person can 'observe' his or her own conscious thoughts and feelings *directly*, in a way which is not available

---

[20] For further discussion of our ability to identify our conscious thoughts and feelings as our own, see my *Subjects of Experience*, ch. 7.

to an 'outside observer', who is always compelled to *infer* what another person is thinking and feeling from observations of that person's bodily behaviour – and that this is why each person is especially authoritative about his or her own conscious thoughts and feelings. But, even leaving aside its questionable assumption that 'direct' observation is somehow especially reliable, this suggestion seems to treat thoughts and feelings as necessarily *private* objects of 'inner' observation in a way which is vulnerable to severe criticism.[21] If my own thoughts and feelings are items which I alone can observe directly, how can I even comprehend the proposition that other people besides myself may have their own thoughts and feelings? If I try to think of 'their' thoughts and feelings by analogy with my own, then – according to the observational model – I shall have to think of them as items which other people can observe directly but which I necessarily cannot. But what would entitle me to call such hypothetical items *thoughts* and *feelings* when they are, by hypothesis, items which I cannot conceivably compare for likeness with my own thoughts and feelings? It seems impossible for me to acquire perfectly general concepts of thought and feeling, applicable to other people as well as to myself, purely from some queer kind of mental self-observation, and yet this is what the observational model of the sources of self-knowledge appears to demand.

But what alternative is there to the observational model? A first step towards one possible alternative is to focus on the point that it is only one's own *conscious* thoughts and feelings concerning which one seems to have an especially reliable and authoritative form of knowledge. For – recalling our discussion of consciousness in chapter 3 – it may be suggested that the fact that a mental state is a *conscious* one is just a matter of its being the object of another, higher-order mental

---

[21] Criticism of views which treat thoughts and feelings as 'private objects' owes much to the work of Wittgenstein: for exposition and discussion of the relevant parts of Wittgenstein's work, see Malcolm Budd, *Wittgenstein's Philosophy of Psychology* (London: Routledge, 1989), ch. 3.

state. Just as I can believe that p, so, apparently, I can believe that I believe that p – and, on the view now being canvassed, this is really all there is to the fact that my belief that p is a 'conscious' one. Similarly, on this view, all there really is to the fact that a certain feeling of mine, such as a pain, is a 'conscious' one is that I not only have it, but *believe* that I have it. Some creatures, it may be suggested, are capable of having only 'first-order' beliefs and consequently lack conscious thoughts according to this model: but we humans are conscious thinkers because we also have 'second-order' beliefs – beliefs about our first-order beliefs.[22]

If the fact that a belief that p is a conscious one is just a matter of its subject believing that he believes that p, then it may seem unmysterious why subjects should have especially reliable and authoritative knowledge of their own conscious beliefs. For it is apt to strike us as an obviously correct principle that if S believes that he believes that p, then, indeed, S believes that p. If this principle is correct, however, then whenever S believes that he believes that p, his belief that he believes that p will be *true*, and so will constitute *knowledge* (on the assumption that reliably produced true belief is knowledge). However, even if this principle does strike us as being obvious, what we really need to ask is *why* it is correct, if indeed it is so: why should it be the case that if S believes that he believes that p, then, indeed, S believes that p? Aren't we just taking for granted here the very phenomenon of self-knowledge which we are seeking to explain? Perhaps, though, we are at least now looking in the right place for a solution to our problem, which, very arguably, we were not doing while we were tempted by the observational model. It may be suggested, for instance, that one can explain on evolutionary grounds why a creature's beliefs about its own beliefs, if it has them, should generally be highly reliable – namely, because any creature which frequently believed that it had

---

[22] One recent defence of a higher-order thought theory of consciousness is by Peter Carruthers: see his *Language, Thought and Consciousness: An Essay in Philosophical Psychology* (Cambridge: Cambridge University Press, 1996), chs. 5, 6 and 7.

beliefs which it did not in fact have could be expected to exhibit such self-defeating behaviour that its survival would be unlikely. According to this suggestion, then, the principle that if S believes that he believes that p, then S believes that p, while not a logical or *a priori* truth, closely approximates to a psychological law: it may have counterexamples, but we have reason to expect them to be few and far between.

MOORE'S PARADOX AND THE NATURE OF CONSCIOUS BELIEF

However, there are also difficulties with this alternative approach to the problem of self-knowledge. For one thing, it is far from clear that an account of consciousness in terms of higher-order mental states is wholly satisfactory, as we began to see in chapter 3. How could a belief be conscious just in virtue of its subject having a belief about that belief? Surely, that a belief is a *conscious* belief has something to do with the intrinsic nature of that mental state, rather than anything to do with its being the object of another belief of the same subject. If it makes sense to suppose that there might be a subject *all* of whose beliefs were unconscious – which the view now under scrutiny seems to presuppose – then why shouldn't some of those beliefs happen to be about other beliefs of that same subject? And yet the view in question rules this out as impossible, since according to that view those beliefs about which this subject had beliefs would for that very reason qualify as *conscious* beliefs.

But, in any case, one may come to feel suspicious, upon reflection, about the very notion of 'higher-order' belief, at least in the sense which is now at issue. For one thing, there do not seem to be any circumstances in which someone could sensibly assert 'I believe that I believe that p'. Suppose I ask you whether or not you believe that p. You may answer 'Yes, I do believe that p', or 'No, I don't', or even, perhaps, 'I'm not sure'. But what could you possibly mean by answering 'I *believe* that I believe that p'? Notice, however, that there is no similar difficulty in understanding what you might mean by saying 'I believe that I *used* to believe that *p*', or 'I believe that I *shall* believe that *p*', where you are commenting on your own past or anticipated mental state. Similarly, there is no difficulty in understanding what you might mean by saying 'I believe that *you* believe that *p*', where you are commenting on another person's present mental state.

These observations seem to be connected with what is known as *Moore's paradox* – the fact that it apparently makes no sense for someone to assert 'I believe that *p* but it is not true that *p*', even though it makes perfectly good sense for someone to assert 'I *used* to believe that *p* but it is not true that *p*' or '*You* believe that *p* but it is not true that *p*'.[23] One lesson which we might think that we should draw from this fact is that to assert 'I believe that *p*' is not to report that one has a certain belief, but is rather to assert that *p*, albeit in a somewhat tentative way. Then we can understand why it should seem virtually contradictory to assert 'I believe that *p* but it is not true that *p*', because this would be both to assert that *p* (albeit tentatively) and to assert that it is not true that *p*. But, whether or not we endorse this analysis, we may at least be persuaded by Moore's paradox to question the assumption that one's own current beliefs are items towards which one can take a cognitive stance, that is, that they are items about which one can have concurrent beliefs. This doubt may be reinforced by the following consideration. When one is asked whether or not one believes that *p*, one does not attempt to determine the answer to this question by thinking about *oneself*, but rather by thinking about the proposition that *p*. If one feels persuaded that there is good evidence in favour of the truth of *p*, then one will be inclined to judge that it is true that *p* and consequently one will answer the question that has been posed affirmatively. Neither any process of introspection nor the formation of any

---

[23] Moore's paradox (named after its discoverer, G. E. Moore) and its implications for the concept of belief are discussed by Jane Heal in her 'Moore's Paradox: A Wittgensteinian Approach', *Mind* 103 (1994), pp. 5–24. See also Arthur W. Collins, 'Moore's Paradox and Epistemic Risk', *Philosophical Quarterly* 46 (1996), pp. 308–19.

'higher-order' belief seems to be involved in one's arriving at such an answer. One's concern is entirely with the truth or falsehood of the proposition that *p* and the evidence which may bear upon its truth or falsehood.

But if, as the foregoing considerations suggest, knowing what one is thinking or feeling is not a matter of having true beliefs, reliably formed, about what one is thinking or feeling, then what *is* it? Perhaps it is simply a matter of *how* one is thinking or feeling, namely, *consciously*. Even more so than the previous proposal, this makes it unmysterious why it should be our *conscious* thoughts and feelings about which we have especially authoritative knowledge, for now we are suggesting that a subject's having 'knowledge' of this kind simply consists in his relevant thoughts and feelings being conscious ones. This, of course, is to presuppose the notion of consciousness rather than to explain it, as the higher-order thought theory attempts to do. But we already have reason to think that the notion of consciousness may be so fundamental that no non-circular explanation or analysis of it is available.

EXTERNALISM AND SELF-KNOWLEDGE

This is a convenient point to mention another problem concerning our knowledge of our own conscious thoughts, one which is connected with the debate over *externalist* and *internalist* accounts of mental content discussed in chapter 4. The externalist holds that the propositional contents of a thinker's thoughts are, in general, partly determined by features of the thinker's environment which exist independently of the thinker. For instance, according to externalism, my thought that the glass in front of me contains *water* has the content it does in part because my physical environment contains a certain kind of substance, H_2O. If my physical environment had not contained that substance, then even if it had contained another kind of substance, XYZ, which looked and tasted just like water, I could not, according to the externalist, have had a thought with precisely the same content as the one I actually have concerning this glass. But the problem, now, is this. I seem to have authoritative knowledge about *what* it is that I am thinking – the propositional content of my thought – when I have the conscious thought that this glass contains water. And yet I may have no knowledge of chemistry and, in particular, no knowledge of the difference between H_2O and XYZ, for the latter kind of knowledge is empirical and scientific. My knowledge of what it is that I am thinking, by contrast, appears to be neither empirical nor scientific, but immediate and *a priori*. However, knowledge implies truth: if I know that I am thinking that this glass contains water, it follows that that is indeed what I am thinking – and if that is indeed what I am thinking, then this in turn implies, according to externalism, that H_2O rather than XYZ exists in my physical environment. So an empirical, scientific truth seems to be implied by my non-empirical knowledge of what I am thinking together with the truth of a philosophical doctrine, the doctrine of externalism. And yet this is surely impossible, in which case we must apparently either abandon externalism or else abandon the claim that I know non-empirically what I am thinking, that is, that I have especially authoritative knowledge of the contents of my own thoughts.

Perhaps, however, a problem is posed here only for the 'observational' model of the sources of self-knowledge. If my knowing what I am thinking is supposed to be a consequence of my inwardly inspecting my own mental states, then the fact, if it is a fact, that the contents of those states are partly determined by features of my physical environment does appear to present a difficulty: for the supposed processes of inward inspection can hardly be supposed to reveal anything about those environmental features. On the other hand, if my having a conscious thought or belief that this is a glass of water is simply a matter of my believing that I believe that this is a glass of water, as the higher-order thought theory contends, then there would seem to be no problem, because the content of such a second-order belief will surely be determined in the same way as the content of the first-order belief which is its object. Thus, if my belief that this is a glass of water has its content determined, in part, by the fact that my physical environment contains H_2O, then so, too, will my second-order belief that I believe that this is a glass of water have its content determined, in part, by the fact that my physical environment contains H_2O: the contents of the two beliefs cannot apparently come apart in any way. This seems to relieve the difficulty. Although my second-order belief is not one that I have formed on empirical or scientific grounds, its having the content that it does implies, according to externalism, that my physical environment contains H_2O, for exactly the same reason that this is implied by the content of my first-order belief. And yet there appears to be no unwelcome suggestion that I could somehow use my knowledge of what it is that I believe to arrive at non-empirical knowledge of the scientific truth in question.[24]

If such a solution works for the higher-order thought theory, however, then it seems that a similar solution will likewise work for the view that knowing what one is thinking is simply a matter of *how* one is thinking – namely, consciously – for on this view also the contents of one's conscious thoughts can be determined by environmental features without this appearing to imply that one can somehow acquire non-empirical knowledge of what those features are. But I should emphasise that the issues raised in this section continue to be the subject of vigorous and complex debate and that no consensus concerning them has yet emerged.

---

[24] Two important papers attempting to reconcile self-knowledge with externalism, in part by rejecting the observational model of self-knowledge, are Donald Davidson, 'Knowing One's Own Mind', *Proceedings and Addresses of the American Philosophical Association* 60 (1987), pp. 441–58 and Tyler Burge, 'Individualism and Self-Knowledge', *Journal of Philosophy* 85 (1988), pp. 649–63, both reprinted in Cassam (ed.), *Self-Knowledge*. The issue is also discussed in several of the papers in Crispin Wright, Barry C. Smith and Cynthia Macdonald (eds.), *Knowing Our Own Minds* (Oxford: Clarendon Press, 1998). For extremely clear and helpful discussion, see John Heil, *The Nature of True Minds* (Cambridge: Cambridge University Press, 1992), ch. 5. An interesting new solution to the problem of self-knowledge is advanced by André Gallois in his *The World Without, the Mind Within: An Essay on First-Person Authority* (Cambridge: Cambridge University Press, 1996).

SELF-DECEPTION

The opposite side of the coin of self-knowledge is *self-deception*, which is quite as puzzling a phenomenon. Sometimes people seem to deceive themselves about what they truly believe or desire. For example, a mother may refuse to confront the fact that her soldier son has been killed in action, despite having received and read official letters reporting his death. She wants to believe that he is still alive and in some sense *does* believe that he is still alive, even though in another sense she clearly must know that he is dead. We may speak of such a person as 'deceiving herself', but it is difficult to interpret this description of her situation literally. One person may deceive *another* person, but only because the former knows something which the latter does not know. In the case of the mother in our example, it appears that she does 'really' know that her son is dead: so it does not seem to make literal sense to describe her as keeping this knowledge from herself, in the way in which one may keep some knowledge from another person. Nor will it really help to suggest that *part* of her mind knows that her son is dead and keeps this knowledge from another part of her mind, for this is to treat self-deception as merely being, in effect, a kind of other-deception, which it plainly is not. Quite apart from anything else, there seems to be something intrinsically irrational about self-deception, which is not the case with other-deception. On the other hand, we should not confuse self-deception with mere wishful thinking, which is also irrational. Wishful thinking is believing something because one wants it to be true, rather than because one has any evidence for its truth. The mother in our example does not simply fall under this description, however, since she has good evidence for the *falsity* of what she wants to believe and yet, in some sense, still believes it in the teeth of that evidence, while at the same time 'really' knowing that it must be false.

It is difficult to decide how one should even begin to describe such a case appropriately.[25] One lesson of this may

---

[25] For more on self-deception, see David Pears, *Motivated Irrationality* (Oxford: Clarendon Press, 1984), ch. 3 and Alfred R. Mele, 'Real Self-Deception', *Behavioral*

be that our everyday talk of 'belief', 'knowledge' and 'desire' has a complexity which has so far eluded the attempts of philosophers to provide it with a clear theoretical foundation. We need not necessarily conclude, with the eliminative materialists, that propositional attitude states are a fiction born of a scientifically inadequate 'folk' theory of the mind (see again chapter 3). But perhaps we should view with a more sceptical eye the comfortable assumption that beliefs and desires are straightforwardly 'states' of persons, or of their minds, by analogy with such physical states of their bodies as shape, mass and velocity.

CONCLUSIONS

In this final chapter, we have covered a great deal of difficult territory, some of it necessarily in a rather perfunctory way. Our reflections on the nature of ourselves and of our knowledge of ourselves have been unsettling rather than comfortable and reassuring. We seem to know less about ourselves than we might have imagined at the outset of our inquiries. We are even uncertain, now, about what *kind* of thing we are and about our own persistence-conditions. Memory, which we rely on for our knowledge about our pasts, turns out to be a complicated and controversial affair. And even our ability to know what we are consciously thinking and feeling seems difficult to understand. These uncertainties, however, should not lead us to despair of making progress in the philosophy of mind. On the contrary, they demonstrate how important the philosophy of mind is as a corrective to the complacency which often characterises both everyday thinking about the mind and the theoretical assumptions of empirical psychologists and cognitive scientists.

and Brain Sciences 20 (1997), pp. 91–136. The latter contains an extensive bibliography.

Bibliography

Anscombe, G. E. M., 'Causality and Determination', in Anscombe, *Metaphysics and the Philosophy of Mind*.

Intention, 2nd edn (Oxford: Blackwell, 1963).

Metaphysics and the Philosophy of Mind: Collected Philosophical Papers, Volume II (Oxford: Blackwell, 1981).

'The First Person', in Guttenplan (ed.), *Mind and Language*, reprinted in Anscombe, *Metaphysics and the Philosophy of Mind*.

Armstrong, D. M., 'Perception, Sense Data and Causality', in G. F. Macdonald (ed.), *Perception and Identity* (London: Macmillan, 1979).

Universals: An Opinionated Introduction (Boulder, CO: Westview Press, 1989).

Aune, B., *Reason and Action* (Dordrecht: D. Reidel, 1977).

Austin, J. L., *Sense and Sensibilia*, ed. G. J. Warnock (Oxford: Clarendon Press, 1962).

Ayer, A. J., *Language, Truth and Logic*, 2nd edn (London: Victor Gollancz, 1946).

The Foundations of Empirical Knowledge (London: Macmillan, 1940).

Baker, G. and Morris, K. J., *Descartes' Dualism* (London: Routledge, 1996).

Baker, L. R., *Saving Belief* (Princeton, NJ: Princeton University Press, 1987).

Barwise, J. and Perry, J., 'Scenes and Other Situations', *Journal of Philosophy* 78 (1981), pp. 369–97.

Situations and Attitudes (Cambridge, MA: MIT Press, 1983).

Beauchamp, T. L. and Rosenberg, A., *Hume and the Problem of Causation* (New York: Oxford University Press, 1981).

Bechtel, W. and Abrahamsen, A., *Connectionism and the Mind: An Introduction to Parallel Processing in Networks* (Oxford: Blackwell, 1991).

Benacerraf, P., 'Mathematical Truth', *Journal of Philosophy* 70 (1973), pp. 661–80, reprinted in Benacerraf and Putnam (eds.), *Philosophy of Mathematics*.

Benacerraf, P. and Putnam, H. (eds.), *Philosophy of Mathematics: Selected Readings*, 2nd edn (Cambridge: Cambridge University Press, 1983).

Bermúdez, J. L., *The Paradox of Self-Consciousness* (Cambridge, MA: MIT Press, 1998).

Bermúdez, J. L., Marcel, A. and Eilan, N. (eds.), *The Body and the Self* (Cambridge, MA: MIT Press, 1995).

Block, N., 'On a Confusion about a Function of Consciousness', *Behavioral and Brain Sciences* 18 (1995), pp. 227–87.

'Troubles with Functionalism', in C. W. Savage (ed.), *Perception and Cognition: Issues in the Foundations of Psychology, Minnesota Studies in the Philosophy of Science, Volume 9* (Minneapolis: University of Minnesota Press, 1978), reprinted in Block (ed.), *Readings in Philosophy of Psychology, Volume 1*.

'What is Functionalism?', in Block (ed.), *Readings in Philosophy of Psychology, Volume 1*.

Block, N. (ed.), *Imagery* (Cambridge, MA: MIT Press, 1981).

Readings in Philosophy of Psychology, Volume 1 (London: Methuen, 1980).

Readings in Philosophy of Psychology, Volume 2 (London: Methuen, 1981).

Block, N. and Fodor, J. A., 'What Psychological States are Not', *Philosophical Review* 81 (1972), pp. 159–81, reprinted in Block (ed.), *Readings in Philosophy of Psychology, Volume 1*.

Boden, M. A., 'Escaping the Chinese Room', in Boden (ed.), *The Philosophy of Artificial Intelligence*.

Boden, M. A. (ed.), *The Philosophy of Artificial Intelligence* (Oxford: Oxford University Press, 1990).

Boolos, G. S. and Jeffrey, R. C., *Computability and Logic*, 3rd edn (Cambridge: Cambridge University Press, 1989).

Braddon-Mitchell, D. and Jackson, F., *Philosophy of Mind and Cognition* (Oxford: Blackwell, 1996).

Brown, R. and Herrnstein, R. J., 'Icons and Images', in Block (ed.), *Imagery*.

Bruce, V. and Green, P., *Visual Perception: Physiology, Psychology and Ecology* (London: Lawrence Erlbaum Associates, 1985).

Budd, M., *Wittgenstein's Philosophy of Psychology* (London: Routledge, 1989).

Burge, T., 'Individualism and Psychology', *Philosophical Review* 95 (1986), pp. 3–45.

'Individualism and Self-Knowledge', *Journal of Philosophy* 85 (1988), pp. 649–63, reprinted in Cassam (ed.), *Self-Knowledge*.

'Individualism and the Mental', *Midwest Studies in Philosophy* 4 (1979), pp. 73–121.

'Marr's Theory of Vision', in Jay L. Garfield (ed.), *Modularity in Knowledge Representation and Natural-Language Understanding* (Cambridge, MA: MIT Press, 1989).

Byrne, A. and Hilbert, D. R. (eds.), *Readings on Color, Volume 2: The Science of Color* (Cambridge, MA: MIT Press, 1997).

Campbell, J., *Past, Space, and Self* (Cambridge, MA: MIT Press, 1994).

Carruthers, P., *Language, Thought and Consciousness: An Essay in Philosophical Psychology* (Cambridge: Cambridge University Press, 1996).

Cartwright, N., *How the Laws of Physics Lie* (Oxford: Clarendon Press, 1983).

Cassam, Q. (ed.), *Self-Knowledge* (Oxford: Oxford University Press, 1994).

Chater, N. and Heyes, C., 'Animal Concepts: Content and Discontent', *Mind and Language* 9 (1994), pp. 209–46.

Cheney, D. L. and Seyfarth, R. M., *How Monkeys See the World: Inside the Mind of Another Species* (Chicago: University of Chicago Press, 1990).

Chisholm, R. M., *Perceiving: A Philosophical Study* (Ithaca, NY: Cornell University Press, 1957).

Person and Object: A Metaphysical Study (London: George Allen and Unwin, 1976).

'The Agent as Cause', in Myles Brand and Douglas Walton (eds.), *Action Theory* (Dordrecht: D. Reidel, 1976).

Chomsky, N., 'Chomsky, Noam', in S. Guttenplan (ed.), *A Companion to the Philosophy of Mind* (Oxford: Blackwell, 1994), pp. 153–67.

Language and Mind, 2nd edn (New York: Harcourt Brace Jovanovich, 1972).

Language and Problems of Knowledge (Cambridge, MA: MIT Press, 1988).

Churchland, P. M., 'Eliminative Materialism and the Propositional Attitudes', *Journal of Philosophy* 78 (1981), pp. 67–90, reprinted in Lycan (ed.), *Mind and Cognition*.

Matter and Consciousness, revised edn (Cambridge, MA: MIT Press, 1988).

The Engine of Reason, the Seat of the Soul: A Philosophical Journey into the Brain (Cambridge, MA: MIT Press, 1995).

Clark, A., *Microcognition: Philosophy, Cognitive Science, and Parallel Distributed Processing* (Cambridge, MA: MIT Press, 1989).

Cohen, L. J., 'Can Human Irrationality be Experimentally Demonstrated?', *Behavioral and Brain Sciences* 4 (1981), pp. 317–70.

Collins, A. W., 'Moore's Paradox and Epistemic Risk', *Philosophical Quarterly* 46 (1996), pp. 308–19.

Cosmides, L., 'The Logic of Social Exchange: Has Natural Selection Shaped How Humans Reason? Studies with the Wason Selection Task', *Cognition* 31 (1989), pp. 187–276.

Crane, T., 'An Alleged Analogy between Numbers and Propositions', *Analysis* 50 (1990), pp. 224–30.

'The Nonconceptual Content of Experience', in Crane (ed.), *The Contents of Experience*.

Crane, T. (ed.), *The Contents of Experience: Essays on Perception* (Cambridge: Cambridge University Press, 1992).

Cummins, D. D. and Allen, C. (eds.), *The Evolution of Mind* (New York: Oxford University Press, 1998).

Cummins, R., *Meaning and Mental Representation* (Cambridge, MA: MIT Press, 1989).

Dancy, J. (ed.), *Perceptual Knowledge* (Oxford: Oxford University Press, 1988).

Danto, A. C., *Analytical Philosophy of Action* (Cambridge: Cambridge University Press, 1973).

'Basic Actions', *American Philosophical Quarterly* 2 (1965), pp. 141–8.

Davidson, D., 'Actions, Reasons, and Causes', *Journal of Philosophy* 60 (1963), pp. 685–700, reprinted in Davidson, *Essays on Actions and Events*.

'Agency', in R. Binkley, R. Bronaugh and A. Marras (eds.), *Agent, Action, and Reason* (Toronto: University of Toronto Press, 1971), reprinted in Davidson, *Essays on Actions and Events*.

Essays on Actions and Events (Oxford: Clarendon Press, 1980).

'Freedom to Act', in T. Honderich (ed.), *Essays on Freedom of Action* (London: Routledge and Kegan Paul, 1973), reprinted in Davidson, *Essays on Actions and Events*.

'How is Weakness of the Will Possible?', in J. Feinberg (ed.), *Moral Concepts* (Oxford: Oxford University Press, 1970), reprinted in Davidson, *Essays on Actions and Events*.

Inquiries into Truth and Interpretation (Oxford: Clarendon Press, 1984).

'Intending', in Davidson, *Essays on Actions and Events*

'Knowing One's Own Mind', *Proceedings and Addresses of the Amer-*

ican *Philosophical Association* 60 (1987), pp. 441–58, reprinted in Cassam (ed.), *Self-Knowledge*.

'Mental Events', in L. Foster and J. W. Swanson (eds.), *Experience and Theory* (London: Duckworth, 1970), reprinted in Davidson, *Essays on Actions and Events*.

'On the Very Idea of a Conceptual Scheme', in Davidson, *Inquiries into Truth and Interpretation*.

'Thought and Talk', in Guttenplan (ed.), *Mind and Language*, reprinted in Davidson, *Inquiries into Truth and Interpretation*.

Davies, M., 'Function in Perception', *Australasian Journal of Philosophy* 61 (1983), pp. 409–26.

Davies, M. and Stone, T. (eds.), *Folk Psychology: The Theory of Mind Debate* (Oxford: Blackwell, 1995).

Davis, L. E., *Theory of Action* (Englewood Cliffs, NJ: Prentice-Hall, 1979).

Dennett, D. C., 'A Cure for the Common Code?', in Dennett, *Brainstorms*, reprinted in Block (ed.), *Readings in Philosophy of Psychology, Volume 2*.

Brainstorms: Philosophical Essays on Mind and Psychology (Hassocks: Harvester Press, 1979).

'Cognitive Wheels: The Frame Problem of AI', in C. Hookway (ed.), *Minds, Machines and Evolution* (Cambridge: Cambridge University Press, 1984), reprinted in Boden (ed.), *The Philosophy of Artificial Intelligence*.

Consciousness Explained (Harmondsworth: Penguin Books, 1991).

Content and Consciousness (London: Routledge and Kegan Paul, 1969).

Darwin's Dangerous Idea (London: Penguin Books, 1995).

Elbow Room: The Varieties of Free Will Worth Wanting (Oxford: Clarendon Press, 1984).

'Intentional Systems in Cognitive Ethology: The "Panglossian Paradigm" Defended', *Behavioral and Brain Sciences* 6 (1983), pp. 343–90, reprinted in Dennett, *The Intentional Stance*.

'Quining Qualia', in A. J. Marcel and E. Bisiach (eds.), *Consciousness in Contemporary Science* (Oxford: Clarendon Press, 1988), reprinted in Lycan (ed.), *Mind and Cognition*.

The Intentional Stance (Cambridge, MA: MIT Press, 1987).

Descartes, R., *The Philosophical Writings of Descartes*, ed. J. Cottingham, R. Stoothoof and D. Murdoch (Cambridge: Cambridge University Press, 1984).

De Sousa, R., *The Rationality of Emotion* (Cambridge, MA: MIT Press, 1987).

Devitt, M. and Sterelny, K., *Language and Reality: An Introduction to the Philosophy of Language* (Oxford: Blackwell, 1987).

Donald, M., *Origins of the Modern Mind: Three Stages in the Evolution of Culture and Cognition* (Cambridge, MA: Harvard University Press, 1991).

Dretske, F. I., *Seeing and Knowing* (London: Routledge and Kegan Paul, 1969).

Eells, E. and Maruszewski, T. (eds.), *Probability and Rationality: Studies on L. Jonathan Cohen's Philosophy of Science* (Amsterdam: Rodopi, 1991).

Evans, G., *The Varieties of Reference* (Oxford: Clarendon Press, 1982).

Evans, J. St. B. T., *Bias in Human Reasoning: Causes and Consequences* (Hove: Lawrence Erlbaum Associates, 1989).

Evans, J. St. B. T., Newstead, S. E. and Byrne, R. M. J., *Human Reasoning: The Psychology of Deduction* (Hove: Lawrence Erlbaum Associates, 1993).

Evans, J. St. B. T. and Over, D. E., *Rationality and Reasoning* (Hove: Psychology Press, 1996).

Field, H., 'Mental Representation', *Erkenntnis* 13 (1978), pp. 9–61, reprinted in Block (ed.), *Readings in Philosophy of Psychology, Volume 2*.

Realism, Mathematics and Modality (Oxford: Blackwell, 1989).

Science Without Numbers: A Defence of Nominalism (Oxford: Blackwell, 1980).

Fodor, J. A., 'A Modal Argument for Narrow Content', *Journal of Philosophy* 88 (1991), pp. 5–26.

Concepts: Where Cognitive Science Went Wrong (Oxford: Oxford University Press, 1998).

'Methodological Solipsism Considered as a Research Strategy in Cognitive Psychology', *Behavioral and Brain Sciences* 3 (1980), pp. 63–109, reprinted in Fodor, *Representations*.

Psychosemantics: The Problem of Meaning in the Philosophy of Mind (Cambridge, MA: MIT Press, 1987).

Representations: Philosophical Essays on the Foundations of Cognitive Science (Brighton: Harvester Press, 1981).

The Elm and the Expert: Mentalese and its Semantics (Cambridge, MA: MIT Press, 1994).

The Language of Thought (Hassocks: Harvester Press, 1976).

The Modularity of Mind (Cambridge, MA: MIT Press, 1983).

'The Present Status of the Innateness Hypothesis', in Fodor, *Representations*.

Fodor, J. A. and Pylyshyn, Z. W., 'Connectionism and Cognitive Architecture: A Critical Analysis', *Cognition* 28 (1988), pp. 3–78, reprinted in Macdonald and Macdonald (eds.), *Connectionism*.

Gallois, A., *The World Without, the Mind Within: An Essay on First-Person Authority* (Cambridge: Cambridge University Press, 1996).

Garber, D., 'Mind, Body, and the Laws of Nature in Descartes and Leibniz', *Midwest Studies in Philosophy* 8 (1983), pp. 105–33.

Garrett, B., *Personal Identity and Self-Consciousness* (London: Routledge, 1998).

Geach, P. T., *Truth, Love and Immortality: An Introduction to McTaggart's Philosophy* (London: Hutchinson, 1979).

George, A. (ed.), *Reflections on Chomsky* (Oxford: Blackwell, 1989).

Gibson, J. J., *The Ecological Approach to Visual Perception* (Hillsdale, NJ: Lawrence Erlbaum Associates, 1986).

Gigerenzer, G., 'Ecological Intelligence: An Adaptation for Frequencies', in Cummins and Allen (eds.), *The Evolution of Mind*.

Gigerenzer, G. and Murray, D. J., *Cognition as Intuitive Statistics* (Hillsdale, NJ: Lawrence Erlbaum Associates, 1987).

Ginet, C., *On Action* (Cambridge: Cambridge University Press, 1990).

Glover, J. (ed.), *The Philosophy of Mind* (Oxford: Oxford University Press, 1976).

Greenwood, J. D. (ed.), *The Future of Folk Psychology: Intentionality and Cognitive Science* (Cambridge: Cambridge University Press, 1991).

Grice, H. P., *Studies in the Way of Words* (Cambridge, MA: Harvard University Press, 1989).

'The Causal Theory of Perception', *Proceedings of the Aristotelian Society*, Supp. Vol. 35 (1961), pp. 121–52, reprinted in Grice, *Studies in the Way of Words* and in Dancy (ed.), *Perceptual Knowledge*.

Guttenplan, S. (ed.), *Mind and Language* (Oxford: Clarendon Press, 1975).

Haack, S., *Philosophy of Logics* (Cambridge: Cambridge University Press, 1978).

Hamilton, A., 'Anscombian and Cartesian Scepticism', *Philosophical Quarterly* 41 (1991), pp. 39–54.

'A New Look at Personal Identity', *Philosophical Quarterly* 45 (1995), pp. 332–49.

Hardin, C. L., *Color for Philosophers* (Indianapolis: Hackett, 1988).

Heal, J., 'Moore's Paradox: A Wittgensteinian Approach', *Mind* 103 (1994), pp. 5–24.

Heil, J., *Philosophy of Mind: A Contemporary Introduction* (London: Routledge, 1998).

The Nature of True Minds (Cambridge: Cambridge University Press, 1992).

Heyes, C. and Dickinson, A., 'Folk Psychology Won't Go Away: Response to Allen and Beckoff', *Mind and Language* 10 (1995), pp. 329–32.

'The Intentionality of Animal Action', *Mind and Language* 5 (1990), pp. 87–104.

Hinton, J. M., *Experiences: An Inquiry into some Ambiguities* (Oxford: Clarendon Press, 1973).

Hornsby, J., *Actions* (London: Routledge and Kegan Paul, 1980).

Howe, M. J. A., *Fragments of Genius: The Strange Feats of Idiots Savants* (London: Routledge, 1989).

Hume, D., *A Treatise of Human Nature*, ed. L. A. Selby-Bigge and P. H. Nidditch (Oxford: Clarendon Press, 1978).

Jackson, F., 'Epiphenomenal Qualia', *Philosophical Quarterly* 32 (1982), pp. 127–36, reprinted in Lycan (ed.), *Mind and Cognition*.

Perception: A Representative Theory (Cambridge: Cambridge University Press, 1977).

Jeffrey, R. C., *Formal Logic: Its Scope and Limits*, 2nd edn (New York: McGraw-Hill, 1981).

Johnson-Laird, P. N. and Byrne, R. M. J., *Deduction* (Hove: Lawrence Erlbaum Associates, 1991).

Kay, P. and McDaniel, C. K., 'The Linguistic Significance of the Meanings of Basic Color Terms', *Language* 54 (1978), pp. 610–46, reprinted in Byrne and Hilbert (eds.), *Readings on Color, Volume 2*.

Kenny, A., *Action, Emotion and Will* (London: Routledge and Kegan Paul, 1963).

Will, Freedom and Power (Oxford: Blackwell, 1975).

Kim, J., *Supervenience and Mind: Selected Philosophical Essays* (Cambridge: Cambridge University Press, 1993).

Köhler, W., *The Mentality of Apes*, 2nd edn (New York: Viking, 1959).

Kosslyn, S., *Image and Brain: The Resolution of the Imagery Debate* (Cambridge, MA: MIT Press, 1994).

'The Medium and the Message in Mental Imagery: A Theory', in Block (ed.), *Imagery*.

Kosslyn, S. M., Pinker, S., Smith, G. E. and Shwartz, S. P., 'On the Demystification of Mental Imagery', *Behavioral and Brain*

Sciences 2 (1979), pp. 535–81, partly reprinted in a revised form in Block (ed.), *Imagery*.

Kripke, S. A., *Naming and Necessity* (Oxford: Blackwell, 1980), first published in G. Harman and D. Davidson (eds.), *Semantics of Natural Language* (Dordrecht: D. Reidel, 1972).

LePore, E. and McLaughlin, B. (eds.), *Actions and Events: Perspectives on the Philosophy of Donald Davidson* (Oxford: Blackwell, 1985).

Lewis, D., 'Mad Pain and Martian Pain', in Block (ed.), *Readings in Philosophy of Psychology, Volume 1*, reprinted in Lewis, *Philosophical Papers, Volume I*.

Philosophical Papers, Volume I (New York: Oxford University Press, 1983).

Philosophical Papers, Volume II (New York: Oxford University Press, 1986).

'Veridical Hallucination and Prosthetic Vision', *Australasian Journal of Philosophy* 58 (1980), pp. 239–49, reprinted in Lewis, *Philosophical Papers, Volume II* and in Dancy (ed.), *Perceptual Knowledge*.

Libet, B., *Neurophysiology of Consciousness* (Boston, MA: Birkhaüser, 1993).

'Unconscious Cerebral Initiative and the Role of Conscious Will in Voluntary Action', *Behavioral and Brain Sciences* 8 (1985), pp. 529–66, reprinted in Libet, *Neurophysiology of Consciousness*.

Locke, J., *An Essay Concerning Human Understanding*, ed. P. H. Nidditch (Oxford: Clarendon Press, 1975).

Loux, M. J., *Metaphysics: A Contemporary Introduction* (London: Routledge, 1998).

Lowe, E. J., 'An Analysis of Intentionality', *Philosophical Quarterly* 30 (1980), pp. 294–304.

'Indirect Perception and Sense Data', *Philosophical Quarterly* 31 (1981), pp. 330–42.

Kinds of Being: A Study of Individuation, Identity and the Logic of Sortal Terms (Oxford: Blackwell, 1989).

Locke on Human Understanding (London: Routledge, 1995).

'Objects and Criteria of Identity', in B. Hale and C. Wright (eds.), *A Companion to the Philosophy of Language* (Oxford: Blackwell, 1997).

'Personal Experience and Belief: The Significance of External Symbolic Storage for the Emergence of Modern Human Cognition', in C. Scarre and C. Renfrew (eds.), *Cognition and Culture: The Archaeology of Symbolic Storage* (Cambridge: McDonald Institute for Archaeological Research, 1998).

'Rationality, Deduction and Mental Models', in Manktelow and Over (eds.), *Rationality*.

Subjects of Experience (Cambridge: Cambridge University Press, 1996).

'The Metaphysics of Abstract Objects', *Journal of Philosophy* 92 (1995), pp. 509–24.

The Possibility of Metaphysics: Substance, Identity and Time (Oxford: Clarendon Press, 1998).

'There are No Easy Problems of Consciousness', *Journal of Consciousness Studies* 2 (1995), pp. 266–71, reprinted in Shear (ed.), *Explaining Consciousness*.

'What Is a Criterion of Identity?', *Philosophical Quarterly* 39 (1989), pp. 1–21, reprinted in Noonan (ed.), *Identity*.

Lycan, W. G. (ed.), *Mind and Cognition: A Reader* (Oxford: Blackwell, 1990).

Macdonald, C. and Macdonald, G. (eds.), *Connectionism: Debates in Psychological Explanation, Volume 2* (Oxford: Blackwell, 1995).

Malcolm, N., 'A Definition of Factual Memory', in N. Malcolm, *Knowledge and Certainty: Essays and Lectures* (Ithaca, NY: Cornell University Press, 1963).

Manktelow, K. I. and Over, D. E., *Inference and Understanding: A Philosophical and Psychological Perspective* (London: Routledge, 1990).

Manktelow, K. I. and Over, D. E. (eds.), *Rationality: Psychological and Philosophical Perspectives* (London: Routledge, 1993).

Marr, D., *Vision: A Computational Investigation into the Human Representation and Processing of Visual Information* (New York: W. H. Freeman and Company, 1982).

Martin, C. B. and Deutscher, M., 'Remembering', *Philosophical Review* 75 (1966), pp. 161–96.

McClelland, J. L., Rumelhart, D. E. and Hinton, G. E., 'The Appeal of Parallel Distributed Processing', in Rumelhart and McClelland (eds.), *Parallel Distributed Processing, Volume 1*.

McCulloch, G., *The Mind and its World* (London: Routledge, 1995).

McDowell, J., 'Criteria, Defeasibility, and Knowledge', *Proceedings of the British Academy* 68 (1982), pp. 455–79, reprinted in Dancy (ed.), *Perceptual Knowledge*.

Mind and World (Cambridge, MA: Harvard University Press, 1994).

McGinn, C., *Mental Content* (Oxford: Blackwell, 1989).

The Subjective View: Secondary Qualities and Indexical Thoughts (Oxford: Clarendon Press, 1983).

Melden, A. I., *Free Action* (London: Routledge and Kegan Paul, 1961).

Mele, A. R., 'Real Self-Deception', *Behavioral and Brain Sciences* 20 (1997), pp. 91–136.

Mellor, D. H., 'I and Now', *Proceedings of the Aristotelian Society* 89 (1989), pp. 79–94, reprinted in Mellor, *Matters of Metaphysics*.
Matters of Metaphysics (Cambridge: Cambridge University Press, 1991).

Merricks, T., 'A New Objection to A Priori Arguments for Dualism', *American Philosophical Quarterly* 31 (1994), pp. 80–5.

Millikan, R. G., *Language, Thought and Other Biological Categories: New Foundations for Realism* (Cambridge, MA: MIT Press, 1984).

Mills, E., 'Interactionism and Overdetermination', *American Philosophical Quarterly* 33 (1996), pp. 105–17.

Nagel, T., 'Brain Bisection and the Unity of Consciousness', *Synthese* 22 (1971), pp. 396–413, reprinted in Nagel, *Mortal Questions*.
Mortal Questions (Cambridge: Cambridge University Press, 1979).
'What is it Like to be a Bat?', *Philosophical Review* 83 (1974), pp. 435–50, reprinted in Nagel, *Mortal Questions*.

Nelkin, N., *Consciousness and the Origins of Thought* (Cambridge: Cambridge University Press, 1996).

Newstead, S. E. and Evans, J. St. B. T. (eds.), *Perspectives on Thinking and Reasoning: Essays in Honour of Peter Wason* (Hove: Lawrence Erlbaum Associates, 1995).

Noonan, H. W., *Personal Identity* (London: Routledge, 1989).

Noonan, H. W. (ed.), *Identity* (Aldershot: Dartmouth, 1993).

O'Brien, D. P., 'Mental Logic and Human Irrationality: We Can Put a Man on the Moon, So Why Can't We Solve those Logical-Reasoning Problems?', in Manktelow and Over (eds.), *Rationality*.

Olson, E. T., *The Human Animal: Personal Identity Without Psychology* (New York: Oxford University Press, 1997).

O'Shaughnessy, B., *The Will: A Dual Aspect Theory* (Cambridge: Cambridge University Press, 1980).

Papineau, D., *Philosophical Naturalism* (Oxford: Blackwell, 1993).
Reality and Representation (Oxford: Blackwell, 1987).

Parfit, D., 'Personal Identity', *Philosophical Review* 80 (1971), pp. 3–27, reprinted in Glover (ed.), *The Philosophy of Mind*.
Reasons and Persons (Oxford: Clarendon Press, 1984).

Peacocke, C. A. B., *Holistic Explanation: Action, Space, Interpretation* (Oxford: Clarendon Press, 1979).
'Scenarios, Concepts and Perception', in Crane (ed.), *The Contents of Experience*.
Sense and Content: Experience, Thought, and their Relations (Oxford: Clarendon Press, 1983).

Pears, D., *Motivated Irrationality* (Oxford: Clarendon Press, 1984).

Penfield, W., *The Excitable Cortex in Conscious Man* (Liverpool: Liverpool University Press, 1958).

Premack, D., ' "Does the Chimpanzee have a Theory of Mind?" Revisited', in R. Byrne and A. Whiten (eds.), *Machiavellian Intelligence: Social Expertise and the Evolution of Intellect in Monkeys, Apes, and Humans* (Oxford: Clarendon Press, 1988).

Prichard, H. A., 'Acting, Willing, Desiring', in H. A. Prichard, *Moral Obligation: Essays and Lectures* (Oxford: Clarendon Press, 1949).

Pullum, G. K., *The Great Eskimo Vocabulary Hoax and Other Irreverent Essays on the Study of Language* (Chicago: University of Chicago Press, 1991).

Putnam, H., *Mind, Language and Reality: Philosophical Papers, Volume 2* (Cambridge: Cambridge University Press, 1975).

Representation and Reality (Cambridge, MA: MIT Press, 1988).

'The Meaning of "Meaning" ', in K. Gunderson (ed.), *Language, Mind and Knowledge: Minnesota Studies in the Philosophy of Science, Volume 7* (Minneapolis: University of Minnesota Press, 1975), reprinted in Putnam, *Mind, Language and Reality*.

'The Nature of Mental States', in Lycan (ed.), *Mind and Cognition: A Reader*.

Pylyshyn, Z. W., *Computation and Cognition: Toward a Foundation for Cognitive Science* (Cambridge, MA: MIT Press, 1984).

'The Imagery Debate: Analog Media versus Tacit Knowledge', in Block (ed.), *Imagery*.

Pylyshyn, Z. W. (ed.), *The Robot's Dilemma: The Frame Problem of Artificial Intelligence* (Norwood, NJ: Ablex, 1987).

Ramsey, W., Stich, S. P. and Garon, J., 'Connectionism, Eliminativism, and the Future of Folk Psychology', in J. E. Tomberlin (ed.), *Philosophical Perspectives, 4* (Atascadero, CA: Ridgeview Press, 1990), reprinted in Ramsey, Stich and Rumelhart (eds.), *Philosophy and Connectionist Theory* and in Macdonald and Macdonald (eds.), *Connectionism*.

Ramsey, W., Stich, S. P. and Rumelhart, D. E. (eds.), *Philosophy and Connectionist Theory* (Hillsdale, NJ: Lawrence Erlbaum Associates, 1991).

Rips, L. J., 'Mental Muddles', in M. Brand and R. M. Harnish (eds.), *The Representation of Knowledge and Belief* (Tucson: University of Arizona Press, 1986).

Robinson, H., *Perception* (London: Routledge, 1994).

Rumelhart, D. E. and McClelland, J. L., 'On Learning the Past Tenses of English Verbs', in Rumelhart and McClelland (eds.), *Parallel Distributed Processing, Volume 2*.

Rumelhart, D. E. and McClelland, J. L. (eds.), *Parallel Distributed Processing: Explorations in the Microstructure of Cognition, Volume 1: Foundations* (Cambridge, MA: MIT Press, 1986).
  Parallel Distributed Processing, Volume 2: Psychological and Biological Models (Cambridge, MA: MIT Press, 1986).
Russell, B., *The Analysis of Mind* (London: George Allen and Unwin, 1921).
Ryle, G., *The Concept of Mind* (London: Hutchinson, 1949).
Sacks, O., *Seeing Voices: A Journey into the World of the Deaf* (Berkeley and Los Angeles: University of California Press, 1989).
Saunders, B. A. C. and van Brakel, J., 'Are There Nontrivial Constraints on Color Categorization?', *Behavioral and Brain Sciences* 20 (1997), pp. 167–228.
Searle, J. R., *Intentionality: An Essay in the Philosophy of Mind* (Cambridge: Cambridge University Press, 1983).
  'Minds, Brains, and Programs', *Behavioral and Brain Sciences* 3 (1980), pp. 417–24, reprinted in Boden (ed.), *The Philosophy of Artificial Intelligence*.
  The Rediscovery of the Mind (Cambridge, MA: MIT Press, 1992).
Segal, G., 'Seeing What is Not There', *Philosophical Review* 98 (1989), pp. 189–214.
Sellars, W., 'The Structure of Knowledge II', in H. N. Castañeda (ed.), *Action, Knowledge, and Reality: Critical Studies in Honor of Wilfrid Sellars* (Indianapolis: Bobbs-Merrill, 1975).
Shear, J. (ed.), *Explaining Consciousness: The Hard Problem* (Cambridge, MA: MIT Press, 1997).
Shepard, R. N. and Metzler, J., 'Mental Rotation of Three-Dimensional Objects', *Science* 171 (1971), pp. 701–3.
Shoemaker, S., 'Functionalism and Qualia', *Philosophical Studies* 27 (1975), pp. 291–315, reprinted in Shoemaker, *Identity, Cause, and Mind*
  Identity, Cause, and Mind: Philosophical Essays (Cambridge: Cambridge University Press, 1984).
  'Persons and their Pasts', *American Philosophical Quarterly* 7 (1970), pp. 269–85, reprinted in Shoemaker, *Identity, Cause, and Mind*.
  Self-Knowledge and Self-Identity (Ithaca, NY: Cornell University Press, 1963).
  'Self-Reference and Self-Awareness', *Journal of Philosophy* 65 (1968), pp. 555–67, reprinted in Shoemaker, *Identity, Cause, and Mind* and in Cassam (ed.), *Self-Knowledge*.
Simons, P., *Parts: A Study in Ontology* (Oxford: Clarendon Press, 1987).
Smith, N. and Tsimpli, I.-M., *The Mind of a Savant: Language Learning and Modularity* (Oxford: Blackwell, 1995).

Smolensky, P. 'On the Proper Treatment of Connectionism', *Behavioral and Brain Sciences* 11 (1988), pp. 1–74, reprinted in Macdonald and Macdonald (eds.), *Connectionism*.

Snowdon, P., 'Perception, Vision, and Causation', *Proceedings of the Aristotelian Society* 81 (1980–1), pp. 175–92, reprinted in Dancy (ed.), *Perceptual Knowledge*.

Stalnaker, R. C., *Inquiry* (Cambridge, MA: MIT Press, 1984).

Stich, S., *The Fragmentation of Reason: Preface to a Pragmatic Theory of Cognitive Evaluation* (Cambridge, MA: MIT Press, 1990).

Strawson, G., *The Secret Connexion: Causation, Realism, and David Hume* (Oxford: Clarendon Press, 1989).

Strawson, P. F., *Individuals: An Essay in Descriptive Metaphysics* (London: Methuen, 1959).

Sutton, J., *Philosophy and Memory Traces: Descartes to Connectionism* (Cambridge: Cambridge University Press, 1998).

Taylor, R., *Action and Purpose* (Englewood Cliffs, NJ: Prentice-Hall, 1966).

Thalberg, I., *Perception, Emotion and Action* (Oxford: Blackwell, 1977).

Thomson, J. J., *Acts and Other Events* (Ithaca, NY: Cornell University Press, 1977).

'The Time of a Killing', *Journal of Philosophy* 68 (1971), pp. 115–32.

Turing, A. M., 'Computing Machinery and Intelligence', *Mind* 59 (1950), pp. 433–60, reprinted in Boden (ed.), *The Philosophy of Artificial Intelligence*.

Tversky, A. and Kahneman, D., 'Causal Schemata in Judgements under Uncertainty', in M. Fishbein (ed.), *Progress in Social Psychology, Volume 1* (Hillsdale, NJ: Lawrence Erlbaum Associates, 1980).

Tye, M., *Ten Problems of Consciousness: A Representational Theory of the Phenomenal Mind* (Cambridge, MA: MIT Press, 1995).

The Imagery Debate (Cambridge, MA: MIT Press, 1991).

The Metaphysics of Mind (Cambridge: Cambridge University Press, 1989).

van Gelder, T., 'What Might Cognition Be, If Not Computation?', *Journal of Philosophy* 92 (1995), pp. 345–81.

van Inwagen, P., *An Essay on Free Will* (Oxford: Clarendon Press, 1983).

Vermazen, B. and Hintikka, M. B. (eds.), *Essays on Davidson: Actions and Events* (Oxford: Clarendon Press, 1985).

Watson, J. B., *Behaviourism*, 2nd edn (Chicago: University of Chicago Press, 1958).

Weiskrantz, L., *Blindsight: A Case Study and Implications* (Oxford: Clarendon Press, 1986).

Whorf, B. L., *Language, Thought and Reality: Selected Writings of Benjamin Lee Whorf*, ed. J. B. Carroll (Cambridge, MA: MIT Press, 1956).

Wilkes, K. V., *Real People: Personal Identity Without Thought Experiments* (Oxford: Clarendon Press, 1988).

Williams, B., *Problems of the Self* (Cambridge: Cambridge University Press, 1973).

'The Self and the Future', *Philosophical Review* 79 (1970), pp. 161–80, reprinted in Williams, *Problems of the Self*.

Wilson, R. A., *Cartesian Psychology and Physical Minds: Individualism and the Sciences of the Mind* (Cambridge: Cambridge University Press, 1995).

Wittgenstein, L., *Philosophical Investigations*, trans. G. E. M. Anscombe, 2nd edn (Oxford: Blackwell, 1958).

The Blue and Brown Books, 2nd edn (Oxford: Blackwell, 1969).

Wollheim, R., *The Thread of Life* (Cambridge: Cambridge University Press, 1984).

Woolhouse, R. S., 'Leibniz's Reaction to Cartesian Interactionism', *Proceedings of the Aristotelian Society* 86 (1985/86), pp. 69–82.

Wright, C., Smith, B. C. and Macdonald, C. (eds.), *Knowing Our Own Minds* (Oxford: Clarendon Press, 1998).

Yourgrau, P. (ed.), *Demonstratives* (Oxford: Oxford University Press, 1990).

Index